THE ISRAELI SUPREME COURT AND THE HUMAN RIGHTS REVOLUTION: COURTS AS AGENDA SETTERS

This book explains the reciprocal relations between the Supreme Court and the Israeli political system. It is based on a unique approach that contends that the non-governability of the political system and an alternative political culture are two key formal and informal variables affecting the behavior of several political players within the Israeli arena. The analysis illustrates the usefulness of such a model for analyzing long-term socio-political processes and explaining the actions of the players. Until this model changes significantly, the decisions of the High Court of Justice express the values of the state and enable Israel to remain a nation that upholds human rights. The court's decisions determine the normative educational direction and reflect Israel's democratic character with regard to the values of human rights.

Dr. Assaf Meydani is a Senior Lecturer in the School of Government and Society at the Academic College of Tel-Aviv–Yaffo. His research interests include public policy, politics and law, and political economy. Dr. Meydani has been a Visiting Scholar at the Center for New Institutional Science at Washington University in St. Louis, Missouri, and the Institute of Management, Innovation, and Organization at the University of California at Berkeley. He is the author of *Political Transformations and Political Entrepreneurs: Israel in Comparative Perspective* (2009). His articles have appeared in journals such as *Israel Studies*, *Israel Law Review*, *Policy and Society*, *Constitutional Political Economy*, *Rationality and Society*, and *Land Use Policy*.

The Israeli Supreme Court and the Human Rights Revolution

COURTS AS AGENDA SETTERS

Assaf Meydani

School of Government and Society, The Academic College of Tel-Aviv–Yaffo

CAMBRIDGE
UNIVERSITY PRESS

CAMBRIDGE UNIVERSITY PRESS
Cambridge, New York, Melbourne, Madrid, Cape Town,
Singapore, São Paulo, Delhi, Tokyo, Mexico City

Cambridge University Press
32 Avenue of the Americas, New York, NY 10013-2473, USA

www.cambridge.org
Information on this title: www.cambridge.org/9781107012622

First published 2011

Printed in the United States of America

A catalog record for this publication is available from the British Library.

Library of Congress Cataloging in Publication data

Meydani, Assaf.
The Israeli Supreme Court and the human rights revolution : courts as agenda setters / Assaf Meydani.
p. cm.
Includes bibliographical references and index.
ISBN 978-1-107-01262-2 (hardback)
1. Courts of last resort – Israel. 2. Political questions and judicial power – Israel. 3. Constitutional law – Israel. 4. Human rights – Israel. I. Title.
KMK3466.M49 2011
347.5694′035 – dc22 2011009809

ISBN 978-1-107-01262-2 Hardback

To Marit, Romy, and Alma with love and appreciation.
To Lea and Ben-Zion Meydani – thank you for always being there.

Contents

Figures and Tables

FIGURES

TABLES

Acknowledgments

This book reflects the efforts of a decade of research and study about law and politics in Israel. Parts of its rationales and ideas have appeared in journals such as *Israel Studies*, *Israel Law Review*, *Policy and Society*, *Constitutional Political Economy*, *Rationality and Society*, *Land Use Policy*, *Democracy and Security*, and *Contemporary Security Policy*. Portions of the book have also been presented at conferences held by the Law and Society Association (LSA), the American Political Science Association (APSA), the Association for Israel Studies (AIS), and the International Political Science Association (IPSA). I would like to thank Gideon Doron, Shlomo Mizrahi, David A. Frenkel, Gad Barzilai, Arye Naor, David Nachmias, Shimon Shetreet, Daphne Barak-Erez, Pablo T. Spiller, Barak Medina, Ronen Shamir, Raanan Sulitzeanu-Kenan, Yoav Dotan, Menachem Hofnung, Itzhak Galnoor, Yoram Rabin, Suzie Navot, Ilan Saban, Udi Sommer, and Guy Seidman for their advice and collaboration. I would also like to thank Naomi Chazan for her time and support. Thanks, too, to the Academic College of Tel-Aviv–Yaffo for generous support, especially Israel Zang, Nehemia Friedland, and Dror Amir. I would also like to thank The Citizens' Empowerment Center in Israel for their support.

The manuscript would never have achieved its final form but for the editorial skill and dedication of Diane Romm. In addition, I would like to thank John Berger, my editor at Cambridge University Press, for his useful advice and support. Finally, my thanks to the anonymous readers for their useful remarks.

1

Introduction

In recent decades, the role of supreme courts in designing and determining institutional changes has been studied from various angles (Schubert, 1965; Jabbari, 1992; Tate and Vallinder, 1995; Gilman, 1996–1997; Baum, 1997; Flemming and Wood, 1997; Feeley and Rubin, 1998; Cornell and Gillman, 1999). The variety of research includes sociological explanations (Parsons, 1962; Nonet, 1976), strategic interactions (Landes and Posner, 1975; Mishler and Sheehan, 1993; Kilwein and Brisbin, 1997; Voight and Salzberger, 2002), and static game models (Gely and Spiller, 1990; Eskridge and Ferejohn, 1992; Segal and Spaeth, 1993; Epstein and Walker, 1995; Epstein and Knight, 1998; Segal, 1997).

In his book, *The Hollow Hope – Can Courts Bring about a Social Change?* Gerald Rosenberg (1991) questions the validity of the commonly accepted axiom that the Supreme Court of the United States is able to affect widespread social change. Critics maintain that Rosenberg's argument ignores the implications of court decisions for future actions that created more direct change (see, for example, Lawrence, 1992; Viscusi, 2002; Gavison, 2009). Such critics have rarely created a dynamic model that illuminates the impact of supreme courts on policy or institutional changes from a historical perspective. However, in *Towards Juristocracy*, Ran Hirschl (2004) shows that the trend toward constitutionalization is not really driven by politicians' genuine commitment to democracy, social justice, or universal rights. Rather, it is best understood as the product of a strategic interplay among hegemonic yet threatened political elites, influential economic stakeholders, and judicial leaders. This self-interested coalition of legal innovators determines the timing, extent, and nature of constitutional reforms. Hirschl demonstrates that whereas judicial empowerment through constitutionalization has a limited impact on advancing progressive notions of distributive justice, it has a transformative effect on political discourse. The global trend toward juristocracy, Hirschl argues, is part of a broader process whereby political and economic elites, while professing support for democracy and sustained development, attempt to insulate policy making from the vicissitudes of democratic politics. However, Hirschl pays less attention to the role of the supreme court in this process.

In this book, we develop such a dynamic model using the concepts of shared mental models and policy entrepreneurship. In a similar vein, Powell and DiMaggio (1991) claim that motives of power and interest have received insufficient attention in neo-institutional sociology. They note that little attention has been paid to the question: How do key workers (actors or players) preserve their dominance or respond to threats in times of crisis or instability? The manner in which gifted entrepreneurs implement a multi-institutional strategy has also been neglected.

This book adopts hypotheses and concepts taken from the institutional literature to develop a procedural model for the analysis of formal political rule change in a democratic system. The analysis also stresses the role of supreme courts as political entrepreneurs in designing institutional changes. The model is then applied to a path-dependent analysis of the role of the Supreme Court in Israel between 1948 and 2007. Thus, we integrate rational choice institutionalism and historical institutionalism (Katzelson and Weingast, 2005; Weingast, 2005).

These analytical tools will be applied to the explanation of the role of the Israeli Supreme Court in matters of "who governs?" vis-à-vis the Israeli parliament. Following Rosenberg, Gad Barzilai (2002) distinguished between several political dimensions: the rhetoric of court rulings and possible changes in legal interpretation, minor or secondary social changes, and the dimension that deals with major social alterations. Barzilai concludes that despite minor changes, no major changes in the socio-political characteristics of the state and the public have taken place in Israel.

In this book, we claim that the Supreme Court played a necessary, but not sufficient, role in the design of the institutional changes that occurred in Israel between 1948 and 2007. Specifically, in its decisions on controversial issues, the court served as the shaper of the value of human rights. Whereas at the beginning of this period the Court limited the ability of citizens to appeal in matters concerning decisions of the parliament and the government, by the end of the period it had expanded this ability significantly, thus implementing an informal policy of procedural judicial activism (Mautner, 1993; Barzilai, 1998; Hofnung, 1999;

Hirschl, 2001; Mizrahi and Meydani, 2003; Galnoor, 2004; Cohn and Kremnitzer, 2005). In effect, during this period, the relationship and the institutional equilibrium between the Court and the parliament were significantly transformed, thus enabling an informal institutional change regarding the rule of "who governs?" in controversial issues. The "who governs?" rule is not all-inclusive (Medina, 2007). However, it is an informal channel for shaping the Israeli institutional reality, a channel in which the Supreme Court has a crucial role. This institutional channel of alternative governance enables the Supreme Court to design policies based on the values of human rights and apply them in controversial issues.

Research about the link between law and politics in Israel discusses the relationship between the Israeli High Court of Justice (HCJ) and the political system, the Knesset, and the government at length. Researchers disagree about the HCJ's degree of involvement in public life. For example, Yoav Dotan states that:

> It seems that in Israel of the twenty-first century no words can describe the important role the HCJ plays in public life. I am doubtful if there is another community so affected by and dependent upon the decision making of a judicial forum as the political community in Israel is affected by the HCJ. Similarly, there seems to be no other judicial forum so deeply involved in the economic, political and social arenas. (Dotan, 2004 :161)

In contrast, Barak Medina presents a different position, claiming that the involvement of the HCJ in policy making is overrated:

> I would like to dispute the claim that judges are the de facto rulers. An easy way to examine the issue would be by estimating the role the HCJ played in each of the major social decisions made in Israel since the 1980s during Barak's tenure. Some of the decisions to be discussed: the 1985 economic plan, settlement expansion, the invasion of and retreat from Lebanon, the Oslo agreements, privatization agreements, increases and reductions in the children's allowance, the disengagement plan, the Homat Magen Operation, construction of the separation wall, the implementation of the tax on capital gains, changes in immigration policy, policies implemented during the second Lebanon war etc. All of these decisions were made by the Israeli Knesset without the actual involvement of the HCJ. It did not initiate any one of the aforementioned decisions. They were not made as a result of its decisions, nor as a result of petitions filed. Despite the fact that some of the decisions were discussed in the High Court of Law after being made by the political system, in no case did the HCJ intervene (except with regard to certain aspects of the separation wall's route and the war on terrorism as mentioned later). (Medina, 2007: 410)

This book attempts to shed light on the extent of judicial involvement in political life from a different point of view, one that is based on quantitative examination of the HCJ's rulings and decisions regarding the relationship with the government in Israel. This approach is integrated within a path-dependent analysis of the relationship between the Supreme Court and the political system from 1948 to 2007.

The book develops as follows. Chapter 2 looks at the number of petitions filed in the HCJ against the government between 2000 and 2006, examining the distribution of petitions against ministers and the judicial results of the petitions. Such an empirical, quantitative analysis yields surprising as well as paradoxical results about the intervention of the Supreme Court in Israeli government policy. Some may claim that, contrary to popular belief, the Supreme Court exercises very limited intervention in the decisions of the Israeli government. Others may claim that the Supreme Court exercises a high level of intervention. These findings are mainly descriptive and do not pretend to analyze the reasons for the findings in depth. What the findings do lead us to is an institutional-process analysis of the relationship between the Supreme Court and the Israeli Knesset. As Epstein, Ho, King, and Segal (2005: 110) note, "This institutional-process theory remains the strongest candidate for resolving our paradoxical empirical findings."

Chapter 3 discusses common explanations analyzing the relationship between law and politics, whereas Chapter 4 presents the theoretical framework in which the Supreme Court is analyzed as a political entrepreneur. This analysis is based on a shared mental model and political entrepreneurship. Chapter 5 begins the empirical study by focusing on the characteristics of the Israeli political structure and culture. Chapter 6 continues this discussion by focusing on the non-governability of Israel's political institutions and on Israel's alternative political culture. Both chapters describe the characteristics of the Israeli system that influence the behavior of the political players, among them the role of the Supreme Court in determining and designing institutional change and policy.

Chapter 7 deals with the Supreme Court and the political system in light of social and political processes in Israel from 1948 to 1999. Chapter 8 provides a detailed look at the struggle in 2000 to create a new conservative Constitutional Court, thus redefining the Supreme Court of Israel as an informal alternative form of governance that could oversee the protection of human rights in Israel. Chapter 9 discusses how between 1999 and 2007, the informal rule of "who governs" in Israel enshrined the

Supreme Court as the arbiter of controversial issues concerning human rights in Israel. In a continuation of this analysis, Chapter 10 elaborates on the Supreme Court of Israel as an agenda setter by examining three Israeli legal cases. In that chapter, we elaborate on the role of the Supreme Court in courts that deal with military law in the region. We also analyze the Interrogation Case of 1999 and the case known as the Land Decision Case of 2002. Chapter 11 discusses in detail the debate over the High Court of Justice's relationship with the Knesset (the Israeli parliament) and proposes a multi-level arrangement for the two institutions. Finally, Chapter 12 draws conclusions and outlines the implications of the study.

2

The Intervention of the Israeli High Court of Justice in Government Decisions: An Empirical, Quantitative Study with Paradoxical Results

There is a wide variety of literature about the relationship between the Israeli High Court of Justice (HCJ) and politics in Israel. The legal and political literature examines the role of the HCJ in various contexts: as part of a ruling elite (Unger, 1975; Mackinnon, 1989; Hirschl, 2001; Barzilai, 2003), as an interest group (Cowan, 1958; Schubert, 1985), and as a special kind of bureaucrat within certain structural conditions (Gely and Spiller, 1990; Segal, 1997; Epstein and Knight, 1998; Cornell and Gillman, 1999). Some scholars stress the contribution of the Supreme Court to societal equilibrium (Parsons, 1962; Nonet, 1976), whereas others stress the cultural and political factors that contribute to the limited role played by the Court (Rosenberg, 1991; Barzilai, 1998, 1999).

In the case of Israel, scholars stress the inability to govern, which is characterized primarily by the decline in the power of political parties and the ascendance of individualist values in the public's attitude toward the authorities (Doron, 1986; Edelman, 1994; Barzilai, 1999; Dror, 2001; Arian, Nachmias, and Amir, 2002; Mautner, 2002). Furthermore, the literature also includes studies that used the quantitative empirical method to assess the HCJ's decision making. This line of research began with American researchers who proposed conducting empirical studies to learn about the actual influence of judicial institutions. Several such studies were conducted in the United States (Schubert, 1974; Segal and Spaeth, 1993; Epstein and Knight, 1998) as well as in Israel (Shachar and Gross, 1996; Shachar, Gross, and Harris, 1996; Gross and Shachar 1999; Dotan and Hofnung, 2001; Salzberger, 2003; Shachar, Gross, and Goldschmidt, 2004; Dotan and Hofnung, 2005; Hofnung and Weinshall-Margel, 2010; Sommer, 2010). The goal of the studies was to determine certain aspects of the Court's work such as the extent of response to petitions, the issue of discourse and controversy in rulings, the assigning of judges, and so forth. The chosen methodology was based on quantitative analyses of measurable variables from the rulings and decisions of the HCJ in the belief that such an approach would allow us to base our conclusions on empirical data as opposed to intuition (which cannot be validated) (Shachar, Gross, and Goldschmidt, 2004: 255). Although quantitative research is unable to encompass all of the aspects of the Supreme Court's behavior when it operates as the HCJ, it is nevertheless informative, as Eli Salzberger (2003) claims. Moreover, in reality, only a small number of high-profile rulings receive public attention, far fewer than the number of decisions actually handed down. Rulings that attract such attention do not reflect the full picture of the HCJ's work or its relationships with other authorities. For instance, Eli Salzberger claims that, "A judge seen as having a liberal reputation in penal policy as a result of a sole ruling or a couple of rulings where she adopted the liberal position might actually hold a conservative position in criminal law (statistically speaking)" (Salzberger, 2003: 553).

This book continues the empirical, quantitative line of research regarding the HCJ's intervention in the government's decision making. Literature in Israel on this topic lacks such an analysis – one that uses a quantitative methodology. The measured variables are as follows:

1. The extent of the caseload in the Supreme Court.
2. The number of petitions against the government in the HCJ between 2000 and 2006.
3. The relative percentage of petitions against the government in the HCJ between 2000 and 2006.
4. The distribution of petitions filed with the HCJ against the government (by ministers).
5. The distribution of petitions filed with the HCJ against the government (by judicial results).

Salzberger criticizes Shachar, Harris, and Gross (1996) because they based their research on specific rulings instead of the general collection of the High Court's rulings:

> The database compiled by the lawyers' chamber is a biased collection of High Court rulings. The choice of rulings is based on the conventional attributes (in other words, the rulings chosen are either well-reasoned,

> containing interesting legal disputes, or constitute legal innovations). However, the rulings that are not published and comprise the majority might provide a truer view of the High Court's work. (Salzberger, 2003: 554)

The importance of quantitative data gathering and analysis, albeit partial, was mentioned in Yoav Dotan's research:

> Investigation of the data concerning pre-petitions is not a simple job . . . the existing cases in the HCJ archives lack many details regarding this or that procedure. Nevertheless, we haven't given up on the attempt to draw some quantitative conclusions – partial and lacking as they might be – regarding the pre-HCJ procedures during the research period. This has been done by conducting a sample check of the cases found during the research in the departmental archive. Due to the fact that the sample included only the cases in the departmental archive as well as the lack of information in some of the cases, the data is to be considered preliminary. (Dotan, 2004: 181)

2.1. ON THE METHOD OF THE QUANTITATIVE STUDY

We examined petitions filed against ministers via the HCJ alone as opposed to the ones filed via administrational courts (small HCJ) or the procedures discussed in the Supreme Court in its function as a court of appeals. We began our research with the data published in the courts' report. However, given that the courts' report samples major rulings only, we decided to broaden the sample based on two additional databases, Takdin and Nevo, which include about 90 percent of all rulings as well as the HCJ's petitions. The petitions sampled were the ones in which the answering party was a minister, a minister's representative, or the government (hereinafter: the government).

The sample included a total of 2,869 petitions in the period beginning in 2000 and ending in 2006. This period was chosen for a number of reasons. First, in 2000, the court law was passed, which established administrational courts (small HCJ)[1] intended to reduce the caseload in

[1] The Administrational Courts Law (2000) has given district courts the authority to discuss administrational issues previously discussed in the HCJ (small HCJ). Administrational issues are defined according to paragraph 2 of the law as a dispute between an administrational authority and an individual. Paragraph 5 defines the topics on which the administrational court is authorized to rule. Examples of such topics include administrational petitions against the decision of an authority in cases of appointments according to the first amendment (i.e., property taxes, education, business licensing, local authorities), administrational appeals according to the second amendment (i.e.,

the Supreme Court and the HCJ. Moreover, this was an attempt to institute a new procedure – petitions were to be filed with district courts that functioned as administrational courts – instead of the HCJ. Second, studies conducted by several researchers, including Eran Vigoda-Gadot, Fany Yuval, and Shlomo Mizrahi, demonstrated that from 2000 to 2006, there was a decline in public trust in the Supreme Court (Vigoda-Gadot and Yuval, 2000–2004; Vigoda-Gadot and Mizrahi, 2005–2006). Normally, one would expect this decline to influence the number of petitions filed with the HCJ.[2]

The mean annual number of petitions was 514, approximately 5 percent of the petitions filed in a given year. For instance, in the year 2000, 9,681 petitions were filed to the Supreme Court (according to the courts' report – including civil appeals and criminal appeals, administrative appeals on decisions of administrational courts and petitions to the HCJ); 289 of them were petitions to the HCJ against the government. In 2006, 11,028 petitions were filed to the Supreme Court (according to the courts' report), 537 of them were petitions to the HCJ against the government. Note that we found it hard to locate a single official source. A comparison of preliminary sources – the courts' report, the HCJ's section in the law department, the Nevo database, and the Takdin database – yielded several gaps in information. For instance, according to the courts' report, in 2000, there were 9,681 petitions filed with the Supreme Court, while the Takdin database indicated there were 8,235. Moreover, we found methodological differences between these databases. For instance, according to the statistical data in the courts' report, the column of HCJ procedures includes petitions by prisoners entitled "appeals by prisoner" as well as petitions entitled "different requests HCJ" or "HCJ procedures." The current research attempted to isolate the petitions entitled HCJ, so our sample included a total of 2,869 petitions.

appeals of decisions by communal associations, the appeals committee on sewage taxes, certain decisions about planning and construction law), as well as administrational appeals for civilian aid in cases included in the third amendment such as public tenders. Any administrational issue that is not included in the preceding list is to be discussed in the HCJ. In addition, an administrational court can pass each matter to the HCJ if it seems to be a matter of special public importance.

[2] For a review of explanations regarding the trend in which Israeli parties and individual politicians have often turned to the courts for intervention in national and internal party affairs, government policies, and even in parliamentary procedures, see Yoav Dotan and Menachem Hofnung, "Legal Defeats – Political Wins: Why Do Elected Representatives Go to Court?" *Comparative Political Studies*, vol. 38(1), 2005, pp. 75–103.

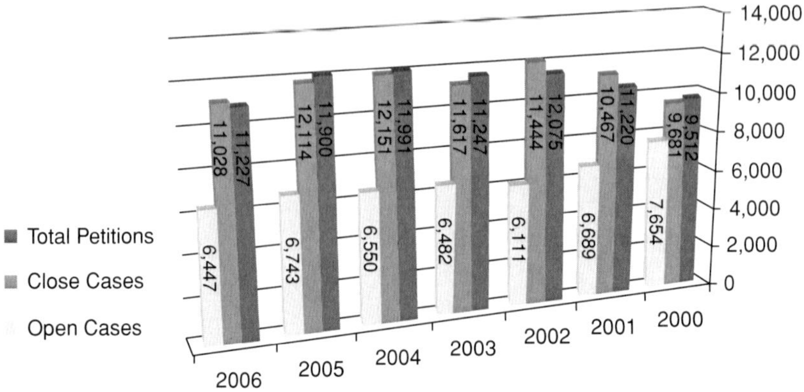

FIGURE 2.1. The extent of the caseload in the Supreme Court.

Figures 2.1, 2.2, and 2.3 are based on the courts' report, which also includes petitions entitled "appeals by prisoner" and "different requests HCJ" under "HCJ procedures." They are also based on the Takdin database, which includes additional cases that reached the Supreme Court, including civil or criminal appeals of which the government or its members are a part. As a result, the number of the petitions discussed in the HCJ against the government includes a total of 3,300 petitions. This sample is larger by 431 petitions than the sample we used in the current research.

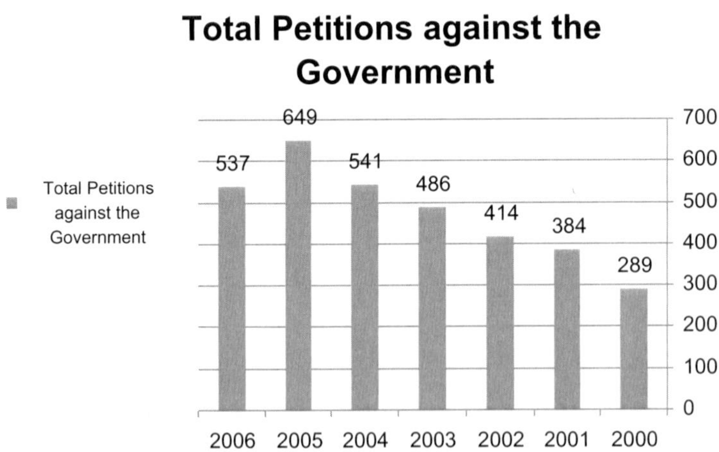

FIGURE 2.2. The number of petitions against the government in the HCJ between 2000 and 2006.

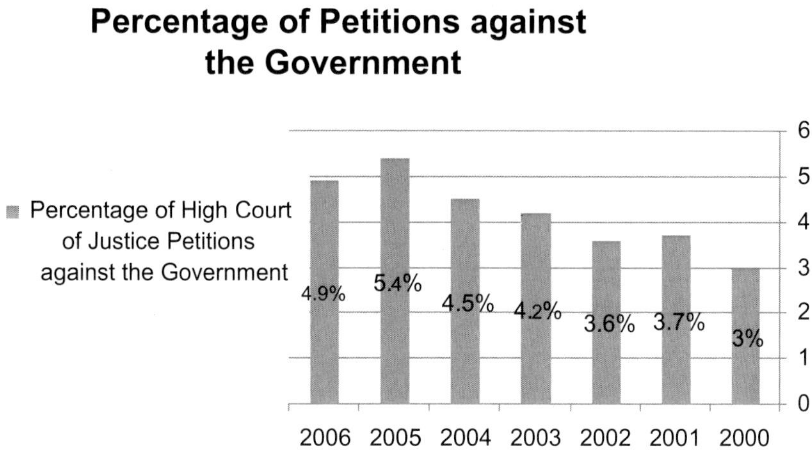

FIGURE 2.3. The relative percentage of petitions against the government in the HCJ between 2000 and 2006, of the total number of cases discussed in the Supreme Court.

2.2 RESEARCH FINDINGS

General

The mean annual caseload during this period was 11,236 petitions. The mean number of open cases annually was 6,542, and the mean number of closed cases annually was 11,336. The data show that the year 2001 marks an increase in the Supreme Court's caseload, which subsequently declined and tapered off. However, in comparison with the year 2000, there is a decline in open cases.

Figure 2.2 presents the total petitions against the Government in the HCJ between 2000 and 2006. The data are taken from the courts' report, from the court's administration, from the Nevo database, and from freely available information. Figure 2.2 presents the number of petitions filed with the HCJ against the government between 2000 and 2006. For instance, in 2000, there were about 300 petitions filed, as opposed to about 704 in 2005. In general, note the increase in cases of this kind discussed in the HCJ between 2000 and 2006.

Figure 2.3 presents the relative percentage of petitions against the Government in the HCJ, between 2000 and 2006, of the total number of cases discussed in the Supreme Court. The data are taken from the Nevo and courts' report databases. These are petitions against the government (petitions responded to by a minister or a deputy minister, or the government). Note the increase in the relative percentage of the petitions against ministers as a percentage of the total number of petitions to the HCJ, despite the fact that during this period district courts had become administrative ones. For instance, in 2000, the percentage of petitions filed with the HCJ against ministers was 3 percent, approximately 289, whereas in 2005, it was 5.4 percent, approximately 649 petitions. In this case, there was an increase in both the number of petitions filed between 2000 and 2006 and the percentage of them that were filed against the government.

The study commenced with the issue of case overload in the HCJ, which has been an ongoing problem. We found that from 2000 to 2006, the number of HCJ cases dealing with government issues rose by 100 percent. This increase is of interest for a number of reasons. First, in 2000, the court law was passed, which established administrational courts (small HCJ)[3] intended to reduce the caseload in the Supreme Court and the HCJ. Moreover, this law was an attempt to institute a new procedure – petitions were to be filed with district courts that functioned as administrational courts – instead of the HCJ. Our data show that this hoped-for improvement was not achieved. Second, studies conducted by several researchers, including Eran Vigoda-Gadot, Fany Yuval, and Shlomo Mizrahi, demonstrated that from 2000 to 2006, there was a decline in public trust in the Supreme Court (Vigoda-Gadot and Yuval, 2000–2004; Vigoda-Gadot and Mizrahi, 2005–2006). One would expect this decline to influence the number of petitions filed with the HCJ, but we found that the opposite was true. For instance, there were 1,700 petitions filed with the HCJ in 2000 out of 9,681 cases opened in the Supreme Court, meaning that 17.5 percent of the cases in the Supreme Court dealt with government decisions.[4] Moreover, about 289 petitions were discussed in the HCJ in 2000, whereas those concerning the government constituted 3 percent of all of the cases discussed in the Supreme Court. In 2005, however, the percentage of petitions against the government was about 5.4 percent of all of the cases discussed in that year, comprising a total of 649 petitions against the government.

The following diagram (Figure 2.4) presents the distribution of petitions filed with the HCJ against the government (by ministers), 2000–2006. The data that appear in Figure 2.4 are based on 2,869 petitions

[3] See footnote 1.

[4] Data obtained from the research department of the court administration.

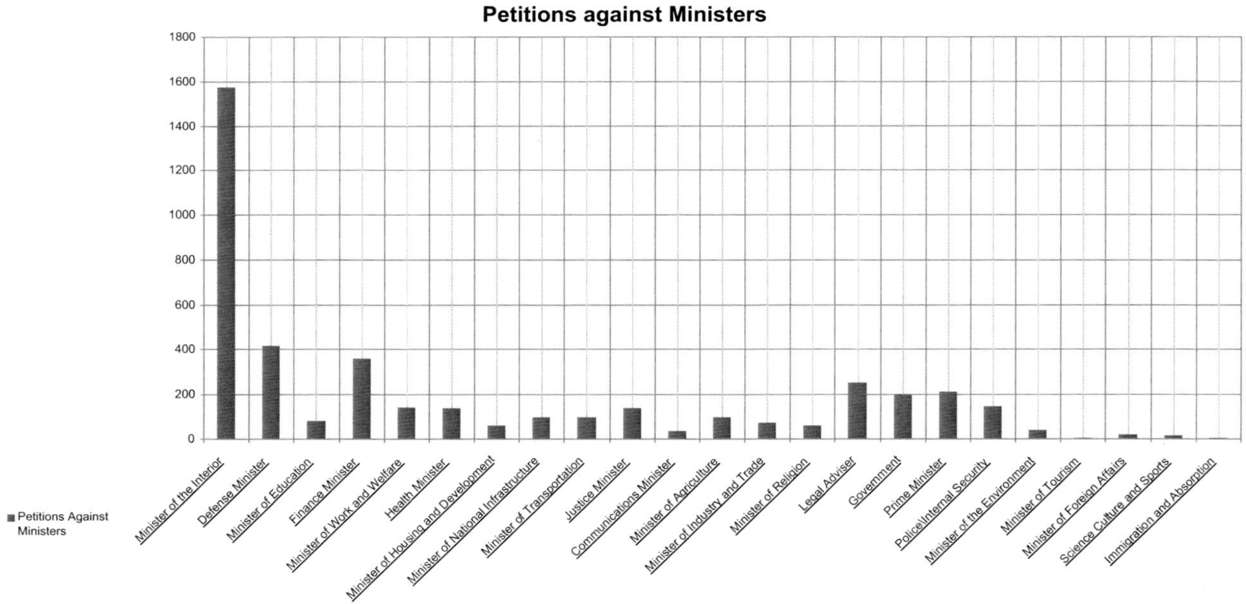

FIGURE 2.4. The distribution of petitions filed with the HCJ against the government (by ministers).

filed with the HCJ against ministers in the years 2000 through 2006. Most of the petitions against ministers are directed at the Minister of the Interior as opposed to other ministers. Petitions against this post pertain to the topics of matrimony, personal status, and citizenship, according to the Law of Return (*Hok haShvut* – in Hebrew). Petitions include instances of family reunions – that is, petitions filed as a result of the Ministry of the Interior's decision not to grant a permanent residence permit to one of the spouses after marriage; this area concerns Jews, Arabs, and people of other religions or nationalities. Similarly, there is the question of granting citizenship to children born to parents of whom one has Israeli citizenship whereas the other does not. Other petitions pertain to local authorities and the Ministry of the Interior's decisions that harmed a given community, either with regard to resource allocation and services or decisions regarding new regulations it implemented. Numerous petitions involved several ministers even when the petition was filed mainly against one or more of them, depending on the context in which the appellants submitted their pleas. For instance, in the case of family reunions, if a prospective bride is an Israeli citizen and the prospective groom is a citizen of a questionable security "region," and they wish to be married, and the Ministry of the Interior refuses because of security issues, the petitioner will usually file a complaint against the Minister of the Interior and the Defense Minister.

The following diagram (Figure 2.5) presents the distribution of petitions filed with the HCJ against the government (by legal outcomes) 2000-2006. The sample includes 2,869 petitions to the HCJ from 2000 through 2006.

The investigation was conducted according to several criteria:

1. Petition Accepted

Petitions accepted include all of the petitions that granted aid to the petitioner, for instance, cancellation, return, compensation, refund, or change of regulations.

2. Petition Retracted

Petitions retracted – on the part of the petitioner or the state – refer to the situation in which one of the sides decides not to continue the suit, usually owing to a settlement that renders the need for a discussion irrelevant.

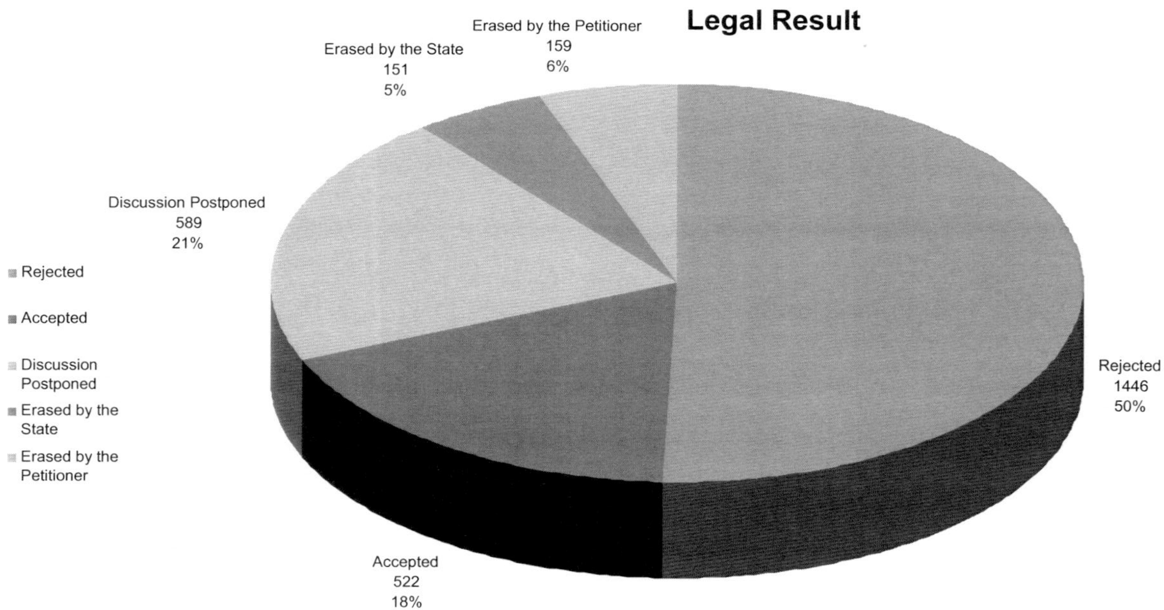

FIGURE 2.5. The distribution of petitions filed with the HCJ against the government (by judicial results).

For instance, a petition for citizenship to the Minister of the Interior was postponed to a later date. During that period, the circumstances changed, rendering the need for a discussion irrelevant, or the Ministry of the Interior approved the request.

3. Petition Rejection

The difference between petition rejection and retraction is that rejection does not allow the petitioner to file the same petition again – the ruling is conclusive. Retraction means that the petitioner may file the same petition again, because the retraction is not initiated by the court.

4. Discussion Postponed

The court may decide to postpone the discussion of a petition, but this does not necessarily constitute a ruling. For instance, the decision to transfer the discussion to a panel of three judges involves postponing the discussion to a later date. (Note that the discussion might be postponed to delay the procedures until a certain condition renders the need for a ruling irrelevant. For example, awaiting the decision of the Ministry of the Interior on the matter of citizenship would result in retraction of the petition). Note that the HCJ rejects approximately 50 percent of the appeals made to it.

We found that despite the increase in petitions against the government, the HCJ intervened less in the government's work than in the past. Only in 18 percent of the petitions did it intervene and accept the petition. One may argue that this 18 percent demonstrates a high level of intervention by the Supreme Court, but, in fact, the court rejected about 50 percent of the petitions that were made to it. Another 21 percent were postponed, and 11 percent were retracted either by the state or by the petitioner.

2.3 FROM A DESCRIPTIVE ANALYSIS TO A PATH-DEPENDENT ANALYSIS: FROM INTERVENTION TO INVOLVEMENT

Given our findings, one might claim that, contrary to popular belief, the Supreme Court exercises very limited intervention into decisions of the Israeli government, even though others may claim that the opposite is true. These findings are mainly descriptive, and we do not pretend to provide an in-depth analysis of the reasons for the findings. Furthermore, the findings do not contribute to a more important question regarding the extent of the involvement of the Supreme Court in social and political affairs. However, they tell us an interesting story. For example, Figure 2.4 demonstrates that most of the petitions against ministers are directed at the Minister of the Interior as opposed to other ministers, and focus on cases of matrimony, personal status, and citizenship, according to the Law of Return (*Hok haShvut* – in Hebrew). Such petitions are not what we call presentational cases, triggering controversies over the role and place of the HCJ in Israel, as did court rulings such as the Interrogation Case (*Public Committee against Torture in Israel v. The State of Israel* – 1999) and the Land Decision Case (*New Discourse Movement et al. v. Minister of National Infrastructure et al.* – 2002). Such paradoxical and, to some extent, contrary results regarding the intervention of the Supreme Court in Israeli government policy lead us to an institutional–process analysis of the relationship between the Supreme Court and the Israeli Knesset as a means of explaining the empirical findings (Epstein, Ho, King, and Segal, 2005: 110).

In recent years, Israeli society and its political system have experienced a deepening crisis evident in increasing social divisions and the inability of the political system to formulate and implement systematic policy plans. This phenomenon, which is often termed *non-governability*, intensifies the public's dissatisfaction with the political system and even with the democratic system. Under these conditions, players adopt strategies that will maximize their own self-interests. One central strategy is intense litigation with the expectation that the HCJ would solve the problem and provide policy decisions. The public turns to the Court because, given its image as a stable and objective entity, it has traditionally enjoyed high levels of trust and legitimacy. However, this process positions the Supreme Court as a central player in the political scene with significant influence on policy-making processes (see, for example, Hofnung, 1997; Barzilai, 1998).

This book describes the systemic crisis in Israeli society as expressed in the problem of non-governability and analyzes its causes and results. The analysis is novel in two important aspects. First, the book offers a theoretical framework, based on shared mental models and political entrepreneurship theory, that explains the political role of the judicial system in general and the Supreme Court in particular, as well as their functions in the policy-making process. Second, the empirical analysis will explain the processes leading to the positioning of the Israeli Supreme Court as a central political player in controversial issues; we will discuss Court rulings and other related issues such as nominating procedures. Moreover, this twofold analysis will allow us to draw conclusions about the future of Israeli democracy and the required social and institutional changes.

3

Law and Politics: Theoretical Aspects

The disciplines of law and politics include a wide variety of concepts and theories, so there are several ways to analyze the relationships between these fields. Hans Kelsen (1945) defines law as a whole set of norms aimed at regulating relations between citizens themselves and between citizens and the authorities. At its core, law is normative, and its origin is the basic norm of the state. The degree to which the law is autonomous relates to the existence of higher values and the extent to which these values impose limitations on the totality of the law. In a similar vein, politics in its original meaning relates to a whole set of phenomena – both social and political – as they existed in ancient Greece.

However, in modern reality, the area of politics is usually interpreted much more narrowly, including only the public sphere. Actually, there are two main approaches to the concept of politics. The institutional approach suggests that all events, phenomena, and roles that have some interaction with the authorities are political. The functional approach distinguishes the aspect of the political role from other social roles, thus defining the political system as the whole set of political roles in society. The uniqueness of the political factor is expressed either in its special characteristics or in its special goal. Weber (1947) defines politics as the aspiration to take part in government or to acquire influence over the division of power. Other definitions of politics are: politics as shaping society and social order, politics as conflict resolution, and politics as responsible for the authoritative division of resources.

It follows that the relationship between the legal and the political fields is not trivial. In effect, there are two basic approaches for analyzing these relations: the formal approach and the inter-disciplinary approach. According to the formal approach, law and politics are two disciplines that are categorically different from one another. The law is an independent, systematic, logical, objective, neutral, and professional entity. It is created based on professional principles that can be evaluated objectively and is therefore free of values. The law and the legal discipline exist in a different sphere than the social sphere, meaning that the principles of law and the legal profession can be transferred from one society to another without the need for special adaptations.

The inter-disciplinary approach views all human and social sciences as a whole. Given that the differences between the sub-disciplines are rather vague, the analysis of human and social reality should consider all of them and the interactions between them. According to this approach, the law and the legal discipline can be understood only in the context of the social and political reality in which they exist.

The relationship between law and politics has been studied since the days of the ancient Greeks, but with various transformations. The traditional literature discussed the place and role of law in human society, usually from a normative perspective. Judges and the judicial system were an integral part of the government, so the academic discussion related to abstract aspects of the law. However, in modern times with the development of the principle of separation of powers, the tension between the political and the judicial systems has increased, so studies have focused on this issue. In the second half of the twentieth century, as law became dominant in daily life, the study of law and politics became a central field in the social sciences. Israeli society is not exceptional in this regard. In recent years it has experienced two parallel processes: the increased dominance of the Supreme Court and the judicial system in political and social reality, and an expansion of the public and academic debate about the interaction between law and politics.

This chapter discusses these issues in three stages. In the first part, we present the normative approaches that connect political and legal thought. In the second part, we critically review the central approaches to the analysis of law and politics. The third part will critique the central arguments about law and politics in Israel. We will argue that neither the formalistic, legal approach nor the sociological approach provides a comprehensive explanation of the socio-politico-legal reality in Israel.

3.1 POLITICAL THOUGHT AND LEGAL THOUGHT

Traditionally, political and legal thought were strongly connected because law was part of the political system. Modern political thought is usually understood as composed of two main streams: the republican orientation and the liberal orientation. Republican thought focuses on laws and constitutions, whereas liberal thought emphasizes the concept of rights. Accordingly, republican thinkers emphasize the concept of citizenship, which is collectivist in its nature, whereas liberal thinkers concentrate on individualism. Historically, republican thought evolved in continental Europe, whereas liberal thought emerged in Britain beginning in the seventeenth century. In the United States, there is an interesting attempt to integrate both approaches through public choice theory, as will be explained in the next chapter. We now discuss the place of law in the republican and liberal approaches.

Republican Thought

Republican thought is founded on the philosophy of Aristotle (1948), who in the fourth century BCE first presented a systematic method for analyzing the state and politics. This method concentrates on an empirical examination using a comparative and relativist approach. These principles also guided thinkers such as Montesquieu (1949) and Tocqueville (1962).

Aristotle based his philosophy on the idea that the law, rather than any human being, is the ultimate sovereign. The ideal state should include democratic components in the sense that it is a community of equal human beings aspiring for the best possible life. The state ceases to be constitutional when the gaps between the community members increase to the degree that they do not have the same virtue. This was the idea from which the concept of citizenship in modern society evolved. According to Aristotle, the law is superior because it represents rationality and objectivity. Therefore, the wise ruler recognizes its superiority rather than regarding the law as being imposed on the ruler.

A constitutional government, according to Aristotle, includes three central elements. First, it serves the public and the general interest. Second, the government rules by constitutional arrangements. Third, the members of the community accept the laws and are willing to obey the authority. The law is central because it represents communal experience and, by implication, the additive wisdom of all of its members. This is also the reason that Aristotle emphasizes the importance of norms, favoring the customary law over the written law. It follows that Aristotle represents a conservative approach in the sense that customary law best represents communal wisdom and therefore should be adopted as much as possible.

In the spirit of Aristotle, thinkers such as Machiavelli (1961), Rousseau (1984), and Burke (1965) can be characterized as belonging to the republican approach. However, Montesquieu and Tocqueville changed the focus of analysis from laws and constitutions to political culture and behavior. In his book, *The Spirit of Law* (1949), Montesquieu developed a methodology that connects the political culture and behavior of a given society to the laws and political institutions that fit this society best. In that way, he proposed a comparative methodology that would enable constitutional reforms depending on the political culture. At the center of this methodology stands the principle of separation of powers, which was based on the British system. The role of the legislator is to transform the general principles of justice into laws. Principles of justice, which may be relative and therefore differ between societies, predate the positive law, meaning that the spirit of laws should correspond to the social, economic, political, and religious atmosphere in a given society. Thus, Montesquieu developed a methodology for analyzing and composing a whole constitutional framework that includes both formal and informal conduct.

These methodological principles guided Tocqueville (1962) in his philosophical-anthropological study of American society. He identified the sovereignty of the people as a guiding principle in the society and constitution. The separation of powers, the federal structure, and various interest groups comprise the rule of the people. Furthermore, Tocqueville identifies three important characteristics of the judicial authority. First, the American judge rules only when there is disagreement. Second, the American judge rules in isolated cases. Third, he or she does not initiate appeals, but judges only cases brought before him or her. Thus, the strength of American judges lays in the constitution, which is the basis of their decisions. Tocqueville also recognizes that the spirit of the constitution corresponds to important characteristics of American society.

Liberalism

Liberal thought emphasizes the role of individuals in social, political, and economic processes. Originally, liberal philosophers attempted to develop a normative theory of the state using deductive reasoning. A core assumption in this approach is the existence of natural rights. The law puts constraints on these rights and the central normative question concerns the legitimate and proper extent of these constraints. Parallel to the development of liberal thought, rational legal thinkers of the seventeenth and eighteenth centuries, who wanted to distance themselves from the church, attempted to base the law on universal rational principles (Perlman, 1984). These attempts were the grounds for the evolution of a formalistic approach in legal studies.

Starting with Hobbes (1588–1679), liberal thought developed the idea that reasons for the law and its limits should be looked for in the "state of nature." Hobbes suggested that natural law is one that evolved from the specter of people warring against one another. In order to avoid such a distasteful prospect, people agree to grant their rights to a powerful Leviathan, or the state, by making a social contract with it. Within this mutual commitment, both the sovereign and the subjects accept the idea of central authority in exchange for security and confidence. Hence, prior to the social state, there was no justice or law, because these are established by society and the state. Justice is a function of the sovereign's rules and legislation (Strauss, 1959; Macpherson, 1962; Hobbes, 1985).

However, with regard to the positive law and the ideal view of its natural origin, Hobbes replaces the idealist view with a much more realistic approach, thus establishing the law on rational foundations rather than religious ones. Rationality is attributed, however, to the sovereign's actions, but Hobbes does not discuss the components and limitations of this rationality.

John Locke (1632–1704) suggests an alternative view of the state of nature to the one suggested by Hobbes. In Locke's theory, the state of nature is characterized by mutual understanding and respect for individual rights, understood as the right to life, freedom, and property. The need for the state arises due to the fact that there may be individuals who deviate from the general harmony, thereby threatening the natural rights of others. Thus, the state's goal is to defend individuals' natural rights from those who threaten them. To guarantee that the state uses its authority properly, Locke developed the idea of separation of powers: the legislative, executive, and judicial authorities. Thus, the judicial system should be separated from the other systems in order to guarantee citizens' natural rights. Montesquieu later developed this aspect of constitutional arrangements (Gough, 1950; Aaron, 1995; Locke, 1997).

In the nineteenth century, liberal thought shifted toward utilitarianism, which was first introduced by David Hume (1711–1776). He criticized the method of deducing certain principles from the hypothetical state of nature, suggesting instead that guiding principles be discerned from reality. Hume identified the principle of utility, arguing that because people follow this principle, a given social reality reflects social utility.

Therefore, there was no need to advance revolutionary changes. Hence, Hume's approach is conservative one.

Jeremy Bentham (1748–1832) and James Mill (1773–1836) saw the utilitarian approach as a proper tool for advancing political reforms. At the core of their approach stands the observation that individuals will do whatever causes happiness and will avoid actions that cause pain. The application of this principle on the macro level leads to the guiding utilitarian principle of maximum happiness for the maximum number of people in the formation of public policy and legislation. Thus, on the one hand, there are no natural rights. On the other hand, the law does not represent just some general ideas disconnected from society. The law is simply the outcome of a utilitarian calculation, and as such, it is a tool for achieving maximum happiness. However, because not all parameters in human life are measurable, the qualitative approach to utilitarianism was developed.

John Stuart Mill (1806–1873; 1984) developed the idea that society must include qualitative parameters rather than solely quantitative ones in its utilitarian considerations. He suggested the principle that a liberal state must be founded on a liberal society. He also attempted to identify the necessary conditions for the development of a liberal society: the principle of freedom of speech and the broad participation of individuals in public life. These mechanisms will increase the individuals' ability to maximize their utility, so that the society and the state will be both stable and efficient. These principles are not natural rights but rather the necessary conditions for a stable and healthy society. Therefore, the state must establish and defend them through a constitution.

To conclude, the various streams in political thought are characterized by a certain methodological approach – either individualistic or structural – and by normative conclusions – either liberal or conservative. However, there is no complete match between the methodologies and the normative conclusions, meaning that such categorizations may sometimes be confusing. Such confusion may arise particularly in inter-disciplinary approaches such as public choice theory, which is used extensively in this book. As will be explained in the next chapter, this theory combines methodological individualism and structural aspects in its positivistic analysis. Hence, public choice theory does not intuitively fall into one of the normative orientations discussed earlier. In the following section we discuss the major approaches for analyzing the relationship between law and politics since the Enlightenment era.

3.2. MAJOR APPROACHES FOR ANALYZING THE RELATIONSHIP BETWEEN LAW AND POLITICS

Until the end of the eighteenth century, legal systems were based on the rules of nature, which provided universal moral guidelines for what was called "Natural Law" (Rubinstein, 1996). However, these guidelines were too general to direct the daily functioning of human society and to handle the emergence of competing values such as private property and equality (Mensch, 1990). Therefore, the early nineteenth century saw the establishment of legal definitions and practices taken from positive law and compiled into old English Law. This positive law was based on common conventions and agreements that resulted from many court rulings, ultimately comprising Common Law. This collection of rules and laws that was based on common sense provided the practical rules that were missing in the Natural Law. Collections of rulings and interpretations such as those of Brakton (thirteenth century), Kook (seventeenth century), and Blackstone (eighteenth century) became the basis of English Common Law (Barzilai, 2003).

The rise of the Enlightenment movement in the seventeenth and eighteenth centuries and the development of liberal thought also affected the legal field. People began to view the law as a tool for advancing their interests. From the nineteenth century onward, the law was developed as a combination of Natural Law and Common Law, meaning that morality and utility were mixed. This approach is characterized as "legal positivism" where the law and the legal system are tools for neutral conflict resolution (Foeler, 1964; Ganz, 1989).

Legal positivism views the legal system as an autonomous system that should advance social coordination. The impartiality of the court, unaffected by social or political influences, gives judges the freedom to examine and criticize the other authorities. Judgment is made based on existing rulings, precedents, and laws, meaning that the role of judges is narrowed mainly to the interpretation of the legislators' intentions. The law is impersonal, hence, its legitimacy. Indeed, Hans Kelsen (1945) defined the principles of legal positivism within the framework of "pure legal theory," which deals only with the question of what the law is rather than what it should be like. Judicial norms are legal arrangements that are obligatory because they are established on the normative foundations of the system. However, Kelsen also suggested modifying classic legal positivism in the direction of what he termed the "literal interpretation school." This school also sees the law as a scientific theory, but it gives judges the freedom to choose between various interpretations of the law as long as the interpretation does not deviate from the original frame of the law (see also Hart, 1961; Posner, 1972; Blackstone, 1979; Dworkin, 1980; Treib, 1985). In effect, this school represents a transformation of legal positivism due to the freedom given to judges in interpreting the law. The interpretive role of judges thus requires us to analyze the factors influencing judges' decisions. The best tool for accomplishing this goal is a sociological analysis.

Sociological Approaches

The sociological approaches see the law and the legal system as social phenomena that should be analyzed using sociological methods. Such approaches range from those who view the law and the legal system as part of the instruments of the ruling class (Marxism), to those who view them as originating from common social rules independently of the state (Ehrlich, 2002), to others who view them as decisions made by state institutions (Llewellyn, 1962; Holmes, 1984). Generally, sociological studies of the law examine the efficiency of the positive law given the legislators' goals and social interests (Pound, 1999), compare the essence of legal norms with the practical behavior of those who execute the law (functionalism), and examine the law vis-à-vis social conflicts or divisions (Himma, 1998).

Within the formalistic sociological approaches we may distinguish between two central streams of thought: the institutional and the legalistic-functional. The institutional approach suggests that the analysis of legal documents, such as constitutions, will allow us to determine the relationship between the different authorities in a state. This approach was popular in the early stages of sociological analyses and does not consider many aspects and variables of reality (Durkheim, 1958).

The legalistic-functional approach suggests that the courts, the legal system in general, and lawyers in particular are integrated into a professional and structural solidarity, a solidarity that usually characterizes political systems. Such a structure contributes to social harmony and stability. In practice, however, courts do not necessarily stabilize social and political entities (Kelsen, 1945; Weber, 1947; Schmidhouser, 1992; Edelman, 1994). Furthermore, while this approach challenged the autonomous status of the court and the law, it did not challenge the superiority and sovereignty of the law.

Others view the Supreme Court as an interest group that attempts to advance its own sectorial goals (Schubert and Danelsky, 1969; Tapp and Levine, 1974; Schubert, 1985). From a sociological perspective, the Supreme Court is often viewed as contributing to a certain social equilibrium (Parsons, 1962; Becker, 1964; Black, 1972; Nonet, 1976). Parsons (1962) argues that because Supreme Court rulings are often on controversial issues, politicians and interest groups may try to restrain it. Indeed, Turk (1976) argues that the Supreme Court does not solve conflicts but, rather, creates and even intensifies existing conflicts. He identifies various conditions under which the law creates conflicts. Thus, most of the sociological literature does not regard the Supreme Court as a political player with an independent agenda. Such a view is more coherent in the approach of legal realism.

Legal Realism

The legal realism approach criticizes the theory of rights, arguing that the legal system cannot defend individual rights because, more often than not, they conflict with rather than complement one another. Therefore, defending rights is all about setting priorities that are neither universal nor objective, but, rather, are strongly connected to social, political, and historical reality. Hence, the judicial area is similar to other social systems where the law is a social and political product reflecting these influences (Barzilai, 2003).

According to legal positivism, judges hand down rulings that are neutral and objective and based on strict absolute rules. In contrast, legal realism suggests that judges not only describe reality but also influence and even change social reality through their rulings. Furthermore, judges have to prioritize rights on a certain scale that may not conform to an abstract theory of rights. Thus, the "truth" is relative to each case. Reality is interpreted and therefore newly created every time a decision is rendered. Given that judges are central players in this process, researchers have gradually concentrated on the personalities, history, ideological inclinations, and positions of judges regarding substantive issues in the legal field. This approach also influenced political science, thus encouraging the research on law and politics (Constable, 1994).

Therefore, according to legal realism, the judicial system is a necessary, complementary element of the legislative authority that has both judicial and political functions – to create harmony between judicial decisions based on legislation and the common views in a given social context (Perlman, 1984). This institutional hegemony derives its broad social and political legitimacy from three main sources: 1) symbolic legitimacy as understood in the ideal type of democracy; 2) diffuse legitimacy, meaning the structural and functional aspects of the court; and 3) public legitimacy. In order to keep this legitimacy, the Court prefers to rule according to the interests of the dominant political coalition and the majority will. By doing so, the Court adopts a policy of self-restraint and denies itself full autonomy (Barzilai, 1999).

Thus, legal realism rejects the existence of "objective truth" because the legal texts are relative to specific social-historical contexts. The judicial system is not superior to other systems in terms of stability. In other words, the court can be understood as a political institution aspiring to increase its political power. The law is shaped in accordance with the power of social groups acting to maximize their interests (Galanter, 1974; Grossman et al., 1998; Edelman and Suchman, 1999).

Post-Realism – Structural Emphasis

Like legal realism, post-realism also assumes that the judicial system is not objective but rather interacts with social reality. However, given this basic assumption, post-realist advocates take a critical approach, which views the judicial system as an integral part of the ruling elite and therefore serving specific interests rather than representing just and moral values (Barzilai, 2003).

Within the post-realist approach we can identify two major streams: judicial behavioralism and critical legal studies. Judicial behavioralism attempts to explain court rulings by analyzing the character and behavior of judges. Researchers in this tradition apply quantitative methods to analyze the background of judges, measuring variables such as education, religious inclination, political orientation, and other relevant characteristics (Epstein et al., 1994; Epstein and Knight, 1998). Naturally, the focus of this approach is on the individual judge.

In comparison, critical legal studies suggest that ruling bodies, groups, and individuals gain legitimacy through judicial institutions such as the Supreme Court (Unger, 1975; Kairy, 1990; Jabbari, 1992). The law and the judicial system are used by the ruling elite to institutionalize social norms that guarantee the elite dominance. It follows that maintaining dominance by legislation is possible as long as the law and the legal system are understood as objective entities free of any normative social context. Hence, the ways in which the law and the judicial system actually maintain social hegemony are covered by objective legal discourse (Hirschel, 1992). The Supreme Court is therefore understood as part of the ruling elite and serving the interests of that group (Mackinon, 1989). This means that the court acts to stabilize the system rather than serving as an agent of change. Furthermore, from time to time the Court rules in a way that opposes the interests of groups within the ruling elite. Such rulings often have significant public repercussions, enabling the Court to re-establish its legitimacy. In other words, the general public gets the impression that the Court is an independent and autonomous organization, increasing the Court's power and ability to rule in favor of the ruling elite. To conclude, the critical legal studies approach, which views the Court as an integral part of the ruling elite, attempts to expose the illusions embodied in concepts such as objective law and rulings (Barzilai, 2003).

Post-Realism – Individualistic Emphasis

The approaches analyzed so far generally suggest a sociological point of view. As will be explained in the next chapter, these approaches have two main shortcomings. First, by assuming that social structures determine individual behavior these approaches significantly marginalize the role of individuals and their impact on social reality. Second, this marginalization promotes a deterministic analysis. For example, according to the critical legal studies approach, the Court's rulings are completely determined by structural factors such as the composition of the ruling elite. If a specific judge deviates from this general line, this deviation is explained as instrumental for maintaining the power and legitimacy of the ruling elite. Thus, reality is used to justify the theory rather than vice versa. In the next chapter we develop an approach that emphasizes methodological individualism.

Indeed, those researching law and politics have gradually moved toward an individualistic approach. This tradition began with the studies of Pritchett (1948) and Murphy (1964), but only during the 1990s became central in the field of law and politics (Segal and Spaeth, 1993; Epstein et.al., 1994; Epstein and Walker, 1995; Barzilai and Sened, 1997; Baum, 1997; Epstein and Knight, 1998; Gilman, 1996–1997; Feeley and Rubin, 1998; Smith, 1998). These studies combine judges' preferences and strategies with extra-judicial structural and institutional influences, thus explaining the ways in which institutional structures shape judicial policy.

Researchers using the individualistic approach suggest both a positive and normative analysis of judicial independence. The positive analyses attempt to explain why judicial independence exists in democratic regimes, and the normative analyses try to explain why such judicial independence is required and justified (Salzberger, 2003). The traditional approach combines the positive and normative analyses, arguing that judicial independence exists because it prevents the misuse of state power. Judicial independence balances itself between the legislative and executive authorities, thus also reducing the rent-seeking activity of interest groups (Epstein, 1987; Macey, 1987). In contrast, the revisionist approach argues that judicial independence helps politicians increase their benefits by exchanging legislation for support from interest groups, a procedure that benefits both groups (Landes and Posner, 1975).

With regard to the traditional approach, it is not clear why politicians, who usually want to maximize their own interests, would delegate authority to the judicial system in a way that might reduce their power. With regard to the revisionist approach, it is not clear why independent judges would be loyal to the interests of legislators. Salzberger (2003) suggests that politicians delegate authority to the judicial system only when it helps them share responsibility or solve social problems and when the costs of such delegation are less than the benefits. This book discusses the tension between these approaches and suggests an explanation of the central role of the Supreme Court as a policy maker by combining structural, cultural, and individual parameters.

The individualistic-economic approach also studies judges' preferences and positions. From an individualistic (or rational choice) perspective, Supreme Court judges may certainly have interests independent of those of certain social groups or elites. Given that they are part of a bureaucratic organization, judges are most likely interested in preserving their organization's power and authority. However, due to the separation-of-powers principle that gives the Supreme Court a monopoly on interpreting the law, the Supreme Court is not an ordinary bureaucratic organization. Rather, due to its unique role vis-à-vis politicians and citizens alike, the Supreme Court is often a political player – either because the rules of the game define it as such, as for example in the United States, or as a result of sociopolitical processes that create incentives for the Supreme Court to become an active political player, as, for example, in Israel. Given that the Court's authority and the structure of the system differ from one country to another, it is difficult to make generalizations about the Court's behavior without referring to the structural variables in a given setting.

New positive theories of the judiciary suggest two widely accepted conceptions of Court behavior (Segal, 1997; Hausegger and Baum, 1999).

The "attitudinal model" argues that the justices vote for the positions most consistent with their personal policy preferences, because the institutional structures facing the Court allow for sincere voting (Segal and Spaeth, 1993). In contrast, rational choice theory views the High Court justices as players who act strategically to advance their preferences (Gely and Spiller, 1990; Eskridge and Frickey, 1994; Schwartz, Spiller, and Urbiztondo, 1994; Hausegger and Baum, 1999). To minimize the possibility of congressional override, justices often adjust the Court's doctrinal positions and do not vote according to their sincere preferences. Within this framework, Yadlin (2002) regards judicial activism as a strategic judicial move that attempts to increase the Court's independence and strengthen the norms derived from the Court's rulings.

Epstein and Knight (1998) found that in more than 50 percent of cases, judges change their decisions in ways that do not reflect their personal preferences. They conclude that judges generally follow their personal preferences but they are constrained by various structural factors – both intra-organizational interests such as the necessity to build coalitions and extra-organizational strictures such as the limitations placed on them by state players and the general public. Overall, however, judges strive to maximize their interests. In contrast to this study, Feeley and Rubin (1998) suggest that judges may change their attitudes and preferences due to structural and institutional influences.

Using a variety of tests, Segal (1997) compares the sincere and sophisticated models of voting behavior by Supreme Court justices by examining the votes of U.S. Supreme Court justices in statutory cases decided between 1947 and 1992. He finds some evidence of sophisticated behavior, but most tests suggest otherwise. Segal then concludes that justices overwhelmingly engage in rationally sincere behavior. In other words, justices are not sincere players by nature or due to their unique personality. Rather, when they adopt sincere behavior, it is because the institutional structures allow them to do so and still keep their interests unharmed. Segal limits his conclusions to the U.S. Supreme Court, noting that

> Courts in diverse institutional settings, however, may evidence precisely the type of behavior predicted by the models. One can readily imagine a spectrum along which the separation-of-powers model may be relatively true (a parliamentary system with strong party control over members and a single majority party; a judiciary without constitutional

> powers; judges without life tenure) or relatively false (a congressional system with decentralized power; a constitutional court; judges with life tenure). In sum, we should hardly be surprised if institutional structures matter. (Segal, 1997: 42)

It is thus clear how differences in structural conditions can explain differences in the behavior of Supreme Court judges.

It follows from Segal's distinctions that there is a whole spectrum of judicial behavior that depends on structural conditions. At one end of the spectrum, judges adopt a totally strategic behavior given extreme structural conditions of a parliamentary system with strong party control over party members, a single majority party, a judiciary without constitutional authorities, and judges without life tenure. Under such structural conditions, judges are so weak that they have to adjust their rulings to the politicians' preferences in order to retain their minimal power. Practically, the Supreme Court avoids judicial activism and restrains itself. At the other end of the spectrum, judges adopt a totally rationally sincere behavior given a congressional system with decentralized power, a constitutional court, and judges with life tenure. Under such structural conditions, judges are so strong that they can afford to behave sincerely without the fear of congressional override. Thus, in practical terms, the Supreme Court adopts judicial activism, meaning that it intervenes in political decisions that do not match its own views. Between both ends of the spectrum are a wide variety of structural combinations that can explain the level of judicial activism adopted in a given country.

However, the analysis presented so far does not consider the social and cultural factors influencing the relationship between politicians and the Supreme Court. The importance of these factors can be exemplified through a rough comparison between the United States and Israel. The structural conditions in the United States are close to the second end of the spectrum mentioned earlier, meaning that the U.S. Supreme Court adopts rationally sincere behavior that leads to judicial activism (Segal, 1997). In contrast, the structural conditions in Israel are close to the first end of the aforementioned spectrum. Israel has a parliamentary system with strong party control over its members. For many years it had a single majority party, and the judiciary does not have constitutional powers (Shetreet, 1994; Mautner, 2002). However, given these conditions, even though we would expect the Israeli Supreme Court to adopt strategic behavior and restrain itself, since the 1970s it has adopted an approach of judicial activism, increasing its involvement in policy making and in politicians' decisions. We argue that this behavior can be explained by socio-political processes and developments in Israeli political culture.

3.3. THE SUPREME COURT AND THE POLITICAL SYSTEM IN ISRAEL

The Israeli Supreme Court is one of the most significant political power groups in the country, yet its actual power is weaker than its potential power. In recent decades, the Supreme Court has gradually increased its involvement in public and political issues, taking a much more activist approach during the 1990s (Barzilai, 1999; Hofnung, 1999; Mautner, 2002). The number of appeals and bills of rights initiated by judges grew significantly, thus triggering controversies over the role and place of the High Court of Justice in Israel. This trend can be exemplified by Court rulings in cases such as the Interrogation Case (*Public Committee against Torture in Israel v. The State of Israel* – 1999) and the Land Decision Case (*New Discourse Movement et al. v. Minister of National Infrastructure et al.* – 2002). Furthermore, in many cases politicians themselves appeal to the Supreme Court, calling for its intervention in the activity of the legislative and executive branches. By doing so, they actually weaken the political system and ultimately their own power. This behavior seems to contradict politicians' self-interest.

Specifically, Court rulings in cases such as the Moshavim Case (*United Mizrahi Bank v. Migdal Cooperative Village* – 1995), the Israel Investment Managers' Case (*The Israel Investment Managers' Office v. The Minister of Finance* – 1997), and the Zemach Case (*Zemach v. The Minister of Defense* – 1999) illustrate the transformation in the delicate relations between the legal and the political systems. In these cases the Supreme Court, which does not have constitutional authority of any kind, decided to abolish a parliamentary law, thus signaling its activist approach. This activism was also expressed in the flexible attitude toward the question of standing and the Court's willingness to hear appeals in areas that had been left to social bargaining in the past. This willingness also led to several debated rulings including the cases of Ka'adan (*Ka'adan v. Israel Land Authority* – 1999), Alice Miller (*Miller v. The Minister of Defense* – 1994), and the recruitment of yeshiva students (*Ressler v. The Minister of Defense* – 1998).

Thus, the central questions to be discussed in this book are: Why has the Supreme Court felt obliged to engage in such activism? Why has the Court changed its policy of self-restraint toward activism? Finally, why has the political system permitted such activism and political intervention by the Court? In this section we discuss the answers that the legal and sociological analysts provide to these questions. In the next chapter we suggest an alternative analysis based on public choice theory.

Explanations of Judicial Activism in Israel – the Legal Approach

The question of judicial activism in Israel stirs up major controversy among legal scholars who concentrate on formalistic aspects of the system. A central claim maintains that the Israeli Supreme Court (or High Court of Justice – HCJ) is not activist but rather adopts an approach of self-restraint. This claim is supported by the fact that the HCJ has abolished only two clauses in two laws since the beginning of what the Court's president, Aharon Barak, has called the "constitutional revolution." One clause was abolished in the law regarding investment consultants and the other in the law pertaining to courts martial. Many of the legal scholars in Israel argue that this small number of legal abolishments signifies an approach of self-restraint rather than activism.

This behavior is usually explained by the fact that the Court defined a "substantive damage" in fundamental rights or values as a major criterion for abolishing a law. Segal (2000) argues that this formal criterion actually demonstrates that the Court actually avoids legal criticism on legislation. However, this argument does not explain why the HCJ defined this criterion in the first place, nor does it consider the interpretive role of the Court (see also Barak, 1987; Barak, 1992; Barak, 1998; Barak, 2000). In practice, the HCJ defined this criterion, and the interpretation whether a certain case falls in this definition will be done also by the Court. In other words, legal terminology can be interpreted by the Court according to its interests or ideology, so that the Court's behavior is determined by one legal term or another. Good examples are the legal terms "standing" and "justice-ability," which were interpreted conservatively in the past, but since the 1980s have been liberally interpreted. The term "standing" refers to the right to be heard by the HCJ. During the 1950s and 1960s, people who filed a petition were required to show that they had a real and direct personal interest in the issue, and the courts were very strict in interpreting this requirement. Similarly, the Court interpreted the question of whether a given appeal could be judged in court very strictly, often deciding that it was a matter for political decision making. As mentioned, since the 1980s, these two criteria have been interpreted very broadly, meaning that they no longer serve as an effective filtering mechanism (Gavison, Kremnitzer, and Dotan, 2000).

Another legal argument maintains that the Israeli parliament (Knesset) adopts an approach of legislative restraint supervised by the parliament's legal adviser. Rubinstein (Shahar, 2001) argues that many conflicts between the HCJ and the Knesset are avoided because the parliament's legal adviser supervises legislation by checking its compatibility with the basic laws. Therefore, the important stage of checking the constitutionality of laws is actually done in the parliament prior to the enactment of the legislation, thus marginalizing the role of the HCJ. Rubinstein suggests that legislative restraint in cases such as the bill regarding the construction of the trans-Israel highway (1994), the bill regarding real estate agents (1992), as well as the bill regarding motorized vehicle insurance (1996) created a situation where the HCJ did not have enough opportunities to intervene in legislation. Therefore, it engaged in what was de facto judicial restraint.

However, the public discourse regarding judicial activism is much broader than the question of abolishing laws. Most of the appeals and the controversial rulings deal with social and political issues that have been traditionally solved through political or social bargaining. Examples of such issues include the recruitment of yeshiva students (HCJ 910/86. *Ressler v. Minister of Defence;* HCJ 3267/97. *Ressler v. Minister of Defence*; Tal Commission, 2000), the closing of Bar-Ilan Street in Jerusalem on Saturdays and holidays (1999), the recruitment of women for a flight course in the army (HCJ 4541/94. *Alice Miller v. Minister of Defence*), the right of women to pray as they choose at the Western Wall (1999), and of the rights of Arab citizens to acquire property in Jewish communities (HCJ 698/95. *Ka'adan v. Israel Land Administration*). In such cases, the involvement of the parliament's legal adviser is irrelevant, whereas the issues were much more controversial than the examples cited by Rubinstein.

The arguments suggested by legal scholars may be also understood in a social-political context. Politicians and social activists alike who see judicial activism as damaging the rule of law as well as the principle of separation of powers often call for the establishment of a constitutional court. According to this view, such a court is expected to represent the various sectors in society as well as the proper balance between democratic and Jewish values. Given this atmosphere, the judicial system attempts to defend the status of the Supreme Court, thus shaping an approach of "defending the judiciary." By arguing that the Supreme Court has not adopted an activist approach but rather an approach of self-restraint, legal experts attempt to show that no constitutional reform is required. Furthermore, some of them call on the Court to adopt a much more activist approach (Shahar, 2001).

Such legal arguments may also damage the legitimacy of the Supreme Court because they create antagonism and the impression that there are hidden agendas (Shamir, 1995). The problem intensifies when legal scholars interpret these arguments differently, creating the impression that their main goal is defending the Court using any possible justification, regardless of its consistency. The damage inflicted by this antagonism is evident in the drop in the public's trust in the Court and the numerous calls to restraint the HCJ (Gavison, 1998; Shahar, 2001). Are the sociological explanations of judicial activism more insightful?

Explanations of Judicial Activism in Israel – the Sociological Approach

The sociological analysis of Israeli reality does not provide comprehensive explanations of judicial activism. Researchers tend to focus on the efficiency of the positive law as expressed in the Court rulings vis-à-vis the legislators' intent, the behavior of policy implementers, and social interests and conflicts. Three emphases can be identified: an emphasis on social values and partisan-structural factors, an emphasis on relationships and interests among the ruling elite, and an emphasis on cultural factors. We will discuss each of these explanations critically.

Barzilai (1998) examines the Court ruling in 1988 regarding the petition filed by Ben Shalom versus the National Elections Committee for the 12th Knesset. The HCJ rejected the petition, thus enabling the Jewish-Arab party list "Progressive list for Peace (PLP)" to participate in the elections. Barzilai explains this decision as an outcome of the development of liberal values in Israeli society since the 1960s, combined with transformations in the partisan structure. As he writes:

> At the end of the 1980s Israeli society was influenced by the rhetoric of individual rights including freedom of speech and freedom of association. Martial law over the Arab population was abolished in 1966, and the Arab minority was intensively involved in political life. In this context,

> disqualification of an Arab party was much more complex and difficult than it was in the 1960s. (Barzilai, 1998)

Barzilai emphasizes both social values and partisan-structural parameters in explaining judicial activism. On the one hand, the Court is understood as a passive player that reflects social attitudes as well as the interests of the political system (for further elaboration regarding the Supreme Court and social change, see Rosenberg, 1991). On the other hand, the Court is understood as an active player that attempts to maintain its public legitimacy as a means of retaining its institutional hegemony (Barzilai, 1999).

Shamir (1994a) suggests a similar argument in which the Court's intervention is understood as a means of establishing the status of "expert judges" who determine the extent to which a certain political decision is reasonable. Indeed, the "reasonability" of policies and decisions has become a major criterion for determining their legality. In other words, the "reasonability" test equates the subjective interpretation of judges with legality, thus providing the Court with a powerful tool for influencing public policy. In that sense, both Barzilai and Shamir express an individualistic orientation, an approach we will develop further in the next chapter. The second emphasis may rely on the critical legal studies approach in which the judicial system is part of the ruling elite. As such, the Supreme Court seeks to maintain and defend the unequal reality through integration with other power centers in society. However, applying this line of argumentation to Israeli society is problematic for two reasons. First, there is a debate about the existence and character of the dominant ruling elite in Israeli society (Higley, 1980; Shapira, 1984; Etzioni-Halevy, 1997). Second, this approach is highly deterministic, thus providing limited explanatory tools for a complex reality such as the Israeli one. We will argue that there are cases in which the Court serves the interests of one group or another, but any case should be explained relative to its specific conditions rather than by a certain grand theory. Such an alternative approach corresponds to the inter-disciplinary approach that we now discuss.

Mautner (2002) suggests that whereas in the 1950s the HCJ adopted an approach of formalism and judicial restraint due to the collectivist culture that characterized Israeli society, in the 1980s it adopted an activist approach due to the emergence of individual and liberal values. Mautner (2002) emphasizes the rise of an individualistic worldview in Israeli culture in the 1970s and 1980s, arguing that the Court found support for its liberal project among major sectors of Israeli society, as well as among many Israeli elite groups, such as the press, the business community, and the academic community. As he states:

> These sectors and groups were ready to help the Court reinforce Israel's commitment to Western, liberal values. Thus, as the gap between the Court's values and those governing leading sectors in Israel narrowed, the Court felt secure enough to expose and openly discuss the underlying values of its jurisprudence, i.e., the Court felt secure enough in its move from the linguistic and conceptual level of the law to the level of the law's underlying normative foundations. (Mautner, 2002: 196).

Furthermore, Mautner argues that due to socio-political processes throughout the 1980s, the groups that sought to make Israel a more secular, liberal, and democratic state controlled many positions in civil society, such as the press, academia, the arts, the professions, and the business sector. However, they failed to gain control over the political institutions of the State and its administration. According to Mautner, the fact that this group could not advance its interests and views through the political system led them to seek the help of the HCJ, which had similar views to its own. The Court, in return, adopted an activist approach in order to "...openly and forcefully proclaim its values, confronting those who sought to scuttle this and catalyze its supporters" (Mautner, 2002: 201). In other words, Mautner argues that the Court took a stand in the cultural, social, and political debate to defend liberal values against significant groups that challenged these values, counting on the support of sympathetic sectors in Israeli society.

Mautner's argument, which is supported by various researchers, actually means that the HCJ has been a channel for specific groups in Israeli society to advance their liberal values over the values held by many other sectors and systems of Israeli society (Edelman, 1994; Barzilai, 1998; Avnon, 1998; Hirschl, 2001; Shafir and Peled, 2002). We challenge this argument on two counts. First, it is not clear at all that only the "liberal elite" has turned to the Court. There are many others, with different characteristics, who have turned to the Court to advance their interests. For example, Dotan and Hofnung (2001) show that the impression that mainly left-wing parties turn to the Court is baseless; in fact, both right-wing and left-wing parties turn to the Court with similar frequency, but the right-wing appeals get less media coverage than those of the left-wing parties.

Second, regarding the motivations of those who turn to the Court, including elite groups, we argue that their main goal is to advance their own interests, whether in terms of social status or policy outcomes, rather than simply strengthening liberal values in Israeli society. For example, in many cases, human rights organizations, which are considered a part of the liberal elite, become the legal representatives of private people who file an appeal. However, in addition to advancing liberal values throughout society, they also advance their own social status as fighters for liberal values. Given that they derive clear and meaningful benefits from such activity, they succeed in overcoming the collective action problem (Meydani and Mizrahi, 2006). To achieve their interests, large parts of Israeli society adopt semi-legal strategies that express their dissatisfaction with Israeli society and political system. However, by adopting a quasi-exit strategy of turning to the Court, they also express a lack of respect for the law, thus potentially weakening democratic values as well the judicial system itself (see also, Gavison, 1997). Furthermore, we argue that the Court itself takes part in this process by adopting an activist approach.

This line of argumentation is partially supported by Dotan and Hofnung's (2001) explanation of why elected representatives go to Court. As mentioned, they show that the political position of the plaintiffs as members of the coalition or the opposition, rather than their attitudes as liberals or non-liberals, explains the number of appeals. Regarding the motivations of Members of the Knesset (MKs) for turning to the Court, Dotan and Hofnung first refer to the structural factors and socio-political processes that characterized Israeli society during the 1970s and 1980s. In particular, they mention the decline of party discipline and the emergence of more direct representation. As a result, Israeli MKs have been interested in getting media coverage – something that they could achieve via appeals to the HCJ. In that way, they use the Court to advance their political interests. We argue that they are not alone; actually all players on the scene are motivated by a certain self-interest and make cost-benefit calculations in deciding whether to use the Court to advance their interests. In the next chapter we present this approach in detail.

3.4. SUMMARY AND CONTRIBUTION

The traditional literature has discussed the role and place of law in human society, usually from a normative perspective. Sociological approaches developed in the second half of the twentieth century see the law and the legal system as social phenomena that should be analyzed using sociological methods (see, for example, Llewellyn, 1962; Holmes, 1984). Others view the Supreme Court as an interest group that attempts to advance its own sectorial goals (Schubert and Danelsky, 1969; Tapp and Levine, 1974; Schubert, 1985). From a sociological perspective, the Supreme Court is often viewed as contributing to a certain social equilibrium (Parsons, 1962; Becker, 1964; Black, 1972; Nonet, 1976). Parsons (1962) argues that because Supreme Court rulings are often on controversial issues, politicians and interest groups may try to restrain it. Indeed, Turk (1976) argues that the Supreme Court does not solve conflicts but rather creates and even intensifies existing conflicts, identifying the conditions that contribute to such situations. Thus, most of the sociological literature does not regard the Supreme Court as a political player with an independent agenda.

These approaches have two main shortcomings. First, by assuming that social structures determine individual behavior, these approaches significantly marginalize the role of individuals and their impact on social reality. Second, this marginalization of the impact of individuals on outcomes leads to a deterministic analysis. In this book we develop an approach that emphasizes methodological individualism and the role of political entrepreneurs in designing institutional changes.

Indeed, researchers of law and politics have gradually been moving toward the individualistic approach. This tradition began with the studies of Pritchett (1948) and Murphy (1964) but became central in the field of law and politics only during the 1990s (Segal and Spaeth, 1993; Epstein et al., 1994; Epstein and Walker, 1995; Baum, 1997; Epstein and Knight, 1998; Gilman, 1996–1997; Smith, 1998; Feeley and Rubin, 1998). These studies combine judges' preferences and strategies with extra-judicial structural and institutional influences, thus explaining the ways in which institutional structures shape judicial policy.

From an individualistic (or rational choice) perspective, Supreme Court judges may certainly have interests independent of those of certain social groups or elites. Given that they are part of a bureaucratic organization, they are most likely interested in preserving their organization's power and authority (Weber, 1962; Downs, 1967; Bendor, 1990; Breton, 1995). Yet, due to the separation-of-powers principle that gives the Supreme Court a monopoly on interpreting the law, the Court is not an ordinary bureaucratic organization. Rather, due to its unique role, the Supreme Court is often a political player – usually as a result of socio-political processes that create incentives for the Court to become an active political player (see, for example, Epstein and Knight, 1998).

Given that the authority of the Court and the structure of the system differ from one country to another, it is difficult to make generalizations about Court behavior without referring to the structural variables in a particular setting.

New, positive theories of the judiciary suggest two widely accepted conceptions of Court behavior (Segal, 1997; Hausegger and Baum, 1999). The "attitudinal model" suggests that justices vote for the positions most consistent with their personal policy preferences, given that the institutional structures allow sincere voting (Segal and Spaeth, 1993). In contrast, rational choice theory views High Court justices as players who act strategically to advance their goals (Gely and Spiller, 1990; Eskridge and Frickey, 1994; Schwartz, Spiller, and Urbiztondo, 1994; Hausegger and Baum, 1999). To minimize the possibility of congressional override, justices often adjust the Court's doctrinal positions and do not vote according to their sincere preferences.

Epstein and Knight (1998) found that in more than half of the cases, judges change their decisions in a way that does not reflect their personal preferences. They conclude that judges generally follow their personal preferences but they are constrained by various structural factors – both intra-organizational interests, such as the necessity to build coalitions, and extra-organizational factors, such as the limitations placed on them by state players and the general public. Overall, however, judges strive to maximize their interests. In contrast to this study, Feeley and Rubin (1998) suggest that judges may change their attitudes and preferences due to structural and institutional influences.

Segal (1997) compares the sincere and sophisticated models of voting behavior by Supreme Court justices using a variety of tests on the votes of U.S. Supreme Court justices in statutory cases decided between 1947 and 1992. He finds some evidence of sophisticated behavior, but most tests suggest otherwise. Segal then concludes that justices overwhelmingly engage in rationally sincere behavior. That is, justices are not sincere players by nature. Rather, when they adopt sincere behavior, it is because the institutional structures allow them to do so and still keep their interests unharmed. Segal limits his conclusions to the U.S. Supreme Court, making it clear how differences in structural conditions can explain differences in the behavior of Supreme Court judges.

In comparison, Israel has a parliamentary system with strong party control over its members. For many years, the country had a single majority party, and the judiciary does not have constitutional powers (Shetreet, 1994; Mautner, 2002). Yet, although the Israeli Supreme

Court is expected to adopt strategic behavior and restrain itself, since the 1970s it has adopted an orientation of judicial activism, increasing its involvement in policy making and in politicians' decisions (for example, Mautner, 2002).

The Israeli literature does not provide analytical explanations of the role of the Israeli Supreme Court in the complicated process of designing institutional change in Israel. The concept of shared mental models and political entrepreneurs will explain these transformations.

4

The Supreme Court as a Political Entrepreneur in the Process of Institutional Change – an Analysis Based on Shared Mental Models and Political Entrepreneurship

This chapter will survey the literature relevant to the processes of formal institutional change, present the central claims on which the book is based, and develop a new theory that combines shared mental models and policy entrepreneurship. We will then use this theory to explain the design of institutional change and identify the role of the Supreme Court as a political entrepreneur in creating this institutional change. In the first part of this chapter, we shall present the tenets of the institutional theory, including its sociological facets as well as the facets arising from studies about social choice theory. We will stress the comparative lack of analysis of the specific aspects pertaining to institutional change making. The second part of the chapter will expand on the claims that underpin the book's central theme, namely shared mental models and political entrepreneurship.

4.1. INSTITUTIONAL THEORY

The book examines the process of basic institutional change using a method called *institutional theory*, a unique approach to the study of social, economic, and political phenomena encompassing a range of meanings in a variety of disciplines such as economics, organizational theory, political science, history, sociology, and social choice. Within these fields there are different emphases as well – micro or macro, cognitive and normative – related to the creation and dissolution of organizations.

The meaning of the concept "institution" varies due to the different methods adopted by scholars in a given field. For instance, according to sociologists, an institutional change is a change in the ordinary manner of conduct (Powell and DiMaggio, 1991). However, political economy scholars define institutions as interactions between individuals and believe they serve as a basis for the understanding of social phenomena. Thus, according to Jack Knight (1995), institutions are rules that design social interactions in ways that allow the players to profit from cooperation. We shall survey two perceptions of the institutional theory: sociological and political-economic (specifically, social choice theory).

4.2. THE SOCIOLOGICAL PERSPECTIVE OF INSTITUTIONAL THEORY

The study of institutional theory is the renaissance of sociology. It is the reaction to the behavioral revolution that interpreted political collectivism and economic behavior as the sum of the results of individual choices, a kind of individual property rights collection that neglected the social, political, and economic contexts (Peters, 1999). The traditional sociological attitude saw institutions as limiting the ability of players to act according to their interests (Selznick, 1949, 1957; Perrow, 1986). It regarded institutional change as a local occurrence, as part of local interactions (Selznick, 1957).

Formal historical changes and the transition from the micro to the macro level influenced the study of institutions too (Peters, 1999). In the 1970s, a new branch of research called the *neo-institutional approach* began to develop in the field of institutional studies. According to this approach, the influence of the environment is more complex than previously believed, affecting the organization and its structure, as well as the actions and thoughts of its constituents (Peters, 1999). The institutional process is a cognitive one, taking place on the social-sectoral and inter-organizational levels (Powell and DiMaggio, 1991).

According to Alexander (1987), the transition from the traditional institutional approach to the neo-institutional approach lacks a deeper multi-dimensional theory. The institutions are first and foremost the product of human behavior and the rules are to be understood as the outcome of conflict and contest (Burns and Flam, 1987). Similarly, Powell and DiMaggio (1991) claim that the motives of power and interest have not received appropriate attention from neo-institutional sociology. According to them, little attention has been paid to the question, "How do key workers preserve their dominance or respond to threats in times of crisis or instability?" Little is known, as well, about the way gifted entrepreneurs implement multi-institutional logic as a strategy (Powell and DiMaggio, 1991).

This book stresses the role of political elements and coping strategies as key elements in the analysis and understanding of how formal institutional changes are designed and implemented. It emphasizes the factors that underlie power within the institution and the manner in which various political entrepreneurs make use of structural conditions to advance their own interests. Thus, the book attempts to combine political strategies and social-structural patterns in order to explain institutional changes (Pridham and Vanhanen, 1994; Colomer, 1995).

4.3. INSTITUTIONAL THEORY AS PERCEIVED THROUGH SOCIAL CHOICE STUDIES

In an effort to understand social phenomena, political economy scholars (who subscribe to the notion of rational choice) offer a variety of definitions for the interactions between individuals (Riker, 1980; Williamson, 1985; North, 1986; Ostrom, 1986; Shepsle, 1986). According to Knight (1995), institutions are rules that design social interactions in a way that enables the players to profit from cooperation. Douglas North (1995) differentiates between formal and informal rules, and defines institutions as limitations enforced on human interactions. Institutions include formal rules (constitutions, laws, accepted court rulings, regulations) and informal ones (conventions, norms, codes of behavior).

Social choice literature, which deals with the analysis of the rules of the game, differentiates between political rules and policy regulations. Policy regulations are rules that regulate everyday life. Political rules are rules that define the framework of political discussion, meaning the rules of the process of decision making and the rules that define how policy regulations can be changed (Buchanan, 1990; Doron and Sened, 2001). This book focuses on formal institutional change of the political rule type.

Rational choice literature presents a number of theories of institutional change. All of these begin with the initial supposition that social players are interested in achieving optimal results at minimal cost. The analytic tradition that started with the works of Coase (1937, 1960) and continued with Williamson (1985) took a turn in the road in the writings of economic historians such as North (1981), scholars of law and economics such as Posner (1981), game theory theoreticians (Schotter, 1981), and organizational economists (Alchian and Demsetz, 1972; Nelson and Winter, 1982). This turn is known as the neo-institutional economy. The neo-institutional approach added a measure of realism to the standard assumptions about the micro-economy, recognizing that individuals attempt to maximize their profit inside a constant and consistent limit of priorities. However, they are hampered in this effort by their limited information and the difficulty of controlling and enforcing agreements.

The neo-institutional literature developed a number of theories about the appearance of social institutions (see, for example, Knight, 1995). In all of these theories, the process of rule design and change reflects complex interactions between various players, all of whom understand the importance of basic, stable rules. Therefore, the consideration system that usually guides the players will tend to be long-term. The theories all include the claim that the appearance of institutions is a result of the interactions between players in society. The strategic issues arising from social interaction are characterized and solved by multiple equilibriums. Each equilibrium constitutes a solution to one interaction, and the players should be able to identify a general equilibrium (Riker, 1980; Shepsle, 1986; Shepsle and Weingast, 1981).

Terry Moe criticized the social choice institutional approach for the emphasis it places on the formalist mechanism of the legislator. According to him, such an approach ignores the informal, dynamic side of institutions. Moe stresses the influence of both informal norms and professionalism on the relationships between players that lead to institutional changes (Moe, 1987: 291). The sociologists Powell and DiMaggio (1991: 6) second Moe: "While some concern is evidenced for how institutions emerge, most of the analyses treat rules and procedures as exogenous determinants of political behavior." This book explores this deficiency.

According to North (1995), the study of institutions is confused due to the vagueness of the concepts that have been used to examine them. He claims that theories regarding institutional changes are impossible to develop as long as the players and the rules of the game are mixed together. The institutions are the rules of the game, whereas the organizations are the players. To understand the way they function, we need a variety of models. The models of institutions examine the limitations placed by people on the human interactions that define the social structure. Models related to organizations deal with all of the issues pertaining to the structure and policy of the entities. When individuals are the players, it is natural that as a part of the organization, they have the ability to make decisions that would change the rules of the game or gradually adopt new, informal limitations. Therefore, the key is the study of the individual and the organization as the main factors in the development of institutions. North adds that institutions affect the power of those that can perform the change. According to him, the neo-classic theory lacks a discussion about the factors that influence the perception of individuals. This lack is manifested in the assumption that a rational human being knows what he or she is doing. North claims that this assumption is wrong, as it fails to acknowledge the fact that the information available to most people in an organization is incomplete. Furthermore, most changes are additive (Wildavsky, 1979). According to North, revolutions are rare. Even when they take place, time eventually shows that they were not real revolutions. Yesterday's choices are at most today's starting point. Moreover, informal limitations imposed by the norms, conventions, and codes of behavior deeply rooted in the culture constitute important sources for path-dependent analysis (Grief, 2006). This book examines a process of general change in the basic rules of the game from the perspective of the individuals who determine the results. However, these individuals do not act in a vacuum, so we will consider the social, cultural, and structural parameters that affect their considerations.

Individual and Collective Learning as a Pathway for an Institutional Analysis

In a recent paper, Mantzavinos, North, and Shariq (2004) explore the cognitive processes of individual and collective learning and tie them to institutional analysis. Referring to individual learning, they adopt an approach that views human learning as related to problem solving, that is, any human activity concerns problem solving, and the individual is constantly engaged in learning ways to solve problems – either existing ones or new ones. Mantzavinos (2001) and Mantzavinos et al. (2004) suggest a theory of learning that can be summarized as follows. The elementary units of knowledge are rules, defined as suggestions that propose the classification of environmental messages or the internal information of the organism in a specific manner. A number of rules and rule clusters organized together in the form of one or more default hierarchies give rise to a mental model, a coherent but transitory set of rules that enables the organism to form predictions about the environment based on the available knowledge. Mental models are flexible knowledge structures created anew each time from the ready-made pool of rules.

A mental model helps the individual formulate solutions to problems. However, when neither the mental model nor other inferential strategies solves the problem, the individual is forced to form new, creative mental models and to try new solutions. A belief is formed when environmental feedback confirms the same mental model so many times that it becomes stabilized, and a belief system is defined as the interconnection of beliefs (Mantzavinos et al., 2004).

It follows that individuals learn existing or new ways to solve problems through direct interaction with the environment. Therefore, norms, values, and ideas transformed by the individual through cultural and educational mechanisms play a significant role in the learning process and the creation of mental models. When individuals communicate with each other to try to solve their problems, the direct result is the formation of shared mental models that provide the framework for a common interpretation of reality and give rise to collective solutions to the problems arising in the environment (North, 1995; Mantzavinos, 2001).

Finally, Mantzavinos et al. (2004) integrate all of the variables into a scheme of institutional change. In the first stage, players all become aware of particular issues, and the shared mental models are applied to solve specific problems. If they are not useful enough, the shared mental models are altered in a process of collective learning until the content of the shared learning is the same or similar for a period of time. When the shared mental models become relatively inflexible, shared belief systems are shaped. Once all of the players have formed the same mental models, the institutional mix may start solving a variety of social problems in a certain way. The institutional framework – that is, the different ways to solve social problems – is learned and applied by all players, thus influencing market interactions and economic performance.

This framework is applied in the current book to explain the evolution of alternative politics in Israel as a continuous mode of behavior that is deeply rooted in the belief system. The specific learning process that laid the groundwork for alternative politics is derived from the specific nature of Israeli political culture. A political culture of a different nature might yield learning processes that would lead to other modes for the alternative provision of public services.

Alternative Politics and the Institutional Change

The phenomenon we attempt to explain in this book is actually a strategy adopted by citizens to bypass the government and find alternative sources for obtaining public services such as health care, education, internal security, and welfare or public policy in general. Specifically, we try to explain what leads ordinary citizens and interest groups to take the initiative to provide public services on their own through alternative channels to those of the government.

Basically, a shortage of public services provided by the government may arise due either to government failure in managing the services, reduced resources due to budget cuts or re-allocation leading to insufficient provision, or external influences such as economic crises. As Hirschman (1970) notes, citizens may respond in two basic ways – voice and exit. The voice option is clearly the most straightforward and widespread in democratic societies, yet there are many situations in which citizens respond by a certain type of exit. The issue of exit has long been discussed in the literature. Scholars now believe that in addition to the original exit strategy of physically leaving the society by emigration, there are other modes of exit behavior that citizens perform while remaining in the society in which they live (Rosbult and Lowery, 1985; Lyons and Lowery, 1986; Lehman-Wilzig, 1991). With the exception of the strategy of neglect, which includes mental withdrawal from caring about social issues, these modes of behavior generally include the alternative provision of public services and often function as a type of voice.

Indeed, there are cases in which citizens cannot or do not want to exit or protest (voice) – generally because they believe that conventional democratic influence channels are blocked. There may be various reasons for the evolution of such a belief, including the decline of traditional power groups such as trade unions due to changing conditions (Pierson, 1996), a direct governmental policy of weakening the opposition (Tarrow, 1995), structural factors such as a high level of centralization that weaken the voice option (Pierson, 1996), and economic crises that significantly reduce the government's ability to respond positively to citizens' demands (Lehman-Wilzig, 1991). The degree to which influence channels are open can be measured by citizens' views about what Tarrow (1994) terms the political opportunity structure. The specific dimensions of political systems that impact the structuring of collective action and protest activity are: 1) the relative openness or closure of the institutionalized political system; 2) the stability of that broad set of elite alignments that typically undergird a polity; 3) the presence of elite allies; and 4) the state's capacity and propensity for repression (Tarrow, 1994).

We suggest that when citizens believe that a given political opportunity structure does not allow conventional democratic channels of influence to materialize, they look for alternative ways to improve policy outcomes and political performance. Expressed in the terms of Mantzavinos et al. (2004), people attempt to find new ways to solve social problems that after a process of collective learning may also lead to the transformation of the belief system. In our context, citizens attempt to find new ways to solve the problem of a shortage of governmental services. Lehaman-Wilzig (1991) suggests defining such behavior by the term "quasi-exit." When people are dissatisfied with policy outcomes but believe that they can neither influence via protest (voice) nor through exit, they create an alternative supply of governmental services through illegal or semi-legal channels.

Empirical evidence shows that in situations similar to those described earlier, people often adopt a do-it-yourself approach, which can also be understood as a quasi-exit strategy. Helmke and Levitsky (2004) point to a set of informal norms (*blat*) that have emerged in the Soviet Union – set up by individuals and personal networks to provide basic needs – which created incentives to behave in ways that alter the substantive effect of formal rules, but without directly violating them. They also characterize substitute informal institutions – such as the alternative provision of public goods in rural northern Peru and in rural China – as aimed at achieving what formal institutions were designed to achieve but failed to do so. Such substitute informal institutions emerge where state structures are weak or lack authority (see also: Zakariah, 1997; Rocamora, 2000; Zweig, 2002).

It follows that the concept of alternative politics attempts to explain four elements that do not necessarily appear in previous conceptualization of such processes. First, it applies to situations in which a do-it-yourself approach (or unilateral initiatives) is widely used by citizens in many areas of life. Second, it is characterized by a complex mix of private and public financing, facilities, provision, and consumption. Third, it applies only in cases where this situation continues for long periods of time (i.e., several decades), meaning that citizens internalize this quasi-exit behavior through learning and socialization processes. Fourth, it becomes a central characteristic of the political culture in a given society, as reflected in its diffusion to all areas and levels of social and political life. For example, in rural China, a quasi-exit behavior helped people solve the shortage of public services, but such behavior did not extend to all sectors in society. In contrast, in the Soviet Union and in Israel, this behavior spread to all sectors of society, including the elite, the administrative agencies, and the political system. In Israel, for example, quasi-exit behavior spread to the judicial arena and became a salient feature of the relations between the public and the Supreme Court (Mizrahi and Meydani, 2003).

Thus, alternative politics is a widespread political culture in which citizens continuously create an alternative supply of governmental services or public goods, often through illegal or semi-legal channels. By doing so, the public solves its immediate shortage and threatens the monopoly held by politicians, thus potentially leading the latter to change policy in accordance with the demands signaled by society. While the standard model of institutionalization explains how institutions and the need for governmental services evolve due to market failures (Mantzavinos et al., 2004), here society responds to a shortage of government services and provides public services via non-governmental or semi-private channels. It is important to emphasize that not just any illegal activity qualifies as quasi-exit behavior or alternative politics. Rather, we refer here to illegal or semi-legal activity that attempts to provide what the government was supposed to provide but failed to do so.

Summary

Mantzavinos, North, and Shariq (2004) suggest that institutional change should be analyzed as part of a process in which a certain institutional reality influences individual and collective beliefs, thus triggering an individual and collective learning process that eventually leads to institutional change, specific policies, and outcomes in terms of economic performance. The learning process depends on finding existing or new methods for solving social problems, that is, shared mental models. This book elaborates on a specific mental model rooted in large parts of the Israeli public that explains the evolution of the "Who Governs?" game in Israel as a means of solving the problem of non-governability in Israel (Dror, 1989). When people are dissatisfied with a particular policy or the level of supply of a public good, they adopt a proactive course of action, seeking an alternative supply source, one that may be illegal or semi-legal. This behavior is part of a widespread, shared mental model that has evolved among the Israeli public and is reflected in many areas of life. However, the book also maintains that the design and determination of institutional change is done by political entrepreneurs.

4.4. POLITICAL ENTREPRENEURSHIP

A political entrepreneur is someone from within the political system such as a politician or a bureaucrat, or from outside the political system such as a member of a social movement or a lobbyist, who has an idea that could change the political status quo and recruits enough people to support this idea. Current literature distinguishes little between types of political entrepreneurs. For example, Doron and Sened (2001: 77) refer to political entrepreneurs as individuals who serve as middlemen between rulers and those they rule (see also, López, 2002; Christopoulos, 2006). This definition conforms to Olson's (1965) definition of a "privileged group," composed of individuals willing to bear the costs of a societal action irrespective of the other individuals also interested in the outcomes of that action. In that sense, supreme courts can serve as political entrepreneurs.

Some political entrepreneurship studies deal with the emergence of political entrepreneurs (Schumpeter, 1942; Dahl, 1961; Salisbury, 1969). Other such as Schneider and Teske (1992) focus on the effect that political entrepreneurs have on policy design. Sheingate (2003: 185), for example, deals with political entrepreneurs as "individuals whose creative acts have transformative affects on politics, policies, or institutions." Another view emphasizes the strategies and actions taken by political entrepreneurs to promote formal institutional change (Kingdon, 1995; Doron and Sened, 2001).

The political entrepreneurs identify the need for a policy design change, define the social problem, and draft a solution to the problem. This solution is defined in this book as "electoral capital," that is, the assets (image, material resources, political support) that politicians may use to help them get re-elected. Following this logic, political entrepreneurs promote the change not only for ideological reasons, but also because of the belief that such action will bring them political support or maximize their public prestige. However, this does not mean that other players will adopt this institutional change as electoral capital; they will do so only if they become convinced that support for the action will allow them to maximize their own public prestige or chances of re-election.

To begin the process of formulating an institutional change, the political entrepreneur *must identify a public need to alter the political rules*. According to Mantzavinos, North, and Shariq (2004), norms, values, and ideas transformed by the individual through cultural and educational mechanisms play a significant role in the learning process and the creation of mental models. Furthermore, when citizens believe that a given political opportunity structure inhibits conventional democratic channels of influence, they look for alternative ways to improve policy outcomes and political performance. In terms of Mantzavinos et al. (2004), people attempt to find new ways to solve social problems that, after a process of collective learning, may also lead to a transformation of the belief system.

This feeling results from a long learning process, during which society comes to understand that to change the situation – that is, to supply the missing policy and solve the problem – they must change the political rules (Mantzavinos et al., 2004). This historical process includes attempts to create policies that rely on existing state rules. When such an attempt fails (for instance, due to political and economic centralization), society may come to believe it is necessary to change the political rule and to adopt an alternative way of solving economic problems and providing economic goods.

4.5. THE POLICY-MAKING PROCESS AND SUPREME COURTS

Public policy is composed of a vast collection of decisions made by the designated authorities in connection with the regulation and management of various areas of life. Each such decision is called a policy decision. The collection of decisions in any particular area constitutes public policy in that area, such as education, health care, and security. For this reason, to provide an empirical explanation of public policy in general, and the policy in specific areas in particular, we must disaggregate the policy into specific policy decisions and analyze the process that gave rise to each such decision. In this part of the chapter, we explain the guiding principles of such a process of analysis as developed by public choice theory. In the next part of the chapter, we integrate the Supreme Court into the analysis.

Figure 4.1 shows the central stages in the process of policy making by presenting policy decisions as the dependent variable and other interactions as the independent variables. Policy decisions are normally expressed in the form of primary or secondary legislation and various types of regulations (Box 6 in Figure 4.1). The final policy decision is usually taken by a group of politicians. Therefore, the internal dynamics in such a group constitute the last stage in the process that we are attempting to explain (Box 6 in Figure 4.1). However, to understand politicians' behavior, we should go back several steps and understand their basic motivations and interests.

The models proposed by public choice theory operate on the assumption that any policy decision made by a politician is underpinned by the reciprocal relations between the politician and the electorate (Box 1 in Figure 4.1). These reciprocal relations are based on the mechanism of supply and demand (Downs, 1957). In other words, the public demands a particular policy, and politicians respond positively (i.e., supply) solely to those demands that increase their odds of being elected. Hence, it is assumed

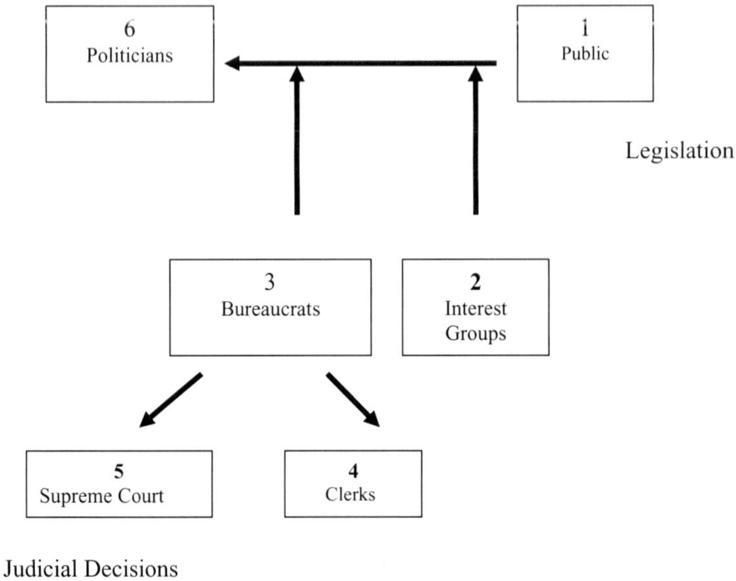

FIGURE 4.1. The policy-making process and Supreme Courts.

that the main interest (and, on occasion, the only interest) of politicians is to maximize their odds of being re-elected. Furthermore, politicians will always prefer the status quo, as long as no public demands are being made on them. This is a partial explanation as to why, in many cases, public policy in any area is not formulated until the situation reaches catastrophic proportions.

The need for state intervention by means of public policy generally emerges when a shortage of a "public good" arises (Weimer and Vining, 1998). Interestingly enough, the same problem that causes this shortage also creates the situation whereby the public often does not demand change until a catastrophe occurs (Box 1 in Figure 4.1). Most people prefer to free-ride on the efforts of others, leading to a collective action problem (Olson, 1965; Taylor, 1987). In fact, we may also regard public policy itself as a public good, because an individual may be affected by a certain decision even though he or she did not take part in bringing it about. If we apply this rationale to the area of law and politics, we can argue that the fairness of laws, the prestige of the justice system, and the idea of stability as a by-product of the positive law are public goods. Thus, self-interest and the possibility of benefiting from a product without participating in its production create the motivation to free-ride on the efforts of others (Olson, 1965; Axelrod, 1984; Taylor, 1987). The result is a shortage of public goods and governmental services on the one hand and a lack of motivation to exert pressure collectively to improve the situation on the other hand.

In the absence of demand by the general public, groups that do manage to overcome the problem of collective action in order to form interest groups have significantly more power (Box 2 in Figure 4.1). The influence of interest groups on public policy and election outcomes, as well as on social welfare, has been widely discussed by political economists (Stigler and Friedland, 1962; Olson, 1965; Peltzman, 1976; Buchanan et al., 1980; Becker, 1964; Mitchell and Munger, 1991). This influence is generally attributed to the exchange between politicians in office and interest groups. The politicians are usually understood to be the suppliers of regulatory services, such as price fixing, subsidies, restriction of entry, promotion of complementary goods, and suppression of substitutes. In exchange for these highly valuable services, the regulated industry – that is, the interest group – can offer politicians campaign contributions, speaking honoraria and the votes of industry employees (Mitchell and Munger, 1991; Austen-Smith, 1998).

In analyzing the influence of interest groups on public policy, political economists tend to agree that the influence of one interest group in a specific policy dimension increases when there are fewer competitors attempting to pursue their interests with politicians. Economists within the Chicago School, such as Stigler and Friedland (1962), Posner (1971), Barro (1973), and Peltzman (1976), theorize that open competition between interest groups working to maximize their own benefits, also termed "rents," will, under certain conditions, maximize market efficiency and social welfare. In contrast, researchers within the Virginia School argue that politicians will give high rents to those interest groups that can guarantee the required number of votes (Buchanan et al., 1980; Ekelund and Tollison, 1980; Coate and Morris, 1995; Lohmann, 1998). The more interest groups competing in a given policy area, the less potential influence peddling by each group. Once politicians are convinced to favor a certain group, its rents will be maximized, thus damaging economic efficiency as well as social welfare.

It follows that according to both previously outlined approaches, as the number of interest groups competing in a given policy area increases, the power and potential influence of each group, individually, decreases. However, the regulatory services won by strong interest groups reduce economic efficiency and social welfare.

A third line of research in studies about the activity of interest groups focuses on the information aspect of their relationship with politicians. As explained earlier, politicians attempt to formulate policy that corresponds to the position of the average voter (Box 1 in Figure 4.1). To do so, they must have some knowledge about the distribution of preferences in society. However, in many cases, the problem of collective action produces passive citizens who do not indicate their positions on most issues unless there is a catastrophe (Box 1 in Figure 4.1). Therefore, the activity of interest groups becomes the politicians' central source of information (Ainsworth and Sened, 1993; Lohmann, 1993; Lohmann, 1995; Lohmann, 1998; Austen-Smith, 1998). Thus, when there are more interest groups acting in a given policy area, politicians have better information and the decision-making process becomes more efficient. In that way interest group activity may contribute to social welfare. In contrast, the Virginia School contends that lack of information about public preferences and the activity of interest groups produce an overall negative impact on social welfare and the efficiency of public policy. Further negative influences are produced by the involvement of bureaucrats in the decision-making process.

The political-bureaucratic structure of a particular system also has a substantial impact on the ability of organized groups to pursue their special interests. The more decentralized the structure, the greater the impact of interest groups on public policy and the more muted the impact of bureaucracy. In centralized systems, the demands of the few interest groups are channeled through the bureaucracy and thus serve to further increase the level of centralization.

This rationale is rooted in formal models of bureaucracy, starting with Niskanen's (1971) budget maximizing model. It is assumed that bureaucrats want to expand the bureaucracy, because maximizing their budget also indirectly maximizes their self-interest and material payoffs (Niskanen, 1971; Hood and Peters, 1994). In contrast, the utility of politicians is a function of their ability to implement a policy that attracts the average voter (Downs, 1957). Therefore, politicians prefer a budget designed to supply the specific demands of their constituency. The fact that politicians and bureaucrats have different, and often conflicting, interests regarding the bureaucracy's budget is the principal source of conflict in their relations (Box 3 in Figure 4.1).

Formal models of bureaucracy explain that the power and ability of bureaucrats to manipulate politicians increases as the number of alternative sources of information and public goods supply decreases (Miller and Moe, 1983; Bendor et al., 1985, 1987a, 1987b; Bendor, 1990). In other words, in centralized political-bureaucratic systems, bureaucrats can control policy-making processes, channeling them toward their own ends (Box 4 in Figure 4.1). In contrast, in decentralized systems, politicians can threaten the monopoly held by bureaucrats by gathering information from, or contracting out projects to, interest groups from the private sector. Such actions are expected to reduce the power wielded by bureaucrats and increase public sector efficiency.

In the event that the interests of bureaucrats are realized, we are then faced with the conflict that maximization of the ministry's budget is not in keeping with maximum economic efficiency. On the other hand, when the interests of politicians are realized, policies become totally subordinate to political considerations, without any essential checks and balances provided by the bureaucratic sector. Such a lack of balance between political and professional considerations also causes harm to social welfare.

Implementing these models, we can conclude that in a decentralized system, where politicians have alternative sources for obtaining information and supplying public services, the ability of bureaucrats to manipulate politicians to favor their own interests is limited when compared to the reality in highly centralized systems. As a result, the power and influence of interest groups on public policy is greater in a decentralized system than in a centralized system. In centralized systems, however, politicians attempt to control bureaucrats by using political appointments and rewards for top administrators (Hood and Peters, 1994). Thus, bureaucrat-politician relations are characterized by the continuous potential for conflict, which leads to negative impacts on social welfare and policy efficiency.

The last stage in the policy-making analysis includes the relations between politicians in the decision-making forums such as the parliament, national government, and city council (Box 6 in Figure 4.1). A politician who wants to enact a given policy should satisfy the interests of a majority of the decision-making forum through political bargaining. This process creates another potential for the inefficient allocation of resources, because each member in the political forum attempts to obtain rents, privileges, and resources for his/her constituency (Riker, 1980; Shepsle and Weingast, 1981; Sened, 1995).

To conclude, the policy-making process is full of obstacles that must be overcome in order to maximize efficiency and social welfare. The various players have many conflicting interests that make it almost impossible to achieve the optimal outcome for the whole society – if such an outcome exists at all. However, a deep investigation of the models suggests that decentralization may improve the policy-making process and its outcomes because such structural changes potentially weaken the power of special interests.

4.6. THE INVOLVEMENT OF THE SUPREME COURT IN POLICY-MAKING PROCESSES

As noted in Chapter 3, the social and political role of supreme courts has been studied from several perspectives. Hereby we elaborate on the sociopolitical and cultural explanation of *judicial activism*, thus leading afterward to the book's outline of the argument.

Sociopolitical and Cultural Explanation of Judicial Activism

The institutional structure and rules under which the Supreme Court operates clearly influence its ability to adopt an activist approach. However, because it operates vis-à-vis a given political system, the nature and functioning of this system also play a key role in explaining the Court's behavior. We argue that the less efficient the political system is in making policy decisions, the more likely the Supreme Court will be willing and able to adopt an activist approach. Although the inefficiency of democratic political systems can be explained in several ways, one of the most common explanations is the existence of social divisions and conflicts that cannot be solved through the political system. Under such conditions, politicians who make choices based only on short-term considerations often prefer the no-decision solution, thus exacerbating the inefficiency of the political system (Dror, 2001).

Taking political inefficiency as a given, citizens tend to adopt a strategy similar to the one adopted when they are dissatisfied with governmental services such as education, health care, the mass media, and security. Based on Hirschman's (1970) model, we can expect that they first demand the supply of such services (voice), and those who can, adopt the exit option. However, when the voice option is exhausted, those who cannot adopt the exit option tend to seek an alternative supply of the governmental services they finding lacking in either quality or quantity. Lehaman-Wilzig (1991) suggests defining such a behavior by the term "quasi-exit." In other words, when people are dissatisfied with policy outcomes but believe that they can neither influence decisions via protest (voice) nor through exit, they create an alternative supply of governmental services through illegal or semi-legal channels. By doing so, the public solves its immediate shortage and threatens the monopoly held by politicians, thereby leading them to change policy according to the demands signaled by society.

Moreover, when a government consistently fails to reach policy decisions, citizens are motivated to search for substitutes for the government, namely alternative centers of power that will provide public policy and solve problems. One such alternative is the military elite. Indeed, in many cases when an inefficient democratic system collapses, a military regime or another form of authoritarian regime based on the support of the military elite is imposed (O'Donnell et al., 1986). Another possible center of power is the Supreme Court – especially in systems where the court's authority is not clearly defined and it enjoys public legitimacy. Under such circumstances, citizens and politicians may regard the Supreme Court as a potential supplier of efficient public policy. As will be demonstrated later, in Israel, the army and the Supreme Court are the most trusted public institutions, whereas the trust in institutions that symbolize the democratic system, such as the government, parliament, and political parties, has declined by 50 percent between 1996 and 2000 (Arian et al., 2002).

Consequently, a political culture characterized by quasi-exit combined with inefficient democratic political systems can cause, and therefore can explain, judicial activism. However, a precondition for the emergence of judicial activism in such political systems is the existence of strong public legitimacy and respect for the judicial system as well as the existence of social divisions and conflicts that cannot be solved either through the civil society or through the political system. In the following section we illustrate this argument by using Israel as a case in point.

An Outline of the Argument

Since the 1970s, Israeli society has been undergoing two central processes. First, the political system has become highly fragmented due to the decline of the Labor Party as a dominant party, as well as the growth of sectorial parties. During the 1990s, a split voting system significantly strengthened the representation of sectorial parties in the legislature, thus weakening the ability of the political system to produce stable policy decisions (Arian and Shamir, 1999, Arian and Shamir, 2002). Second, central characteristics of Israeli political culture, which had been dormant during the 1950s and 1960s, have come to life and to a large extent shaped the place of law and the Supreme Court in Israeli society.

Historically, prior to the establishment of the State of Israel in 1948, the Jewish community in Palestine established its political, social, and economic institutions via semi-legal or illegal channels. The British mandate authorities were faced with new facts and realities that they finally accepted. Moreover, the Jewish institutional setting was highly centralized. When it was transformed into the State of Israel, the result was a highly centralized political, economic, and administrative system that remained that way during the 1950s and 1960s (Horowitz and Lissak, 1990; Arian, 1997; Aharoni, 1998). The combination of highly centralized systems and a tradition of activity via semi-legal channels significantly influenced Israeli political culture. The centralism prevented the development of alternative power centers such as interest groups and significantly slowed the development of a civil society based on liberal values (Mautner, 2002). During the 1950s and 1960s, Israeli society did not exert substantial pressures for change. Such pressures came after the Yom Kippur War in 1973, which revealed the deep dissatisfaction of the Israeli public vis-à-vis the functioning and policy of the Labor Party. To change the ruling coalition and its policy, the Israeli public used legal democratic channels such as elections, demonstrations, strikes, and the mass media. However, toward the end of the 1960s, attempts to influence policy in ways that were illegal started to appear. At first, there were illegal settlements in the occupied territories that forced a certain reality on the government. Over the years, as the public gradually gave up on the legal channels of influence, such semi-legal and illegal activities spread to other areas of life (Lehamn-Wilzig, 1991).

As explained in the previous section, such activities can be termed quasi-exit behavior. People who are dissatisfied with governmental services and either cannot use or do not believe in the influence of the exit or voice options adopt one of two quasi-exit options. One is the passive option, meaning that people distance themselves from public life, concentrating on their personal life as much as possible. The second is the active option, meaning that people try to find alternative channels, often illegal, to obtain the types of services that the government is supposed to supply. By doing so, the public threatens the governmental monopoly, thus forcing policy changes in the direction required by society. In other words, politicians often respond to such pressures by legalizing some of the semi-legal or illegal institutions created by society. This rationale explains the legalizing of illegal settlements in the 1970s as well as the creation of gray markets in medicine, education, mass communications, and the economy in the 1980s. In all of these areas, the government responded to illegal private initiatives by legalizing them and granting them formal status (Lehman-Wilzig, 1991). Thus, quasi-exit behavior is a central characteristic of Israeli political culture and a central explanatory variable of sociopolitical processes.

A similar rationale can explain the process of increasing judicial activism in Israel. As explained, during the 1970s and 1980s, the Israeli public made extensive use of legal democratic means, such as elections, demonstrations, and strikes, to change policy. However, these measures did not lead to significant policy changes. Deep divisions within Israeli society, such as the polarized relations between secular and orthodox Jews, between residents of the center of the country and those in the periphery, between immigrants from Arab and Mediterranean countries and immigrants of European descent, and between Israeli Arabs and Israeli Jews, fractured the country (Horowitz and Lissak, 1990; Ezrahi, 1990). Gradually, a sense of deadlock emerged in which the public felt that there was no way to exert influence on the government. This deadlock was clearly expressed in the formation of two National Unity Governments in the years 1984–1990, leaving no real political alternative. The inability of the political system to produce stable policy decisions, combined with the sense that opportunities to influence the government were blocked, triggered demands to change the electoral rules on the one hand and attempts to find an alternative power center that would provide public policy on the other. The alternative was the Supreme Court, because there are no clear-cut constitutional rules that define its powers (Barzilai, 1999). By appealing to the Court, the Israeli public attempted to create new facts and a new reality through intensive litigation. Like quasi-exit behavior in other areas, in the judicial area as well, such behavior is expected to threaten politicians and lead them to institutionalize the new status quo – either by accepting and legalizing the new balance of power or by redefining the Supreme Court's authority.

It follows that the deep divisions in Israeli society combined with the centralized institutional setting have led to the inability of the political system to handle public policy. In the face of such a deficit, Israeli society has adopted a quasi-exit behavior of intensive litigation in order to produce policy decisions, while also pressuring politicians to make fundamental institutional reforms. Thus, the central role of the Israeli Supreme Court as a policy maker is the result of deep and complex sociopolitical processes rather than that of an elitist system or the personality of a certain judge. In the next chapter, we elaborate on this argument in detail.

5

Israeli Public Law

5.1. PUBLIC LAW AND HUMAN RIGHTS

Public law in Israel reflects the collection of norms that govern the legal relationships between the state and individuals, as well as the relations among governmental agencies concerning the attitude toward human rights. Human rights norms are reflected in constitutional laws such as Basic Law: Human Dignity and Liberty and Basic Law: Freedom of Occupation, and regular laws such as the Prevention of Sexual Harassment Law, 5758–1998; the Annual Leave Law, 5711–1951; the Hours of Work and Rest Law, 5711–1951; the Male and Female Workers Equal Pay Law, 5756–1996; the Male and Female Workers (Equal Retirement Age) Law, 5747–1987; the Equal Rights for People with Disabilities Law, 5758–1998; the Sick Leave Pay Law, 5736–1976; and the Youth Labor Law, 5713–1953. In addition, there are administrative laws that govern the protection of human rights in various bureaucratic departments. Whereas the norms that underpin public law include the protection of human rights, the feasibility of inculcating respect for human rights encompasses other fields such as the regulation of administrative authorities, the oversight and monitoring of how administrative authority is used, as well as the formal and material definition of constitutional norms, the legal status of government agencies, and the administrative process (Meydani, 2007).

5.2. THE CONSTITUTIONAL MECHANISM IN LAW AND PRACTICE

Constitutional law is the body of law that governs the legal status of the basic norms in the Israeli legal system and defines the interrelationships and powers of government agencies and other state entities. The constitutional mechanism is designed around legal norms, each of which has a different status. A formal constitution is generally at the top of this pyramid. Unlike countries such as the United States and Canada that have coherent constitutional documents, Israel does not have a formal constitution. However, over the years, a system of basic laws has been enacted, which are designed to address specific constitutional issues. At some point in the future, they may be compiled into a complete constitutional document. The statutes that constitute the legislation entitled Basic Law: Human Dignity and Liberty, passed in 1992, are recognized as having constitutional status that takes precedence over regular law in Israeli judicial interpretation.[1] The recognition of the Basic Laws as having constitutional status was dubbed the "constitutional revolution" (Barak, 1993c). Thus, Israel now has constitutional norms that override normal statutes and provide the legal basis on which the Supreme Court interprets Israeli legal provisions and conducts a judicial review of primary legislation. The basic laws that have had the most significant impact are Basic Law: Human Dignity and Liberty and Basic Law: Freedom of Occupation, commonly regarded as the "Human Rights Statement" of Israel.

In addition to the provisions of constitutional law, human rights norms also encompass the provisions of administrative law. This legal field regulates the activities of all governmental administrative agencies. Administrative law deals with the structure of the administration and its authorities, the proper conduct of the administrative process, the amount of discretion the authority is allowed, the oversight of the administrative agency, and the degree of freedom of activity the administrative agency has under private law. At the heart of administrative law is the concept that public administration functions as a public trustee and is therefore expected to behave according to higher standards than those applicable to players under private law (Zamir, 1996).

The administrative authorities in Israel generally have a decentralized, hierarchical structure. Thus, for example, there are central administrative authorities (such as the Ministry of the Interior) that have offices around the country (local authorities). Similarly, the different administrative jurisdictions embody various types of authority, among them quasi-judicial, legislative, and executive authorities. The guideline directing the activity of administrative agencies in Israel is the principle of

[1] CA 6821/93 *United Mizrahi Bank v. Migdal Cooperative Village*, in Decisions, vol. 49, section 4, p. 221 (in Hebrew).

legality. The principle stipulates that, as opposed to a private individual who is allowed to do anything that is not explicitly prohibited, administrative agencies begin at a higher standard. Implementation of the principle of legality with respect to the administrative agencies assumes that everything that is not explicitly allowed is prohibited. In other words, the activity of the administrative agency must be stipulated explicitly in the law. Furthermore, administrative agencies are subject to the doctrine of natural justice,[2] which requires fair proceedings in disputes with citizens, including providing a party injured by their action with the right to be heard and to have his or her case reviewed. Administrative agencies are also subject to the test of reason and proportionality stemming from the constitutional philosophy in Israel.[3] Thus, the administrative agency must determine clear, general standards for legislation and is prohibited from enacting legislation that is supposed to apply to an undefined group of people. In addition, the agency must regulate itself internally and create stable legal norms and decisions that must be published and applied from the moment of their enactment.

5.3. ISRAELI CONSTITUTIONAL HISTORY AND THE HUMAN RIGHTS STATEMENT

According to United Nations General Assembly Resolution 181 of November 29, 1947, Israel was to have its Constituent Assembly adopt a constitution. There has been significant legal debate about whether this resolution is still binding on Israel. Indeed, at the beginning of 1949, a Constituent Assembly was elected. However, the Assembly's decision was not to ratify a constitution, but instead to become the legislative body and gradually enact basic laws that together would form the sections of a constitution at some point in the future. This endeavor has still not been completed. To date, the Knesset has passed eleven basic laws. Five basic laws define the activity of government agencies – Basic Law: The President of the State, Basic Law: The Knesset (amended twice), Basic Law: The Judiciary, and Basic Law: The State Comptroller. Three basic laws define national institutions and assets – Basic Law: Israel Lands, Basic Law: The State Economy, and Basic Law: The Army. One basic law defines the status of Jerusalem as the capital of Israel. Two basic laws – Basic Law:

[2] HCJ 5848/99 *Paritzky v. District Planning and Building.* Committee, Jerusalem, 54(3) PD 5.

[3] Har-Zahav, R., Israeli Administrative Law, Shenhav Publishers, 1996; HCJ 6406/00 *Bezeq v. Minister of Communication*, PD 58(1) 433.

Freedom of Occupation (amended once) and Basic Law: Human Dignity and Liberty – define fundamental human rights and are at the heart of all other legislation. These basic laws assert that their purpose is to establish in law the values of the State of Israel as a Jewish and democratic state. By virtue of this act, those very values of the State of Israel as a Jewish and democratic state became the object of judicial interpretation. Moreover, both of these basic laws restrict the authority of the Knesset to enact laws that violate the basic rights that they serve to protect. If a law that infringes on these rights is found to have a worthy purpose and is proportional in its infringement, it is deemed constitutional and does not violate the basic law.

Judicial review of the constitutionality of primary legislation was not explicitly defined in the basic laws, and has developed in Israel on the basis of the Supreme Court's interpretation of the constitutional documents. It is through this process that rights such as the freedom of expression, the freedom of election, and the freedom of protest have been established (Kretzmer, 1997).

In the 1970s and 1980s, the Supreme Court began adopting a strategy of increased intervention in the activities of other government agencies in areas where it had heretofore not inserted itself (Mautner, 1993). At the procedural level, the High Court of Justice began to accept cases without rigorous investigation of the doctrines of "standing" and "justiciability," which in the past had been the cornerstones in determining the Court's willingness to hear appeals (Gavison et al., 2000). In the 1980s and 1990s, the Supreme Court significantly expanded its level of intervention in the activities of administrative agencies. Thus, it ruled that the exemption from military service granted to yeshiva students was not legal. It disqualified interrogation methods used by the General Security Service and, through its intervention, allowed women to be inducted into the Air Force pilot training course. This intervention drew no small amount of criticism from the legal community and members of the public alike. The expression widely used in public and legal discourse to describe these developments is "activism." Among other things, these developments are the result of deep fissures in Israeli society, along with an institutional structure that creates a situation in which the political system finds it very difficult to cope with problems that require the formulation of public policy. The functional failures of the legislative and parliamentary branch lead to an increasing number of appeals to the judiciary branch (Hofnung, 1997; Barzilai, 1998).

The very fact that the Court has the authority to strike down laws is seen by some as dealing a blow to the supremacy of the legislative branch, despite the Knesset's ability to overrule the Court through legislation. However, since the legislation of Basic Law: Human Dignity and Liberty (1992) and Basic Law: Freedom of Occupation (1992), the Supreme Court has invalidated sections of no more than five laws.

5.4. THE SEPARATION OF POWERS: THE ROLE OF THE ISRAELI SUPREME COURT IN DEFENDING HUMAN RIGHTS IN ISRAEL

A fundamental element of the Israeli system of government is the principle of the separation of powers. Over the years, Israel has undergone a change in terms of how the state is perceived by the Court, moving from a pure separation of powers to a model of checks and balances. In the latter model, the Supreme Court recognized its political power and understood that its legitimacy as a partner in the collective social decisions in the State of Israel required it to play a number of roles, including interventional monitoring of the affairs of other agencies. In this regard, the Court was required to intervene in matters that deviated from the traditional pattern of separation of powers, for example, stripping Knesset members of their immunity, overseeing regulations, reviewing political agreements, validating political appointments, and allowing government ministers with indictments pending against them to retain their positions (Claude, 1999).

The judicial branch in Israel has the status of first among equals relative to the other branches of government. Thus, for example, it enjoys a substantial degree of independence from political influence. Judges on the Supreme Court are appointed by the Judicial Selection Committee, composed of representatives of all three branches of government, ensuring a professional and apolitical selection process (Shetreet, 2004).

The Israeli Supreme Court serves a wide variety of functions. First of all, it is the highest court of appeals in the Israeli legal system. Furthermore, it is the first venue in which disputes between individuals and the state are heard. This second role has caused the Supreme Court to be viewed by the general public as the watchdog over the rule of law and the champion in the fight against corruption and the protection of human and civil rights. To reduce the heavy burden of fulfilling this role, a reform has been enacted in which cases brought by individuals against the state will now be heard first by lower courts.

5.5. A JEWISH AND DEMOCRATIC STATE: AN UNDEFINED HUMAN RIGHTS ATTITUDE

The Israeli public has been grappling with the issue of the Jewish character of Israel as a Jewish and democratic state since the founding of the state. The State of Israel's unique character, as well as the history preceding its establishment, testifies to the explicit desire of its founders to establish a Jewish nation with a Jewish character and to make the State of Israel the homeland of the Jewish people. This desire is reflected in the selection of Hebrew as the official language of the country, the recognition of the Jewish holidays and Jewish symbols as the official national symbols, and the establishment of religious services and immigration legislation that show a decisive preference for Jews (Rubinstein and Medina, 2005). That said, no law has been passed stipulating who is a Jew, and the formal definition recognizes a Jew as an individual who is born to a Jewish mother or an individual who has converted. It does not specifically define the type of conversion, whether in accordance with Jewish law, nor does it state whether conversion is possible when conducted under auspices that are not Orthodox. Whereas Israel is the national homeland of the Jewish people, it does not exclude others from becoming citizens; it is, under its laws and founding principles and despite the hostility, war, and terror to which it is subject, a state that is a land of equal opportunity for all of its Arab citizens. Thus, for example, the Court has ordered that the writing on street signs must also appear in Arabic and ruled that Arabs and Jews should be treated equally when purchasing residential property.[4]

Despite these principles, a major social problem in the country is the inability to govern. This deficit has led to an alternative political culture in which the Supreme Court plays a role as the arbiter of controversial issues.

[4] HCJ 4112/99 Adalah, *The Legal Center for the Rights of the Arab Minority in Israel v. Municipality of Tel-Aviv-Jaffa* (not yet published); HCJ 6698/95 Qa'dan v. Israel Land Administration, et al., PD 54 (1) 258.

6

Israel in Light of Structural and Cultural Variables

6.1. THE POLITICAL CULTURE: ISRAEL AND ITS NON-LIBERAL CULTURE OF ALTERNATIVE POLITICS

Violations of human rights in democratic systems are usually case-related rather than the result of a consistent, articulated policy. This is also the situation in Israel, where governmental authorities are required to safeguard the individual's fundamental "natural" rights[1] and the Israeli Knesset (parliament) is required to uphold the fundamental rights outlined in the Basic Laws of 1992, namely Basic Law: Human Dignity and Liberty and Basic Law: Freedom of Occupation.[2] As a result, human rights organizations usually adopt a case-related strategy in which they help people in specific cases defend their rights, rather than attempting to inculcate attitudinal changes in society in support of human rights. This is also the reason why these organizations regard the Court as their natural ally in defending human rights and helping people in litigation. However, in the long run, such an approach may prove ineffective in societies such as Israel, in which the norms of human rights have not been internalized in the political culture. In such societies, the case-specific strategy may achieve results in the short term, but in the long run may create the impression that human rights are the interest of elitist groups rather

[1] See, for example, H.C. 73/53 Kol Ha'am Co. Ltd. v. Minister of Interior 7 P.D. 871 – in which the Supreme Court affirmed the freedom of expression; H.C. 153/87 *Shakdiel v. Minister of Religious Affairs*, (1988) 42(2) P.D. 221 – in which the Supreme Court played a primary role in defending the status of female members of public religious bodies; H.C. 5100/94, Pub. Comm. *Against Torture in Isr. v. Gov't of Israel*, 53(4) P.D. 817 – in which the Supreme Court declared that Israeli law prohibits physical methods of interrogation.

[2] See, for example, C.A. 6821/93 *United Mizrahi Bank Ltd. v. Migdal Coop. Vill.* 49 (4) P.D. 21.

than the whole society. Given that the Court is heavily dependent on the legitimacy granted to it by the public, this process of alienating the public from human rights procedures may lead to a decline in the legitimacy given to the Court in defending human rights. Therefore, human rights organizations in Israeli society must consider these conditions and design a long-term strategy for defending human rights through the internalization of norms in society. A number of significant changes in Israeli political culture in recent decades make the possibility of instilling such norms in society more feasible.

6.2. THE TRANSFORMATION OF ISRAELI POLITICAL CULTURE: FROM A TOP-DOWN TO A BOTTOM-UP ORIENTATION IN DECISION-MAKING PROCESSES

From the mid-1970s, two significant changes took place in Israeli society. First, the Labor Party lost its dominance in the political system, thus creating a two-block system. In the 1980s, this situation gave power to sectoral parties, such as the religious parties. In the 1990s, with the introduction of direct elections for the Prime Minister, the Knesset saw a further rise in sectoral politics. These changes caused the weakening of the legislative authority relative to the judicial authority (see, for example, Mautner, 2002). Second, key features in the political culture in Israel that had been repressed in the 1950s and 1960s came to the fore and largely shaped the relationship between citizens and politicians as well as the place of the law and of the Supreme Court in Israeli society (Mizrahi and Meydani, 2003).

In 1977, the Labor Party lost its dominant position after twenty-nine years of leading the country, and the right-wing Likud Party formed a coalition government. These events revealed the deep fragmentation and divisions in Israeli society, which also found expression in the evolution of mass movements, notably Peace Now and Gush Emunim, which expressed the left-wing and right-wing positions, respectively, regarding the Arab-Israeli conflict. Despite the clear mandate for change, for various reasons, the newly elected government failed to implement reform plans between 1977 and 1983, and Israeli society experienced political, social, and economic crises (Harris et al., 1997; Zalmanovitch, 1998). The political system was transformed into a fragmented system characterized by an increasing number of parties, and it became quite difficult to create coalitions. The unstable situation led to the Likud Party and the Labor Party forming a national unity government in 1984, agreeing on an economic plan and a partial withdrawal from Lebanon. However, they could not reach agreement on many other issues, and thus this government and its successor in 1988 were mired in a political stalemate (Horowitz and Lissak, 1990; Arian, 1997).

These dynamics created the impression among the public that the political system was facing a deep crisis that experts called a governability crisis, that is, the inability to govern efficiently and provide public services (Horowitz and Lissak, 1990; Arian, 1997). Thus, the government continuously failed to provide public services. In addition, the public felt that it could not change the situation because all of the normal channels of influence seemed to be blocked.

Given these structural conditions, large sectors of Israeli society attempted to find an alternative means of providing governmental services. The 1980s were characterized by a significant growth in the black-market economy, particularly regarding illegal trade in foreign currency; gray-market medicine – expressed in the semi-legal private supply of health care services using public facilities; gray-market education – expressed in the hiring of privately paid teachers and the evolution of independent private schools; and pirate cable networks – all of which are alternative methods of obtaining services that the government is supposed to provide (Lehman-Wilzig, 1991, Lehman-Wilzig, 1992). Indeed, during the 1980s, it became clear that unilateral initiatives of this kind were almost the sole means by which people could improve their outcomes. Ultimately, though, most of these initiatives were institutionalized and became part of governmental policy. These rules became much more decentralized – particularly in the fields of foreign currency trade and the communication market (Bruno, 1993). In the fields of education and health care, the government changed the rules in the direction signaled by society and initiated several reform plans aimed at decentralization (Chernichovsky, 1991; Yogev, 1999). These institutionalization processes had a direct impact on specific policies and outcomes, and in the 1990s, Israeli economic and administrative systems became much more decentralized than in previous decades.

Thus, substitute informal institutions evolved as a central strategy of social movements and individuals for solving social problems in Israeli society. They also led the way toward formal institutional changes and the formation of specific policies (Levi-Faur, Sheffer, and Vogel, 1999). These processes intensified during the 1990s, when unilateral initiatives and alternative politics were expanded to a wide variety of fields.

In the field of internal security, the feeling of many Israelis that the police did not provide sufficient security triggered the evolution of privately paid security services, protecting the public against crime and theft in many neighborhoods and small towns (Zinger, 2004). In the field of social welfare, given the growth in socio-economic gaps and the failure of the government to provide sufficient support for the poor, Israeli society has witnessed a tremendous growth in the number of voluntary organizations for helping weaker groups of society, both in terms of financial support and consultation (Gidron, Bar, and Katz, 2003). In the relationship between church and state, given the monopoly of the Israeli religious authorities over marriage and divorce procedures, many Israelis who felt uncomfortable with this monopoly adopted unilateral initiatives of civil marriage procedures outside of Israel – especially in Cyprus (Lehman-Wilzig, 1992). As this became a widespread phenomenon, Israeli authorities and courts had no choice but to recognize these marriages. Thus, the creation of this substitute informal institution led to a formal institutional change that actually created a separation between church and state in a very important area.

The emergence of these informal institutions reflects an even deeper change in the nature of the relationship between citizens and politicians in Israel. In the 1950s and 1960s, this relationship was based on a top-down approach in the sense that policies were decided through a highly centralized system with very limited participation of citizens. By the 1980s and 1990s, this relationship had been transformed and was now based on a bottom-up approach. In this new relationship, citizens identified policy problems and solved them unilaterally by forming substitute informal institutions. In doing so, they actually signaled the required institutional change to politicians. Thus, institutional changes as well as specific policies and outcomes were initiated from the bottom up.

Furthermore, in this process, the legislative and the executive authorities were weakened whereas the Supreme Court, which enjoyed public legitimacy and trust, was strengthened. As explained elsewhere (Mizrahi and Meydani, 2003), the deep rifts within Israeli society, together with the institutional structure, create a situation in which the political system is unable to deal with problems that entail the shaping of public policy. In light of this inability, Israeli citizens have been filing an ever-increasing number of petitions with the Supreme Court, with a twofold purpose: to push for the policy decisions to be made, and to put pressure on the politicians to change the institutional structure, in one way or another. The political role of the Supreme Court in Israel is, therefore, the consequence of deep, complex, political and social processes rather than the result of an elitist mechanism or the personality of a particular judge.

Human rights activists and non-governmental organizations (NGOs) in Israel tend to ignore the shifts in the nature of the relationship between citizens and politicians, but they play a central role in empowering the Supreme Court as a political player and defender of human rights. The main channel of activity for defending human rights is the legal system, as evident, for example, in the public and legal struggle of Shatil, established by the New Israel Fund, to add sixty-one new pre-compulsory kindergartens in the academic year 2000–2001 and to open the first library to serve the Bedouin population in the Negev (Eldar, 2002). In a similar vein, following the petition filed by Bizchut, The Israel Human Rights Center for People with Disabilities, the HCJ ordered an examination of more than 200 new buses to assess their accessibility for people in wheelchairs.[3] Likewise, following the petition filed by the Association for Civil Rights in Israel (ACRI), the HCJ ordered the termination, within two months, of the acceptance proceedings of the Arab Ka'adan family to the Jewish settlement of Katzir.[4] In 1995, the HCJ, accepting a petition filed by ACRI, ordered the revocation of Rule 27 of the Rules of the Israel Bar Association, which had allowed attorneys to retain a client's case files, thus preventing the client from going to another attorney.[5] Similarly, in 1996, another ACRI petition, concerning discrimination in the registration of Arab children in kindergartens in Jaffa, achieved a successful resolution. Under pressure from the HCJ, the criteria were revised for accepting children into kindergartens, and the practice of discrimination was eliminated (Eldar, 2002). All of these examples demonstrate the case-related strategy of human rights NGOs. Long-term strategies of mobilizing mass support for human rights barely exist, despite the fact that given the changing nature of the relationship between citizens and politicians, this may be exactly the time to push for major changes in attitudes and policies toward human rights.

6.3. NON-GOVERNABILITY IN ISRAEL

Since the 1980s, there has been tremendous tension in Israel between society and the government. This process began in the 1970s but was aggravated by a variety of ill-conceived political and economic reforms that were implemented nonetheless. These changes led to the emergence of a

[3] *Shahar Butzer v. Local Authority Macabim-Reut* (High Ct 1993).
[4] *Ka'adan v. The Israeli Administration of Landed Property* (High Ct 1995).
[5] *Farid Ganem v. The Israel Bar* (High Ct 1993).

new generation of more pragmatic, technocratic leaders who felt less obligated to traditional ideologies and partisan mechanisms. Simultaneously, the increasing social and economic gaps between constituent groups in society had an increasing influence on public policy, leading to social fragmentation (Canetti, Frant, and Pedahzur, 2001; Arian, Nachmias, and Amir, 2002). The situation reached a peak in the 1996 elections, whose results vividly demonstrated the political splits along partisan lines. The authority of the prime minister grew and that of the Knesset decreased. These processes led to the exacerbation of the existing contradictions, the deepening of divisions and the lack of cohesiveness in public policy (Doron and Harris, 2000). With no clear mandate from the people, the Knesset lost its ability to fulfill its function effective as a legislative body.

Since the 1970s, the centralized nature of Israel's political and economic systems has made it increasingly incapable of functioning effectively. This phenomenon has been called non-governability. Initially, attempts were made to overcome this deficiency through democratic processes such as protests and exit strategies. When these approaches failed, the public created alternative forms of political participation. In other words, the public sought to supply the missing goods and services they wanted and needed by working around the system instead of through it. In the process, the public came to the realization that there was a need to change the existing political rules. However, economic and political instability, coupled with procedural democratic norms, made the players focus on short-term, immediate considerations or the use of institutional change as a solution to urgent economic and political crises. As a result, public policy on human rights received only minimal attention.

In their book, *Governability and the Executive Authority in Israel* (2002), Arian, Nachmias, and Amir analyzed the split of the Israeli factional system, depicting it as a sign of instability. The parameters they used as a measure for analysis included the extent of electoral change from one election to another inside political blocks and between them, the number and size of new parties, the period of time a specific government and the parliament remained in power, and the frequency of changes in political policy, such as changes in the appointment of members of the parliament.

The political literature divides the changes in the partisan system into three periods during which a meaningful political change took place (Arian, Nachmias, and Amir, 2002; see also, Goldberg, 1994). In the early days of its existence, Israel's partisan system functioned with one dominant party at its center. During this period, the Mapai Party and its successors (Maarach and Avoda – Labor in Hebrew) were at the center of all of the coalitions and governments. During the second period, which began with the Likud's victory in the 1977 elections, the partisan system became more competitive, and control alternated between the Avoda and Likud parties and the parties identified with them. This was the period when unified governments came into being, reflecting electoral equity. During the third period, the direct election of the prime minister was introduced. This period saw an increasing split in the Knesset and a rise in sectoral politics along with a decline in the electoral power of the larger parties (Hazan, 1996). Together, these phenomena reflected the height of political instability. The number of lists of parties competing for a place in the Knesset grew, reaching a peak of thirty-three in 1992. In the 1996 elections, there were twenty parties competing for seats in the Knesset and in 1999, thirty-one parties. The growth in the number of parties competing for the Knesset took place despite the rise of the block percentage in 1992, from 1 percent to 1.5 percent (Arian, Nachmias, and Amir, 2002: 103).

Since 1981, the contest between Likud and the Maarach (Avoda and Mapam) has been a close one. In 1981, both parties garnered about a million and a half votes, with only 10,405 votes separating them. From that point on, however, Avoda began losing votes. This tendency is especially significant if one examines the number of voters. Their number increased in the period between 1969 and 1988 by approximately 900,000 votes. The difference in the number of votes the Avoda Party received in 1988 (685,363) and in 1969 (632,035) was only 53,000 votes, whereas the Likud votes rose from 338,948 in 1969 to 709,305 in 1988 – an addition of 370,000 (Arian, Nachmias, and Amir, 2002: 104).

In the 1990s, the competitiveness of the political system did not decline, but the power of the two largest parties continued to weaken, so that their combined power was less than what it had been in the first years after the state's establishment. In 1999, the weight of the two parties in the Knesset fell even further. The combined number of mandates they both secured was similar to the one a large party would have secured in seven out of ten election campaigns between 1949 and 1981. In the 1999 elections, Israel Achat, which included Gesher and Meimad, secured only 26 mandates, which constituted 670,484 votes (20.3%). Likud fell to 19 mandates, with its number of voters down to 468,103 (14.1%). In the special prime minister elections in 2001, there was an especially low voter turnout: 62.3 percent, compared to the 78.7 percent in 1999, and

TABLE 6.1. *Rae's split measure, 1949–1999*

Value of the split measure	Knesset	Year
0.788	1	1949
0.792	2	1951
0.832	3	1955
0.797	4	1959
0.814	5	1961
0.788	6	1965
0.702	7	1969
0.701	8	1974
0.707	9	1977
0.680	10	1981
0.740	11	1984
0.770	12	1988
0.772	13	1992
0.820	14	1996
0.884	15	1999

Source: Arian A., Nachmias D., and Amir R. (2002). *Governability and the Executive Authority in Israel.* Israeli Institute of Democracy, p. 107.

similar percentages in the previous elections (Arian, Nachmias, and Amir, 2002:108).

The changes in the partisan system of distribution in Israel as well as the increase in political instability are clearly reflected in the Knesset distribution measures documented in Arian, Nachmias, and Amir's book (2002). The researchers present a table with the split measure devised by Rae (1967: 47–58). This measure is calculated as 1, minus the square percentage of the sum of votes in every party. The values of this measure range from 0 to 1. If the parliament has only one party represented in it, the value of the measure would be 0 (no split). The greater the number of parties in the parliament, the closer is the value of the measure to 1. Table 6.1 shows an ever-increasing split between parties in the Knesset, with the highest value occurring in 1999 (0.884).

Another measure that helps describe and explain the changes that the partisan system brought to Israeli government is the measure of centralization (Hirshman, 1970). Its values range between 0 and 1, as well. If the parliament has only one party represented in it, the value of the measure would be 0. The smaller the value of the measure of centralization, the smaller the size of the parties in the parliament.

TABLE 6.2. *The effective number of parties and the measures of centralization, 1949–1999*

Centralization measure	Effective party number	Knesset	Year
0.211	4.73	1	1949
0.207	4.83	2	1951
0.167	5.99	3	1955
0.203	4.92	4	1959
0.158	5.37	5	1961
0.211	4.72	6	1965
0.279	3.58	7	1969
0.298	3.35	8	1974
0.229	4.36	9	1977
0.320	3.13	10	1981
0.259	3.86	11	1984
0.228	4.38	12	1988
0.227	4.39	13	1992
0.178	5.61	14	1996
0.115	8.68	15	1999

Source: Arian A., Nachmias D., and Amir R. (2002). *Governability and the Executive Authority in Israel.* Israeli Institute of Democracy, p. 109.

The final measure that is useful in examining the partisanship of the Israeli Knesset is the effective number of parties (Laakso and Taagepera, 1979). This measurement indicates the hypothetical number of equal-sized parties that might have a similar influence on the split in the political system. The measure equals the sum (in percent) of the seats each party has in the parliament, divided into 1. The measure consists of a whole number as well as a decimal fraction: The whole number represents the number of parties and the fraction represents the distance from another whole number (another effective party). In most election campaigns, the effective number of parties ranges from -1 to $+1$ in relation to the number of parties that won a tenth of the seats in the parliament. Values for the effective number of parties and measures of centralization between 1949 and 1999 appear in Table 6.2.

The findings presented in the table reflect an ever-increasing rise in political instability. As Arian, Nachmias and Amir (2002:110) note

> The Knesset was split since its first days... in the year 1949, the split level was already relatively high (0.79), and there were approximately five

> effective parties. The greater the split became and the higher the number of effective parties, the more complex the job of putting together a coalition became and the less the chance of coalitional stability.

From 1969 on, the findings show that the effective number of parties decreased, while the centralization of the partisan system increased. Since then, there has been a shift from a dominant party to a competitive partisan system. In the 1996 elections, the centralization measure dropped to 0.18, while the effective number of parties went up to 5.61. In 1999, the effective number of parties continued its ascent to an unprecedented rate of 8.68. The result was a much more complex process of putting together a coalition as well as a reduced chance of coalitional stability, confirming the public's perception of political instability.

From 1977 on, negotiations about the distribution of positions and budget allocations in the government became more complex and demanding. The bigger parties responded to the demands and sought to increase the number of government offices. Even though the amendment to the Basic Law: Government passed, limiting the number of ministers to eighteen (including the prime minister), after Ehud Barak was elected prime minister in 1999, due to difficulties in creating a coalition, the law was amended once more, increasing the number of positions available for ministers. This tendency continued and accelerated when the Sharon government was established in 2001 – it had twenty-six ministers and thirteen minister deputies.

In addition, Israel has gone through many periods of economic instability as well. The rate of unemployment has vacillated between 17 percent in the first few years of the state and 2.5–3 percent in the 1970s, and rose back more than 11 percent in the beginning of the 1990s (Meydani, 2009).The effects of privatization and the decline in real wages were reflected mainly in the salaries of uneducated and unskilled workers. Thus, between 1980 and 1997, their salaries – which had been 70 percent of the national average – declined to 55 percent of the average income. The salaries of workers who had eight years or less of education declined during the same period from 74 percent of the average income to 59 percent (in Swirski and Fraenkel, 2001; see also, Moalem and Frisch, 1999). Government mortgages also declined from 38 percent of all mortgages taken out by home buyers in 1994 to 25 percent in 1999. According to Shlomo Swirski and Etty Konor-Attias, the decline reflects the inability of the government mortgage to offer meaningful assistance in purchasing a home. The result is reflected in the decline in the rate of home ownership in the lower tenth of the population, which fell from 52.2 percent in 1987 to 43.3 percent in 1992, and to 24.2 percent in 1997. The ownership rate of the second lowest tenth of the population declined from 58.0 percent in 1987 to 55.6 percent in 1992, and to 53.8 percent in 1997 (Swirski and Konor-Attias, 2000).

Thus, structural variables such as the inability to govern and economic instability create an atmosphere in which politicians' decisions are driven by short-term considerations. This kind of atmosphere makes it hard for policy makers to design long-term policies. In fact, it is this instability and political gridlock that leads to the problem of collective action in which major sections of the public feel it is useless to make their preferences known to policy makers. One of the results of this situation is a lack of public policy on human rights.

6.4. THE ALTERNATIVE POLITICS OF THE STATE ECONOMY ARRANGEMENT LAW

In 1985, politicians passed the State Economy Arrangement Law (SEAL), commonly regarded as part of the budget legislation in Israel. However, this law became an alternative that many groups used to enact policies rather than trying to pass them through the legislative process of the Knesset. This law allowed for an accelerated, flexible regulatory process, but one that lacked any democratic discussion in the Knesset or the intervention of Israeli consumer organizations.

Israel of 1985 was suffering from a severe economic crisis. Inflation rose to hundreds of percents a year; the budget deficit was growing continually, and currency reserves were diminishing. The banking and financial systems had not yet recovered from the major share crisis of 1983. Attempts made by the government, the coordination bureau of the employers' organizations, and the Histadrut (the workers' union) to stabilize the economy with band-aid treatments and package deals proved futile. The situation kept deteriorating. The military policy Israel was following in Lebanon only aggravated the feeling of economic crisis among the public. Furthermore, signals were beginning to emerge from the public demanding the resolution of various social issues (Bruno, 1993; Razin and Sadka, 1993; Bechor, 1996). A comprehensive economic stabilization plan was proposed as early as the beginning of the 1980s, but it was the exacerbation of the economic crisis, combined with the failure of the band-aid solutions, that helped promote the plan among the decision makers.

The National Unity Government was formed in September 1984, headed by Shimon Peres (Maarach-Avoda [Labor Party]) as the prime minister. Toward the end of that year, a small group of experts and high-ranking officials met with the goal of formulating an economic stabilization program, of which the SEAL was to become a part. Some of the political entrepreneurs behind the initiatives were the director general of the treasury at that time, Dr. Emmanuel Sharon, leading representatives of academia such as Prof. Michael Bruno, later the governor of the Bank of Israel, Prof. Eitan Berglas, Mordechai Frenkel from the Bank of Israel, and Amnon Neubach, the economic advisor to the prime minister. The team enjoyed the support of Prime Minister Shimon Peres (Maarach) and the Minister of Finance, Yitzchak Modai (Likud). The discussions were held in secret concurrently with talks with the U.S. administration, which committed to earmarking a special allocation of $1.5 billion to rescue the Israeli economy (Peres, 1995). The team agreed that the only way to emerge from the crisis was with a comprehensive economic program (for the status of Israel's PM, see Arian, Nachmias, and Amir, 2002). Shortly after government approval was received, the necessary actions were brought to the Knesset for approval under the heading "The State Emergency Economic Arrangement Law – 1985." This was the first Arrangements Law, which over the years was transformed into electoral capital for decision makers and into a platform that influenced political and economic processes and gave rise to certain political and professional norms in Israel's political and public system.

The State Economy Arrangement Law (SEAL) was enacted in 1985 as a measure that complemented the economic stabilization program. The program consisted of a host of laws and legislative amendments from numerous areas, which the government of Israel presented to the Knesset for approval as one whole. Conceived as a solution for an emergency situation, SEAL has since become a rooted practice and is brought up for renewed approval by the Knesset every year, concurrently with the budget law. As is customary, the SEAL is presented as a single whole to the Knesset's finance committee, which discusses its various articles in a short, pre-determined period of time. The law is then submitted for final approval by the Knesset's plenum (Nachmias and Klein, 1999).

The literature on the topic emphasizes the instability of the political coalition and the declining ability of the economy to function as the catalysts that promoted the use of the SEAL. Scholars also point to the fact that the law is used as an instrument for minimizing political costs (Nachmias and Klein, 1999). An analysis of the preliminary design of the

SEAL shows that this type of legislation was the subject of criticism even in 1985. In their article, David Nachmias and Eran Klein point out the dissatisfaction that prevailed in the Ministry of Justice at that time and the determined objections of the Attorney General, Prof. Yitzchak Zamir (Nachmias and Klein, 1999). Nachmias and Klein emphasize that despite the Basic Law: State Economy – 1975, the Protection of Investments of the Israeli Public in Financial Assets – 1984, and the Foundations of Budget Law – 1985, all of which limit the government's ability to undertake major economic measures without the approval of the Knesset, the economic program was devised under a veil of secrecy and concurrently with driving the Ministry of Justice off the center stage. The political entrepreneurs' ability to promote the process with the help of the prime minister and the minister of finance resulted in part from non-governability, the crisis atmosphere, and the alternative politics that had developed in Israel since the 1970s and accelerated the personal initiatives of decision makers. With time, this pattern of individual action became a deeply ingrained management norm.

In the years since the implementation of the economic stabilization program, the government has used the SEAL to facilitate the approval of hundreds of laws and legislative amendments in a broad range of areas such as health care and welfare, taxation and investments, municipal taxes and regulatory, and structural reforms of the agriculture, communications, and energy industries.

Certain sectors have also begun using the SEAL as an instrument to advance their own interests. For example, the government uses the law and the coalition majority to support its initiatives. The prime minister and the minister of finance use it to accelerate the legislative process and overcome obstacles and conflicts to strengthen their power. High-ranking officials in the Ministry of Finance regard the SEAL as a vital tool for the design and implementation of socio-economic policies and for promoting structural reforms in Israel's economy. Nachmias and Klein (1999) point out that this group has a strong influence on the public system. Therefore, its backing of the SEAL has special importance, both because of the professional-public stature of its members and because of their extensive experience in working with the political system. Interestingly, high-ranking officials in other ministries object to the SEAL, but the rise of the free market that can supply the economic and social products Israel is short of has turned the treasury officials into opinion leaders who enjoy the support of prime ministers, finance ministries, and senior figures in Israel's economy. Some members of the Knesset also use the SEAL as electoral equity. They supported the law in the belief that the imbalance in the political system necessitates that a governance tool of this kind be left in the hands of the government. Two prominent supporters of the SEAL were Prof. Shevach Weiss (Labor) and Amnon Rubinstein (Meretz) (Nachmias and Klein, 1999). This rationale was also adopted by other groups in Israel's economy that support structural reforms that involve privatization and regard the SEAL as critical for successful implementation of these reforms. Other groups regarded the SEAL as a convenient way to obtain huge budgets for their members.

7

The Supreme Court and the Political System in Light of Social and Political Processes in Israel during 1948–1999

Between 1948 and 1999, the relationship between the Supreme Court and the political system underwent a number of changes. To establish causal relationships between structural factors, such as the nature of the political, economic, and bureaucratic systems, the form of political participation, and the role of the Supreme Court in Israeli society, we will divide the five decades since the establishment of Israel to the end of the twentieth century (1948–1999) into four periods.

The 1950s and 1960s were characterized by a high degree of centralization in all of the systems, by a very low level of political participation in forms other than elections, and by a relatively self-restrained approach in terms of justiciability and standing adopted by the Court.

The 1970s were characterized by a high degree of centralization in the economic and bureaucratic systems, but the political system became much more fragmented. This period saw a high level of political participation in legal channels other than elections, and the beginning of an activist approach adopted by the Court in terms of standing and justiciability. The analysis of this period begins with the Bergman petition (1969) and ends with the Rubinstein petition (1982) – both concerned the laws regulating the financing of political parties. They exemplify the process through which the Court has gradually become more flexible regarding questions of standing.

The 1980s were characterized by a relatively high degree of centralization in the economic and bureaucratic systems, while the political system became very fragmented. This period also saw a high level of political participation in legal forms other than elections combined with quasi-exit behavior and the use of alternative politics. The Court increased its activism in terms of standing and justiciability. The analysis of this period ends with the passage of two basic laws: Basic Law: Human Dignity and Basic Law: Freedom of Occupation.

The 1990s were characterized by a high degree of centralization in the economic and bureaucratic systems, while the fragmentation of the political system reached a peak. This period saw a high level of political participation in the form of quasi-exit behavior and the use of alternative politics also directed at the Court. At the same time, the Court's activism in terms of standing and justiciability became so clear that its attitudes were considered by other players in any policy-making process.

We now discuss the main characteristics of each period to show the process through which the forms of political participation have been transformed, ultimately leading to the quasi-exit behavior of both the Israeli public and the Court. We do not offer a complete analysis of all of the cases brought before the Court, nor do we select a representative sample of these cases. Given that there is a broad agreement that judicial activism in the sense of the Court's accepting petitions for discussion without much concern for justiciability and standing exists, we do not try to explore this observation through case analysis.

7.1. INITIAL STRUCTURAL AND CULTURAL CONDITIONS

Israeli society and political culture were shaped under the rule of the British Mandate in Palestine from 1917 to 1948. These decades have been described and analyzed in numerous books and articles (to mention just a few: Eisenstadt, 1989; Shprinzak, 1986; Migdal, 2001; Horowitz and Lissak, 1990; Lehman-Wilzig, 1992). The main insights suggested by these studies can be summarized as follows.

In the three decades prior to the establishment of the State of Israel in 1948, the Jewish community in Israel had a relatively large measure of autonomy in managing its own affairs in most fields of life. British mandatory authorities enabled the Jewish community to create a political party system based on a form of democratic election, establish economic and industrial organizations, and run autonomous systems of public health, social welfare, and education. This autonomy did not include the permission to freely settle the country, to have an independent military organization, or to enforce the rule of law. The British policy of undermining independent initiatives of the Jewish community in these areas of life became very difficult in the 1930s and 1940s due to the intensifying conflict between the Jewish and Arab populations.

These structural conditions led the Jewish leadership to formulate a twofold strategy that became the hallmark of the Zionist ethos. First, whenever it was possible and authorized by the British Mandate, the Jewish leadership created independent organizations, alternative to those of either the British authorities or the Arab community, to accelerate economic development, provide public services such as health, education, and welfare, and develop infrastructure such as electricity, roads, water supply, industry, and building construction. The Arab community did not utilize such a strategy for reasons not discussed here. Thus, the idea that the Jewish community could not trust others and had to create its own institutions and organizations gradually became a building block of the Zionist ethos. Second, facing significant threats from the Arab population and a British ban on large-scale Jewish immigration, as well as the aspiration to expand Jewish settlement in Palestine to the greatest extent possible, the Jewish leadership gradually built illegal paramilitary forces that had three main goals: fighting the Arab paramilitary forces, organizing illegal Jewish immigration, and establishing and defending illegal settlements. These channels of activity became the strongest building block of the Zionist ethos as well as of the values that were inculcated through the educational system after the establishment of the State of Israel (Horowitz and Lissak, 1990). We should emphasize that these channels of activity were not only alternative but also illegal as far as British mandatory law was concerned. The British mandatory authorities were faced with new facts and realities that they finally accepted.

Based on the learning process presented in the previous chapter, we suggest that the process of Jewish institution building in the pre-state period, which was illegal in several important respects, had a significant influence on the political culture, belief system, and approach to conflict and problem solving in Israeli society after 1948. In other words, the ethos that was imparted to generations of Israelis included the idea that acting via unilateral initiatives on the margins of the system of formal rules and even outside this system is not only permitted, but even serves national goals. To a large extent, this was the modus operandi of Israeli society (Shprinzak, 1986; Migdal, 2001; Lehman-Wilzig, 1992).

Ironically, however, due to a high level of centralization, the Jewish, and later the Israeli, institutional setting enabled politicians to repress similar initiatives directed toward the Jewish, or Israeli, system itself (Shprinzak, 1986; Horowitz and Lissak, 1990; Aharoni, 1998). The Labor Party, which led a coalition government during the 1950s and 1960s, had a socialist orientation and therefore championed the close involvement of the state and public administration in the economic system (Aharoni, 1998). This centralism prevented the development of alternative power centers such as interest groups and significantly slowed down development of a civil society based on liberal values (Horowitz and Lissak, 1990). It had a similar impact on the Supreme Court, which was relatively weak and restrained during the 1950s and 1960s.

7.2. THE 1950S AND 1960S: FROM THE ESTABLISHMENT OF THE STATE TO THE SIX DAY WAR (1948–1967)

In the first period after the State of Israel was established, during the 1950s and 1960s, Israel's political, administrative, and economic systems were highly centralized (Horowitz and Lissak, 1990; Aharoni, 1998), evident in the fact that information was rarely accessible to Israeli citizens (Doron, 1988). In particular, there was intense censorship of information related to "security" issues – a term that was interpreted very broadly. During the 1950s and 1960s, Israelis did not clamor for change. Thus, whereas political participation through voting during these decades was very intense, other forms of political participation hardly existed.

During the 1950s and 1960s, the Israeli Supreme Court was reluctant to accept petitions for discussion without concern for justiciability and standing (Witkon, 1982). According to Dan Horowitz and Moshe Lissak, this restraint made it easy for the Court to avoid having to contend with issues related to values and moral content, which would have set the public and the other authorities against it. By refusing to deal with contentious issues, it could retain the public's trust in the Court and in its rulings (Horowitz and Lissak, 1990; Rubinstein, 1980a). The Court's approach of restraint was expressed mainly in the creation of obstacles to filing petitions with the HCJ – namely justiciability and standing (Rubinstein, 1980b). In matters in which the Supreme Court adopted an approach of restraint, it denied the public the opportunity of having any influence on major issues.

With the establishment of the State of Israel, the Supreme Court faced a difficult task of gaining the public's trust (Rubinstein, 1980a). Indeed, if we read the newspapers from that period, it would appear that there was essentially no law and order in those early days. Although the streets were rife with riots and executions were commonplace, the courts of Jerusalem were closed (Huller, 1997). To make matters worse, the government authorities tended to give broad powers of discretion to the executive branch (Horowitz and Lissak, 1990). The situation was also influenced by the belief that law, as a profession, had no special role in the task of building the new State (Witkon, 1965; Witkon, 1982). Given this state of affairs, the Supreme Court developed an approach of restraint with respect to attempts to criticize laws solely on the basis of their content. Judicial restraint with regard to government policy was expressed in cases such as *Azuz v. Ezer*, *Jabotinsky v. Weizman*, *Merkaz Rehitei Lekol v. The Minister of Trade and Industry*, as well as in *Hugim Leumi'im v. The Minister of the Police*. Amnon Rubinstein (1980b) notes that the judge who handed down the verdict in *Azuz v. Ezer* still referred to the law "which was duly made," thus leaving the question unanswered as to how possible it would be to invalidate a law unduly made. This interpretation shows that although it could have adopted an activist approach, the Supreme Court chose to exercise restraint. Thus, in the State's early years, the Supreme Court developed a closed legal system that permitted it to promote judicial restraint with respect to issues related to security, religion, and government policy. Beginning in the 1970s and 1980s, the Supreme Court adopted an open system to promote judicial activism, gradually achieving an independent attitude on these issues.

Nevertheless, as opposed to the approach of restraint adopted by the Supreme Court with respect to the question of government policy, when it came to adjudicating issues related to the citizen's basic rights and freedoms, it adopted an approach of total activism. This activism was first expressed in the case of Bejerano, a mediator who worked outside the vehicle licensing bureau and received a warrant demanding that he cease work because what he was doing was immoral. Bejerano filed a petition with the HCJ and won on the grounds of the right of freedom of occupation, despite the fact that there was no law guaranteeing freedom of occupation at that time. The HCJ stated that there is a natural freedom of occupation. If a minister wants to challenge that natural freedom, he or she must do so in accordance with a specific law. In this case, no such law existed (*Bejerano v. The Minister of the Police*). This activist approach continued in the case of Dr. Yisrael Sheib, a former leader of the LECHI Organization – Fighters for Israel's Freedom, an underground organization that was engaged in a struggle with the Hagana, the main Jewish underground in British mandatory Palestine headed by David Ben Gurion. In this case, David Ben Gurion, as Prime Minister and Minister of Defense, issued a warrant preventing Dr. Sheib from working as a teacher. The Court ruled against Ben Gurion (*Dr. Yisrael Sheib v. The Minister of Defense*). This activism was also expressed in the issue of freedom of expression in the case of Kol Ha'Am. The case involved the closing of a newspaper of the Communist Party that had published an article criticizing the Israeli government. The newspaper appealed the decision before the Supreme Court, who ruled unanimously that freedom of speech and freedom of information are the cornerstones of Israeli democracy (*Kol Ha'Am v. The Minister of the Interior*). This activism was also evident in the issue of the right to disseminate information in *Ulpanei Hasrata BeYisrael v. Gary and the Council for the Review of Films and Plays*.

However, the Court did not always apply its approach with egalitarian principles: Whenever a particular basic right came up against either the values of security or religion, the Supreme Court adopted judicial restraint. Thus, for example, the petition of Oswald Rufeisen, known as Brother Daniel, was rejected (*Oswald Rufeisen v. The Minister of the Interior*). Rufeisen converted to Christianity and was known as Brother Daniel. He petitioned the Minister of the Interior, seeking to obtain an immigrant's card and be registered as a Jew on his ID card. In the same vein, the Court decided that intervention in the decision of a military court would occur solely in the event of a significant and salient error (*Grossman v. The Military Advocate General*). This approach was also expressed in other judgments concerning security issues such as *Subchi El Yuchi v. The Minister of Defense*, *Jamal Mahmud Atzlan v. The Military Governor and Commander of the Galilee*, *Boganim v. The Chief of Staff* and *Neiman v. Military Governor*.

According to Horovitz and Lissak (1990), refusing to deal with issues relating to values and moral content, which would have set the public and the other authorities against it, allowed the Court to retain the public's trust in it and in its rulings.

The Court's activism in the matter of the citizen's basic rights and freedoms enjoyed the support of the politicians, such as the Minister of Justice, Pinchas Rosen, who was renowned for his fervent advocacy of the independence of the judicial branch. However, the support of the politicians was only partial; it was given to certain subjects only, and in accordance with the conduct of the Supreme Court. Thus, in the case of *Binyamin Shalit v. The Minister of the Interior*, the politicians enacted a roundabout legislation. Benjamin Shalit, an Israeli Jewish naval officer, married a Scottish woman abroad and returned with her to Israel. They had two children. The Shalits wanted to register their children as Jews under the "nationality" designation on their ID cards, while keeping the "religion" category blank. The Ministry of Interior refused. Shalit went to the Supreme Court, which, in 1970, ruled in his favor in a 5–4 decision. The court's decision was based on technical grounds, specifically questioning the legal right of a clerk to question a registrant's application. However, the court recognized that its decision would cause a public debate about the question of "who is a Jew?" In its decision, the court cautioned, "It is in fact a mistake to think that the matter under consideration requires us to determine who is a Jew." Following the decision, in 1970, the National Religious Party introduced legislation in the Knesset to amend the Population Registry Law to read that an individual registering as a Jew by "religion" or "nationality" must be a "person who was born of a Jewish mother or who has converted to Judaism." Following enactment of this change, in 1972, when the Shalits attempted to register their third child as a Jew in the "nationality" category, the Supreme Court referred to this amended law and denied the request.

Needless to say, subsequently the Supreme Court was aware of the possible results of over-intervention, which could give rise to a restriction of its powers by means of suitable legislation (Rubinstein, 1980a; Lahav, 1989). The Supreme Court's approach of restraint was expressed in the creation of restrictive rules such as the rule that the Court would not intervene in questions of government policy but would confine itself to an examination of the legality of the execution of this policy (Merkaz Rehitei Lekol, High Ct 1952); the creation of restrictive doctrines such as the doctrine of independent status, which gives the Supreme Court immunity from external influences (Landau, 1996); and the creation of obstacles to filing petitions with the HCJ, in the form of jurisdiction, justiciability, and standing or *Locus Standi*. In this respect, the Supreme Court acted in accordance with the dictates of a collectivist culture in which the individual is perceived as an instrument for realizing the aims of the State (Shapiro, 1977, 1984; Horowitz and Lissak, 1990; Mautner, 1993; Segal, 2000). As stated earlier, this collectivist culture was also reflected in the legal rules that the Supreme Court chose to adopt.

In matters in which the Supreme Court adopted an approach of restraint, it denied the public the opportunity of having any influence on significant issues. The most salient example was the Lavon Affair (1954), the scandal over a failed Israeli operation in Egypt in which Egyptian, American, and British-owned targets in Egypt were bombed. Pinhas Lavon, the Israeli Defense Minister, was forced to resign because of the incident. Despite what was called "the unfortunate affair" and the ensuing inquiries and public debate, no petition was filed with the HCJ. However, despite being denied a say in this issue, the public was not spurred into forming various interest groups. The centralized nature of the Israeli government prevented the development of alternative centers of power in the form of interest groups and slowed down the development of a civil society with liberal attributes (Eisenstadt, 1989; Shaham, 1998). Furthermore, due to the problem of collective action, the public was not motivated to exert pressure on the government as long as no catastrophes occurred. However, the Six Day War in 1967 brought significant changes to Israeli culture and the political system as well as to the Court's behavior.

7.3. THE 1970S: FROM THE BERGMAN PETITION TO THE RUBINSTEIN PETITION (1967–1982)

A significant change in the development of Israeli political culture came about in 1967 with the Six Day War (Barzilai, 1992; Naor, 2001). It gave rise to nationalistic and religious feelings about the holy places in the West Bank. That change in the atmosphere was also expressed in the attempts of religious people to establish illegal settlements in the West Bank. These events reflected the re-appearance of the mental model that had characterized the pre-state period – solving social problems through unilateral initiatives. The first initiative was in Hebron in 1968 and ended with a local agreement. By the mid-1970s, the creation of illegal settlements had become the core activity of a large grassroots movement – Gush Emunim – the young guard of the mainstream Zionist National Religious Party (Lehman-Wilzig, 1992). In their settlement activity, they applied a strategy similar to that used by the Jewish leadership during the British Mandate, namely well-planned overnight forays. By the time the sun rose in the morning, several families were already living in temporary shelters with the Israeli flag waving over their settlement. At first, there were clashes with the government and the army, but in several instances the government actually gave up and cooperated with these illegal initiatives (Lehman-Wilzig, 1992). Within a few years, the rules of the game regarding settlements in the occupied territories had changed. With the rise of the right-wing Likud Party to power in 1977, settling the West Bank and Gaza Strip with Jewish settlements became formal policy. This led to a situation where more than 200,000 Israeli Jews settled in these territories, distributed such that the situation is almost irreversible (Benvenisti, 1999).

This process can be explained using the framework proposed by Mantzavinos et al. (2004). Given the rise of nationalistic and religious feelings regarding the holy places in the West Bank, several religious sectors viewed the unwillingness of the Labor-led government to settle the territories as a government failure (Shprinzak, 1986). After their prolonged political pressure within their own party and against the broader Labor coalition failed, these religious groups came to believe that the channels of influence were blocked (Lehman-Wilzig, 1992). Formal rules were not effectively enforced due to the relative weakness of the Labor-led government as well as the re-appearance of the Zionist ethos (Horowitz and Lissak, 1990). These conditions pushed the Gush Emunim movement to look for a mechanism to solve the social problem they were facing. They interpreted this problem as similar to those that the Jewish community had faced in the pre-state period (Shprinzak, 1986) and hence viewed it as an "old problem." As Mantzavinos (2001) explains, people in such situations unconsciously use solutions that have worked in the past. In this case, those solutions were unilateral initiatives. Furthermore, in their justifications and terminology, settlers used the Zionist ethos and even called themselves the "true Zionists" (Shprinzak, 1986). We can infer that they were using the shared mental model that had developed during the pre-state period as a useful means of solving social problems. In doing so, they created an alternative way to build settlements, meaning they found an alternative method for providing a public service. The strategy of unilateral (private) initiatives has proven useful for forcing a specific policy on the government, and it has gradually been institutionalized into the formal rules of the game. It has also been translated into specific policies and led to outcomes with significant political implications.

We should emphasize that these unilateral initiatives have the characteristics of a quasi-exit strategy rather than the private provision of services. Settlers provided their basic facilities such as mobile homes and food privately, but they demanded and relied on the public provision of other services such as personal security, electricity, water, and roads. Most of these services, particularly personal security, were provided by the government prior to the legalization of a given settlement. In other words, this mode of alternative provision of services included a complex mix of public and private financing, facilities, and services, many of which in their initial stages were illegal. These factors allow us to characterize this mode of alternative provision of services as a quasi-exit strategy. These events represented the beginning of quasi-exit behavior in Israeli society after it had been suspended for two decades and reflected the government's difficulty in ruling the country.

The intensive pressures directed toward Israeli politicians during the 1970s led them to change their strategy and their view regarding the role of the Court and jurisdiction as a whole. This change was exemplified by the passage of the Act of Inquiry Committees, which enabled politicians to transfer certain governmental problems to an alternative "decision maker" – an Inquiry Committee chaired by a Supreme Court judge. The 1969 Bergman petition was another example of this change (*Bergman v. The Minister of Finance*, High Ct 1969). This petition claimed that a certain change in electoral law regarding the financing of elections contradicted the basic law regarding the parliament and that this change had not been passed by the proper majority. A turning point in this case was evidenced by the behavior of the politicians led by Attorney General Meir Shamgar, who did not claim justiciability and standing, thus enabling the Court to invalidate the law. While the HCJ changed its attitude about the public's ability to have an influence on significant issues, the politicians' actions attested to a tendency to evade personal responsibility and a tendency to seek public support at times when they needed it. Furthermore, Aharon Bergman, as a private person, could have used other forms of influence that are more common in a democratic system such as protest, or lobbying in the parliament. By turning to the Court, knowing that there were no clear rules, Bergman actually adopted a quasi-exit strategy that challenged both the political system and the Court. The Court, on the other hand, chose to hear the case even though it did not have a clear authority to do so. By agreeing to hear the case, the Court also adopted a quasi-exit strategy of creating facts on the ground as a means of strengthening its organizational power.

That change in the relationship between politicians and the HCJ signaled an invitation to the public to attempt to advance their causes through the Court if they did not agree with the actions of the government authorities. This trend was evident in the cases of *Kaniel v. The Minister of Justice*, *Agudat Derech Eretz v. The Broadcasting Authority*, *Ashkenazi v. Minister of Defense*, and *El Asad v. Minister of Interior*. Some of petitions concerned moral issues in matters relating to the actions of the government authorities and others questioned the legality of certain laws. Examples include *Ofek v. The Minister of the Interior*, which dealt with the freedom of the Association of Policemen, and *Katlan v. the Prison Service*, which dealt with prisoners' right to privacy.

The situation after the Yom Kippur War, in which the political system lacked the ability to govern (Dror, 1989; Eisenstadt, 1989; Horowitz and Lissak, 1990; Mautner, 1993; Shaham, 1998) and the public was denied the opportunity to have any influence on significant issues, gave rise to demands to change the electoral system (Rubinstein, 1982). At the same time, there were attempts to find an alternative that would satisfy the desire for a public product – in this case, a public policy. Solutions to both of these problems came in the form of the Supreme Court. Without any clear-cut rules defining its role, the Court felt free to respond to the ever-growing number of petitions filed by a public that was trying to create a new reality by establishing new facts on the ground.

Nevertheless, the Supreme Court continued to display its restraint with respect to two issues: religion and security. Such restraint is evident in its ruling in *Sheikh Suliman Hussein Oda Abu Hilu v. The Government of Israel* that the issue of the defense policy is not justiciable, and in *Motti Ashkenazi v. The Minister of Defense* that the issue of the army's structure and how people function within it is not justiciable (see also, *Barad v. Madar*; *Gonen v. The Commission of Inquiry on the Yom Kippur War*; and *Greenstein v. the Military Advocate General*). In the same vein, in *Wathad v. The Minister of Finance*, the Court rejected a petition against the payment of grants given to discharged soldiers to students studying at religious institutions, thus underscoring the place of Torah study among the Jewish people.

However, the reluctance of the HCJ to rule on issues of security was not absolute. Furthermore, in matters that were not confined solely to security or religious issues, as defined by the Supreme Court, the HCJ applied an activist policy. In this vein, whenever the proprietary rights of Arab residents were infringed on, the HCJ adopted a policy of activism. Thus, for example, the HCJ allowed the petition against the establishment of settlements in Allon Moreh, after it was determined that the Land Expropriation Order had not been issued for purely military needs but rather for political reasons (*Davikat v. The Government of Israel*). Similarly, the HCJ intervened in the decision of the Military Administration regarding the unification of families (*Samarah v. The Commander of the Judea and Samaria Region*) and overturned the rulings of rabbinical courts when reasons were not given for the court's decision and when a child's best interests were at stake (*Biers v. The Rabbinical Court*). However, when the issue was of a purely religious nature, the HCJ also adopted judicial restraint. For example, the Court was generally careful not to intervene in the rulings of the rabbinical courts (*Vicki Levi v. The Tel Aviv-Jaffa District Rabbinical Court*).

Thus, although signaling an open approach during most of the 1970s, the Court remained restrained. This restraint grew out of two main events that expressed and influenced the socio-political processes in Israel: the 1973 Yom Kippur War that triggered strong criticism against the Labor-led government, and the 1977 election in which the Labor Party lost its dominant position after twenty-nine years of leading the country and the right-wing party, Likud, formed a coalition government. These events revealed the deep fragmentation and divisions in Israeli society that were also expressed in the evolution of mass movements – notably Peace Now and Gush Emunim, which expressed the left-wing and right-wing positions, respectively, regarding the Arab-Israeli conflict. To change the ruling coalition and its policy, the Israeli public used legal democratic channels such as elections, demonstrations, strikes, and the mass media. These events also created the potential for structural changes. Given that replacing the entire administration was considered almost impossible, the newly elected government made a certain number of political appointments and initiated a plan for structural reforms aimed at decentralization and privatization (Harris et al., 1997; Zalmanovitch, 1998). However, because the old bureaucracy maintained strong positions of power in all levels of the civil service, those bureaucrats had an interest in sabotaging structural reform while de-legitimizing new political appointments. This rationale may explain the fact that between 1977 and 1983, the government failed to implement its plans.

Thus, during the 1970s, the political system remained relatively unfragmented, the economic and bureaucratic systems were highly centralized, and public dissatisfaction was expressed through regular forms of political participation such as protests, demonstrations, and the activity of interest groups. As a result, there was not enough space or demand for the Court to develop its independence, so it pursued its policy of self-restraint. The significant changes happened in the third period, which is analyzed in the following section.

7.4. THE 1980S: FROM THE RUBINSTEIN PETITION TO THE PASSAGE OF BASIC LAWS: HUMAN DIGNITY AND FREEDOM OF OCCUPATION

Major changes in the forms of political participation as well as in the Court's policy occurred in third period, the 1980s, which witnessed a deepening of the demographic and structural social changes that began in the 1970s. The influence of the religious political parties, particularly that of ultra-Orthodox parties, grew, and the status of religion in public life became stronger. In addition, encouraged by the Likud government, there was an increase in the settlements in Judea, Samaria, and the Golan Heights, both in size and in number. Political life was characterized by a continuous degeneration of the main systems of the political parties and their leadership. In addition, the political wheeling and dealing between the coalition parties continued, and the level of political debate declined drastically. Extra-parliamentary political activities also flourished at this time: the Peace Now movement, various protest movements that evolved in the wake of the Lebanon War, and Gush Emunim and the settlers of Judea and Samaria. All of these movements played a pivotal role in the political arena (Yishai, 1986). The need for various legal commissions, such as the Kahan Commission and the Karp Commission, also remained. The Kahan Commission was set up in the aftermath of the massacre at Sabra and Shatila and leveled fierce criticism at the government. Following allegations that the government displayed inordinate tolerance toward groups of religious and right-wing activists, the attorney general set up the Karp Commission to investigate the question of how the law was enforced with respect to Jews who attacked Arabs in Judea and Samaria.

The public argument between the opposition parties and the coalition parties grew more acute. Left-wing political parties who felt powerless appealed to the HCJ. Having understood the nature of the Court's decisions and being aware that in certain matters other politicians would not object, left-wing politicians increased the frequency of their petitions to the HCJ, thus advancing their interests and their party's interests (Benvenisti, 1999; Benvenisti, *Ha'aretz* 2000; Dotan and Hofnung, 2001). The HCJ benefited from the fact that the politicians sought its authority and was thereby able to improve its status among policy makers.

It was in this climate that the court heard the Rubinstein petition (1982). Like Bergman's petition (1969) M. K. Rubinstein claimed that a certain change in electoral law about the financing of elections contradicted the basic law regarding the parliament. Furthermore, he contended that this change had not been passed by the proper majority. The Supreme Court ruled in favor of Rubinstein and declared the law void (*Rubenstein v. The Knesset Speaker*). Analyzing the decision, Shimon Shetreet claimed it marked the first time the Knesset had accepted the Court's ruling without even trying to amend the law, as it used to do in early petitions (Shetreet, 1994).

The differences between the Likud and the Maarach (the coalition of the Labor and MAPAM parties) became even more acute, and in the wake of a situation in which policy making had become impossible, the decision was made to set up two national unity governments, one in 1984 and its successor in 1988. These governments created a political stalemate (Shaham, 1998). The need for various commissions continued in the wake of certain incidents concerning the actions of the Israeli secret services in Israel and overseas: the Bus 300 Affair (1984), the Pollard Affair (1985), and the Vanunu Affair (1986). The amount of public criticism raised during these events manifested quite clearly the changes that had occurred in the public's ability to influence public affairs. If in the 1950s and 1960s the public's channels of influence had been blocked, in the 1980s the Supreme Court opened its gates and permitted criticism even in these classified areas pertaining to state security (*Vanunu v. The State of Israel*).

A case in point, which illustrates how the Supreme Court signaled the opening of its gates, is the Sarid petition to the HCJ (1981). In this case, the HCJ refused to intervene in the decision of the Knesset Speaker to cut short the debate over a proposed vote of no confidence in the government by a few hours. Nevertheless, the HCJ did articulate its willingness to intervene in internal parliamentary proceedings solely in the event that the issue would do significant damage to the fabric of parliamentary life. This determination was, in effect, a signal to politicians that the HCJ was prepared to intervene in parliamentary issues. Indeed, the HCJ subsequently declared that the Knesset Speaker was not empowered to prevent a one-man faction from submitting a motion for a vote of no confidence in the government (*The Kach Faction v. The Knesset Speaker*).

The HCJ sent out these signals about its conduct in judgments by means of the "Ubiter." In the Rubenstein petition to the HCJ (1982), Judge Shlomo Levin wrote the main decision, which was supported by all five judges:

> As in previous cases, which have discussed the question of equality pursuant to section 4 of the Basic Law: The Knesset, High Ct 98/69 and High Ct 260, 246/81, the Attorney General does not raise the claim of an absence of justiciability... therefore, we were requested by him to reject the petition based on its particular merits. Indeed it is important to note, in parentheses, that the greater the number of cases in which this Court is required to discuss petitions of a constitutional nature of the aforementioned type based on their particular merits, the smaller the chances that this Court will relinquish the adjudication thereof, even if the Attorney General deems it appropriate, in the future, to raise questions such as these, and questions similar to them. (*Rubenstein v. The Knesset Speaker*: paragraph 4)

The feeling of the government's inability to govern, coupled with the opening of channels of influence in the form of the HCJ, enticed the public, with all its diverse groups, and various politicians to seek the services of the HCJ (Sheleg, *BaMachane* 1997). Petitions brought ranged from the right to receive information (*Zichroni v. The Managing Committee of the Broadcasting Authority*) to the freedom to demonstrate (*Levi v. The Southern District Commander of the Israel Police*). The Supreme Court expanded its intervention in Knesset decisions (*Miari v. The Knesset Speaker*) and in issues related to religion and security. In the same vein, the HCJ ordered the defense authorities to provide gas masks that protected people against chemical and biological attack to the Arab residents of the administered territories, just as they did to all Israeli citizens (*Murkus v. The Minister of Defense*). Likewise, the HCJ issued an injunction to prevent the demolition of the home of a terrorist charged with murder, because it would also have entailed the demolition of the home of his brother's family (*Turkman v. The Minister of Defense*). Similarly, with the intervention of the HCJ, the military authorities decided to provide religiously observant Jews with gas masks against chemical and biological warfare that were specially adapted for beards (*Miller v. The Minister of Defense*). The IDF's policy not to accept women in its pilots' course was reversed in *Miller v. The Minister of Defense.* With regard to religious matters, the HCJ authorized the participation of a woman on a religious council (*Shakdiel v. The Minister of Religious Affairs*) and also ruled that the membership of a woman on the committee to elect the City Rabbi could not be disqualified (*Poraz v. The Mayor of Tel Aviv-Jaffa*).

This intervention on the part of the Court was granted political legitimacy due to the fact that politicians preferred placing responsibility on the shoulders of the HCJ (Voight and Salzberger, 2002). In addition, the HCJ also enjoyed public legitimacy at that time (Barzilai, Yochtman-Yaar, and Segal, 1994), although, as we will stress later, public legitimacy was contingent on the issues pending discussion by the HCJ. The Court was well aware of this fact, and as distinct from its approach with respect to petitions concerning equality, if the issues were of a purely military or political nature, the Court would adopt an approach of restraint (Hofnung, 1991; Kremnitzer, 1999). The HCJ rejected petitions concerning government decisions about the release of prisoners and political prisoners (*Federman v. The Minister of Defense*), a petition against holding peace talks with Syria (*The Temple Mount and Land of Israel Faithful Movement v. The Prime Minister*), and a petition concerning the legality of the actions of the government in the establishment of settlements (*Bargil v. The Government of Israel*).

At the same time, the Supreme Court itself, led by Justice Aharon Barak, underwent a transformation. In the Ressler petition (1986) to the HCJ, Barak determined that everything is justiciable, and, in his words, that: "In every case, there is the law, and in every case, there are the varying degrees within the law." Thus, Barak conveyed a message to the public that the doors to the channels of influence had been flung wide open (see also, Bendor, 1988; Dotan, 1996; Mizrahi and Meydani, 2006). Nevertheless, petitions concerning issues of a purely military or political nature and petitions concerning government policy still remained non-justiciable in practice. Thus, the HCJ eventually rejected the petition filed by Attorney Yehuda Ressler concerning the conscription of yeshiva students, citing the reason that a reasonable defense minister may take religious considerations into account. Nevertheless, Justice Barak added that a reasonable decision could become an unreasonable decision when circumstances changed. With such a caveat, the Supreme Court was signaling to interest groups that with respect to the future, its gates remained open on this issue, despite the decision. Emboldened by these pronouncements, interest groups swung into action to bring about a change in the circumstances (Magen, 1998a; Magen, 1998b). Here again, we see an example of the HCJ serving as a political catalyst.

As explained before, the political system has been transformed into a fragmented system characterized by an increasing number of parties and great difficulties to create coalitions (Arian, 1997; Aharoni, 1998; Barzilai, 1998; Hofnung, 1999; Korn and Shapira, 1997). The feeling of its lack of ability to bear any political influence drove the political left wing to the HCJ. Having understood the nature of the Court's decisions and being aware that in certain matters, the other politicians would not object, the left-wing politicians increased the frequency of their petitions to the HCJ, thus advancing their interests and their party's interests (Shamir, 1990; Benvenisti, 1999; Benvenisti, *Ha'aretz* 2000 ; Shetreet, 1994). By turning to the Court, these politicians, who could alternatively advance structural reforms, actually adopted a quasi-exit strategy. Although these and other politicians sought to advance their interests, as argued by several researchers, they gained legitimacy for that move from a political culture of quasi-exit. In an atmosphere where anything goes and everyone seeks (semi-legal) ways to put facts on the ground, the HCJ was regarded as another legitimate channel to do so. The HCJ, on the other hand, benefited from the fact that the politicians sought its authority, and also, in this manner, it established its status among the policy makers (Shamir, 1990). This motivation, in a given environment where all players perform a quasi-exit behavior, led the Court to actually join in and set its own borders of authorities, meaning that the Court also adopted a quasi-exit strategy. This process brought many groups in Israeli society to turn to the Court in the late 1980s and more intensively in the 1990s to defend their goals.

This behavior grew rapidly in the late 1990s and in the years after 2000 (Dor and Hofnung, 2006), leading the Court to hear appeals on a broad range of subjects. Examples of such cases include petitions brought by homosexuals (*El Al v. Danilovitz*), left-wing parties and MKs (*Meretz v. The Jerusalem District Commander*), right-wing MKs (see, for example, the petition filed by M. K. Avraham Ravitz [Yahdut Hatora] to postpone the nomination of Judge Edna Arbel to the Supreme Court and Gilad Ardan's [Likud] petition to put Major General Moshe Mizrahi on criminal trial), professional groups such as The Israel Investment Managers' Office (*The Israel Investment Managers' Office v. The Minister of Finance*), Israeli Jews (*Ressler v. The Minister of Defense*), women's groups (*Women's Lobby v. Government of Israel*), writers and journalists (*Schnitzer v. Chief Military Censor*), Israeli Arabs (*Ka'adan v. Israel Land Authority*), non-Israeli Arabs (*Turkeman v. Minister of Defense*), students (*The Public Committee against Torture in Israel v. The State of Israel*), ultra-Orthodox Jews (*Plonim v. Minister of Defense*; *Rubinstein v. The Minister of Defense*; *Rabbi Igal Shiloh v. Rabbinate Rishon Le'zion*) and non-Orthodox, seculars Jews (*Keren – The Movement for Progressive Judaism v. Minister for Religious Affairs*; *Hoffman v. The Chief of Staff, Office of the Prime Minister*). We should note, however, that this refers only to justifiability and standing. With regard to judicial activism, we can see that the Court's ruling during those years reflected the effect that the multi-cultural society was having on the field of law. The rate of judicial intervention in security, social rights, and religious issues, however, was still relatively limited (Kretzmer, 1997; Kretzmer, 1993; Shamir, 1990; Shamir, 1995; Barzilai, 2002).

Thus, a special form of political participation – quasi-exit behavior – is a necessary condition for judicial activism in the absence of constitutional powers granted to the Court. Court judges cannot adopt an activist approach in the absence of public appeals. The public, in turn, will appeal to the Court only if it feels that all other channels of influence are blocked. In such a situation, the public will adopt its traditional quasi-exit behavior and appeal to the Court. Only after that necessary condition is fulfilled can the Court judges, who must weigh institutional considerations as well, decide whether or not to hear the petition from the public. Thus, political participation is a necessary condition, and institutional considerations are a sufficient condition for judicial activism in the absence of constitutional powers granted to the Court. In other words, despite the fact that the Court does not have powers granted to it by a constitution, the public may essentially delegate such powers to the Court through the quasi-exit strategies it uses to obtain policy decisions that it cannot obtain through any other means. Like quasi-exit behavior in other areas, such behavior in the judicial area is expected to threaten politicians and lead them to institutionalize reality – either by accepting and legalizing the new balance of power or by redefining the authority of the Supreme Court. Furthermore, given that a certain form of political participation causes judicial activism, public attitudes and behavior necessarily affect the success of any institutional change that tries to limit the Court's power. Therefore, the political culture and forms of participation should also be at the heart of any analysis of institutional change. The 1990s witnessed the truth of this observation.

7.5. THE 1990S: FROM THE PASSAGE OF BASIC LAWS: HUMAN DIGNITY AND FREEDOM OF OCCUPATION TO THE ZEMACH PETITION (1992–1999)

In the beginning of the fourth period (the 1990s), the sense of deadlock in the political system triggered the evolution of a mass movement calling for the formation of a written constitution and for changing electoral law (Alon, 1995; Bechor, 1996). At the same time, a do-it-yourself approach continued to dominate public life as a quasi-exit strategy of groups and individuals for solving social problems in Israeli society and for the alternative provision of public services (for example: the evolution of private security services – Zinger, 2004; the growth in the number of volunteer organizations dedicated to helping weaker groups of society – Gidron, Bar, and Katz, 2003; the adoption of unilateral initiatives of civil marriage procedures outside of Israel – particularly in Cyprus – Lehman-Wilzig, 1992).

The year 1992 witnessed a turning point that actually came from the direction of the legislators: the passage of a new electoral law with split voting for the prime minister and the parliament and the beginning of a constitutional reform reflected in the passage of three Basic Laws – The Basic Law: the Government, the Basic Law: Freedom of Occupation and the Basic Law: Human Dignity and Liberty (Meridor, 1995). Two Basic Laws – The Basic Law: Freedom of Occupation and the Basic Law: Human Dignity and Liberty – are usually considered the basis for a future constitution and clearer-than-ever guidelines for the HCJ. However, they do not grant any additional explicit power to the HCJ itself.

From this period onward, the Supreme Court performed a radical volte-face in terms of the extent of its judicial activism. This transformation was led by Aharon Barak, who served as Chief Justice of the Supreme Court beginning in 1995. In his rulings and published articles, Barak revealed his approach to judicial philosophy, judicial activism, and the role of the Supreme Court in a democratic society (Barak, 1993a, Barak, 1993b; Parosh, 1993; Rozen Zvi, 1993; Zamir, 1993a; Zamir, 1993b). This volte-face also received support from some of the members of the legislative branch, primarily those identified with the political left wing (see, for example, The Knesset's Proceedings, Vol. 125, p. 3390, with regard to the draft of the Basic Law: Freedom of Occupation).

The passage of the amendment to the Courts Law in 1992 represented an additional development in the relationship between the Supreme Court and the politicians. The amendment gave the Chief Justice of the Supreme Court a more important role in the management of the court system (see sections 9–10 of the Courts Law). The initiative for the change came from the Ministry of Justice and the then Justice Minister, Dan Meridor. One explanation for Meridor's initiative alleges that Meridor, who identified with liberal positions, and wanted to gain legitimacy in the eyes of the legal system, agreed to delegate his power and to confer power on the Chief Justice of the Supreme Court (see The Knesset's Proceedings, Vol. 125, p. 2762).

At the same time, the inability to govern continued. The number of terrorist attacks constantly increased, reaching a peak in March 1993. The construction sector came to an almost complete standstill. In addition, the activities of the movements protesting Israel's presence in the Golan Heights and Judea, Samaria, and Gaza flourished, and there was a severe escalation in incidents in the Lebanese border area, which reached its peak in Operation Accountability. On September 13, 1993, following the signing of the Oslo agreement, the State of Israel and the Palestinian Liberation Organization (PLO) signed a document that outlined an agreement of principles. There was a dramatic improvement in Israel's political status around the world. However, in the initial period after the signing of the agreement, there were an ever-increasing number of terrorist attacks on both sides. Rabin's government, which included the left-wing Meretz

Party and the right-wing Shas Party, created internal tensions and cast doubt on the government's ability to make difficult decisions. In the summer of 1993, two significant events occurred, both connected to Shas, when two indictments were filed: one, against Minister of the Interior Aryeh Der'i, the other against Deputy Minister Pinchasi. The indictments concerned a breach of trust. The question of their suspension became a point of controversy among the members of the coalition. The government's ineffectuality brought the issue to the gates of the HCJ.

At the same time, the HCJ was discussing the petition of a meat importer, claiming that the government's prohibition on the importing of non-kosher meat was in contravention of the Basic Law: Freedom of Occupation (*Mitral Ltd. et al. v. The Knesset of Israel*). Just as the Court exercised judicial restraint with respect to the question of the legality of Reform conversion (*Pissaro [Goldstein] v. The Minister of the Interior*), so it acted with respect to the meat importer's petition, even though it could be argued, ostensibly, that this issue was not of a purely religious nature. In this case, proprietary rights blended together with religious questions, and the HCJ could have exploited this blend to grant the petition, ruling that this prohibition was in contravention of the Basic Law: Freedom of Occupation. The Court could have taken advantage of the fact that this petition came at a time when the government's ineffectuality was so patently clear, primarily because high up on the public agenda were the indictments of two Shas MKs who were renowned for their extreme opposition to any act that might adversely affect the religious nature of the State of Israel. And yet the HCJ chose to reject the petition unanimously. At the time, the media and the political establishment attached great importance to this decision (Shetreet, 1998).

During this period, the Supreme Court continued to apply a policy of activism regarding the criticism of Knesset decisions. Such activism is evident in the rescission of the Knesset's decision to lift MK Pinchasi's immunity, because it had not been given an appropriate opportunity to examine the relevant material (*Pinchasi v. The Knesset of Israel*). In the same vein, the Supreme Court ordered the prime minister to remove Pinchasi from his office as deputy minister because of the indictment proceedings against him (*Amitai – Citizens for Proper Administration and Integrity v. The Prime Minister*).

In addition, the Supreme Court began to apply a policy of activism through the Basic Laws. It ruled, for example, that discrimination against homosexuals and lesbians is unlawful (*El Al v. Danilovitz*), required the publicizing of agreements between Knesset factions (*Shalit v. Peres*), and once again established the freedom to demonstrate as one of the foundations of the law (*Meretz v. The Jerusalem District Commander*). Nevertheless, the HCJ was careful not to intervene in the actions of the Knesset in its legislation (*Zandberg v. The Broadcasting Authority*; *Segal v. The Knesset Speaker*). This attitude was maintained up until the Bank Mizrahi verdict in 1995 (Civil Appeal 6821/93, Civil Appeal Application 1908/94, Civil Appeal Application 3363/94, *United Mizrahi Bank v. Migdal Cooperative Village*), when the Supreme Court, with an extended composition of nine judges – which in itself attests to the importance of the issue – ruled that while the Arrangements Law in the Agricultural Sector (Amendment) does indeed prejudice proprietary rights, it nevertheless meets the conditions set forth in the Basic Law: Human Dignity and Liberty. Therefore, the Arrangements Law should not be invalidated. However, the verdict also states: "It [the Supreme Court] is given the power to determine that any law is in contravention of the Basic Law: Human Dignity and Liberty, and to declare that the said law, for the said reason, is nullified." With this pronouncement, for the first time, the Supreme Court signaled its future intentions by setting itself on a par with the Knesset. For the first time, the Supreme Court declared that it had the power to nullify a regular law for reasons relating to values and moral content. Furthermore, it stated that any court has this power.

The timing of the decision was perfect. On the one hand, an issue was raised that would not normally have appeared on the public agenda in Israel. On the other hand, the government continued to display ineffectuality in its ability to govern. In 1994, the amendment to the Basic Law: Human Dignity and Liberty and the Basic Law: Freedom of Occupation was passed. This amendment establishes the principles of the Declaration of Independence in law. The passage of this amendment was a clear signal to the public that yet another barrier had been broken down, further facilitating its ability to have an influence in policy making. If in the decision handed down in 1995 the Supreme Court gave a signal about its power, then two years later in 1997, in the petition of the portfolio managers to the HCJ (*The Israel Investment Managers' Office v. The Minister of Finance*) and another two years later in 1999, in the Zemach petition to the HCJ (*Zemach v. The Minister of Defense*), the Court made use of this power. In both cases, however, the Court exercised this power with the caution characteristic of a political player who fears for his position due to the limiting of his powers by the Knesset itself – by instituting a suspension proceeding and transferring the matter to the Knesset to finish the job.

However, the central place of the Supreme Court in the political arena and the fact that its decisions could be in conflict with the political and military elite forced it to adopt restraint and conservatism with respect to the scope of judicial criticism of political and military issues. Thus, the Supreme Court accepted the military's point of view and turned down a request for a personal inscription on a military headstone (*Vickselbaum v. The Minister of Defense*). At the same time, the Court did hand down decisions favoring the military automatically. Thus, in the matter of Brigadier General Nir Galilee, The Supreme Court ruled that he should be barred from promotion to the rank of Major General because he had harassed an eighteen-year-old female soldier under his command (*Plonit v. The Chief of Staff*). Another example of the Court's occasional willingness to intervene in religious issues was its ordering of the government to permit women to pray at the Wailing Wall, wearing a *tallith* (prayer shawl) and reading aloud from the Torah, while granting a six-month extension for an arrangement to be determined for women's prayers at the Wailing Wall (*Hoffman v. The Director-General of the Prime Minister's Office*). Similarly, the HCJ intervened in a decision of a military committee to review the punishment of Rami Dotan, an Israeli Air Force General who confessed to skimming millions of dollars of U.S. military aid from American defense contractors (*The Movement for the Quality of Government in Israel v. The Punishment Review Committee*). The activism of the HCJ was also reflected in its ruling against the use of physical force by the General Security Services (*The Public Committee against Torture in Israel v. The Government of Israel*).

In contrast, the approach of restraint with regard to political and military issues was expressed, for example, in February 1995 when the HCJ eventually rejected the petition to invalidate the coalition agreement between Shas and Labor, thus attempting to maintain the status quo with respect to its relations with the legislators, out of concern that its powers would be curbed (*Wellner v. The Chairman of the Labor Party*). In the same vein, in 1997, the Supreme Court approved the detention of a group of prisoners as a "bargaining chip" in order to receive information about Israeli prisoners and MIAs, including navigator Ron Arad (*Plonim v. The Minister of Defense*). It shall be stressed that almost three years later, in March 2000, the HCJ reversed its decision. It is possible that over the course of time, the Supreme Court realized that the ostensible vitalness of the prisoners as a "bargaining chip" was, in effect, rather insignificant. A major contribution was made by the very removal of this issue from the public agenda (*Plonim v. The Minister of Defense*, Further Hearing 1048/97). Likewise, the Supreme Court handed down a compromise regarding the traffic arrangements on the Sabbath on Bar Ilan Street in Jerusalem (*Lior Horev et al. v. The Minister of Transport*), adopting an approach in this case similar to its stance in the lifting of the immunity of MK Pinchasi. In the Bar'on Affair, the attorney general Elyakim Rubinstein decided to indict the Shas leader, Aryeh Der'i, for allegedly seeking the January appointment of Roni Bar'on as attorney general in exchange for a plea bargain in his own ongoing corruption trial and support for the Hebron redeployment. Rubinstein and State Attorney Edna Arbel did not indict Prime Minister Benjamin Netanyahu, Justice Minister Tzachi Hanegbi, or other top officials, citing lack of sufficient evidence. The HCJ decided not to intervene in the Attorney General's decision, despite the fact that it noted in its decision that a different conclusion could have been reached with respect to the prime minister (*Yahav v. The State Attorney*). Was the Court taking legal considerations into account or, rather, was it afraid that the legislators would curb its powers? Similar judicial restraint was exercised in the amnesty of the GSS officials (*Barzilai v. The Government of Israel et al.*; Dayan, 1995). The same was true in Misgav's petition to abolish the law to dissolve the Knesset and hold elections within four months (*Misgav v. The Knesset*), as was the petition of the manpower agency, Tnufa, to abolish the law allowing the employment of workers by personnel contractors (*Tnufa, Manpower Services v. The Minister of Labor and Social Affairs*). Thus, the 1990s laid the groundwork for the movement to create a new conservative Constitutional Court, thus redefining the Supreme Court of Israel as the informal alternative guarantor of human rights in Israel.

8

The Struggle for a New Conservative Constitutional Court (2000): Redefining the Guarantor of Human Rights in Israel – the Role of the Israeli Supreme Court

In June 2000, the Israeli parliament adopted a proposal introduced by Knesset member Eliezer Cohen (Israel Beytenu Party) to create a constitution. The purpose of this proposal was to make the Knesset the founding authority "that will create a unified, comprehensive and complete constitutional document."[1] Of 120 Knesset members, 44 supported the proposal. In November 2000, Knesset members Cohen and Igal Bibi (Mafdal) proposed a complementary plan to create a constitutional court of law. This proposition was supported by 52 Knesset members out of 120 members of the Knesset. The fact that the idea was raised by members of the religious Mafdal party came as something of a surprise, because the religious parties in the Knesset had opposed the idea of a constitution since the country's establishment. Did the representatives of these parties (Mafdal, Yahdut Hatora, Shas, and others) simply decide at the dawn of the new millennium to change their minds? Or was this what might be called a "heurostatic action" (Riker, 1984; Riker, 1986; Doron, 1996),[2] the purpose of which was not necessarily related to the founding of the institution? What really might have been at stake here was a veiled threat to the High Court to change its ways, or the Knesset would curb its powers.[3] In any case, on January 2, 2002, after strong opposition was

[1] See summary "This week in the Knesset" dated June 7, 2000 on the Knesset's Web site, http://www.knesset.gov.il.

[2] Heurostatics is a doctrine of political manipulation, a presentation of reality so that the results of political interaction will always be for the good of the manipulator.

[3] There are numerous examples of favorable judicial rulings by the Supreme Court that have contributed to enhancing civil rights in matters of religious practice. For example, the Court struck down municipal bylaws that forbade the sale of pork H.C. 117/55; 72/55 *Siegfried Avraham Fraidi v. Tel Aviv-Jaffa Municipality and others*, *Shmuel Mendelsson v. Tel Aviv-Jaffa Municipality*, PD 10(2) 734; The Court recognized the

raised by a number of groups, the Knesset rejected these two proposals. Senior lawyers convinced the Knesset members to rule out the idea of a constitutional court.

8.1. A CONSTITUTION FOR ISRAEL AND A CONSTITUTIONAL COURT: AN ONGOING DEBATE

The discussion within the Israeli literature about the need for a special, constitutional court of law may be divided into three related issues. The first issue deals with the degree of judicial criticism leveled against the Knesset's lawmaking (Barak, 2003).[4] The next issue pertains to the ways in which judges who discuss constitutional issues are appointed. The third issue, the one that is central to this book, is determining the need for a constitutional court of law in the existing legal and institutional climate in Israel. Although many scholars claim that the creation of such a court of law is not needed, each one provides somewhat different explanations to substantiate his claim (Dotan, 1999; Shetreet, 2004: 623).

This book stresses the point of view of public policy. In this context, Galnoor (2004: 355) claims

> Israel has a democratic grain, deep within the political system. When political institutions are unable to cope with prolonged internal and external crises, public trust in those institutions erodes. Due to this fact, a mutual bond has been created between the general Judicialization processes in society . . . and between Judicialization, politics and managing. Moreover, due

right to alternative burial, years before the Knesset set this right into law H.C. 397/88 *Menucha Nechona v. Minister of Religious Affairs* (not published); The Court has also played a primary role in defending the status of female members of public religious bodies (HCJ 153/87. *Leah Shakdiel v. Minister of Religious Affairs et al.* PD 42(2) 221; HCJ 753/87. *Poraz v. Mayor of Tel-Aviv*, PD 42 (2) 309). The Court clarified that the Chief Rabbinate and its associated bodies, including religious court judges and rabbinical courts, are public bodies that are subject to the rule of law and the judicial review of the HCJ, and must therefore abide by non-discrimination laws H.C. 732/84 *Tzaban v. Minister of Religious Affairs*, PD 40(4) 141.

[4] See also Segal, Z. 2003. The use of a Judgment Day weapon in judicial criticism, *Law and Government (Mishpat Umimshal)* 6 (2): 337 (in Hebrew); Mautner, M. 1993. *The Decline of Formalism and the Rise of Values in Israeli Law*. Tel-Aviv: Ma'agalay Da'at (in Hebrew); Barzilai, G., and I. Sened 1997. How Do Courts Accumulate Power and Why They Lose It: An Institutional Perspective (unpublished paper, presented at APSA, Boston; Dotan, Y. and M. Hofnung, 2001). "Interest Groups in the Israeli High Court of Justice: Measuring Success in Litigation and in Out-of-Court Settlements," *Law and Policy*, 23:1–27

> to the dominant position of politics, whatever occurs in it has an empowering effect – or even a formative one – on all spheres of life in Israel. Such widespread and lengthy processes are the ones that caused Judicialization as opposed to the so-called zeal of the courts of law.

Galnoor stresses the importance of focusing on the factors that led the Knesset to raise the issue of a constitutional court of law. Public policy is the result of the interactions among the four main groups: politicians, interest groups, bureaucrats employed by the state, and the public at large (Howlett and Ramesh, 2003). It is in this context that we can appreciate the proposal to create a constitutional court of law. Groups from the religious parties and the settlers' lobby opposed the interference of the High Court in certain issues, such as the drafting of religious college students (1999) or the prohibition on the use of certain interrogation methods by the General Security Service (1999). They went to the press and the Internet and demonstrated in order to express their dissatisfaction with the court's decisions. For example, in February 1999, 250,000 people took part in one of the biggest demonstrations ever in Jerusalem (Doron and Harris, 2000). The struggle that the demonstrators defined as the design and retention of collective and religious values moved to the forefront of the public agenda. The saliency of the issue as well as the raising of it for public debate reflected the desire of the demonstrators to have the policy makers give the issue more attention (Willmore and Carey, 1968).

8.2. THE HIGH COURT AND THE PROCESS OF PUBLIC POLICY MAKING: THE PROPOSAL TO CREATE A CONSTITUTIONAL COURT OF LAW (2000)

In June 2002, the Knesset passed the first reading of a proposal to confer the status of a founding authority on the Knesset. Forty-four Knesset members supported it, including senior MKs from the Labor Party, as well as Knesset members Moshe Katzav and Reuven Rivlin from the Likud. Moreover, the complementary proposal regarding the constitutional court of law gained the support of fifty-two Knesset members. Grounded in the basic principles of Israel as a democratic Jewish state, the essence of the proposal by Knesset members Eliezer Cohen and Igal Bibi was the creation of a constitutional court of law, which would be the only court of law allowed to rule on issues pertaining to constitutional ambiguities. The proposal also included suggestions about determining the composition of this law court (Doron and Meydani, 2007).

8.3. THE LEGAL SYSTEM SUPPORTED BY THE MINISTER OF JUSTICE

The legal system, with the support of Minister of Justice Meir Shetreet (Likud), expressed its objection to the proposal. The main difficulty cited was that providing the Knesset with the authority to appoint the constitutional court judges violated the norms of legal activity. Allowing such appointments to be made might lead to the politicization of the court, because the judges would no longer be appointed according to their abilities but as representatives of different societal opinions (Barak, 2003).[5] The support of Knesset member Shetreet was not surprising. He is a part of the moderate-liberal branch of Likud, and his attitudes regarding the court system mirror those of the public (Alon, *Ha'aretz* 2001).

8.4. POLITICIANS – THE GOAL OF BEING RE-ELECTED

David Mayew compares politicians' motivations in democracies to the profit motive of businesses. Just as businesses engage in behaviors designed to maximize their profits, so too politicians engage in activities designed to get them re-elected (Mayew, 1974; Bueno De Mesqita et al., 2003). On the basis of this assumption, we can understand the behavior of the politicians with regard to the legal proposals outlined previously.

As expected, these proposals created tensions in the relationship between the court and the Knesset. The controversy pertaining to the position of the High Court – especially the legitimacy of its rulings at the time[6] – brought the tension to a head. Thus, the issue was perceived

[5] It is worth noting the role that Prof. Aharon Barak, the President of the Supreme Court, had during this period. In 1992, Barak declared that a constitutional revolution had occurred in Israel. The Knesset passed two new basic laws that year: Basic Law: Human Dignity and Liberty and Basic Law: Freedom of Occupation. Barak argued that these new basic laws must be treated as fundamental legal principles, overriding normal legislation, despite Israel's lack of a written constitution (Barak A. 1993. "The Constitutional Revolution: Protected Human Rights," *Law and Government (Mishpat Umimshal)*, 1 (1): 9–10 (in Hebrew)). In 1995, the Supreme Court, headed by Barak, recognized this principle (CA 6821/93 *United Mizrahi Bank v. Migdal Cooperative Village*, in Decisions, vol. 49, section 4, p. 221 (in Hebrew)). Furthermore, Barak has even personally advocated against the need for a separate constitutional court, both in public and in writing: Barak, A. 2003. "The Supreme Court as a Constitutional Court," *Law and Government (Mishpat Umimshal)*, 6: 315 (in Hebrew); see also his speech in front of the Israeli Democracy Institute on November 1, 2001.

[6] See, for example, HCJ 5100/94, *The Public Committee against Torture in Israel v. The State of Israel*, PD 53 (4) 817. The ruling on the issue of prohibiting the use of torture

as one that had the potential to ignite a political conflict between the parties, a conflict from which the politicians might benefit. For instance, Knesset member Yuli Tamir (Labor), serving at the time as a member of the committee for appointing judges, criticized the judges on the High Court, demanding a more representative composition. Later she even filed a proposal to broaden the committee that appoints the judges and change how it functions.[7] By doing so, Tamir, who usually associated with liberal positions (especially regarding the relationship between religion and the state), sent a message to centrist voters who might vote for Labor. Representatives of the religious parties likened Tamir's position to that of the anti-religious Meretz party, despite her affiliation with Labor. Knesset member David Tal (Shas – a religious Sephardic party) made this point very clear to his party's voters by saying: "The High Court has trampled everything good. It has turned into a tool of Meretz" (Alon, *Ha'aretz* 2001). Eliezer Cohen (Ihud Leumi – rightist party) asked: "What is the High Court of Justice today? Today it is not accepted by half the people because it is political."[8] Another religious Knesset member, Avraham Ravitz, added that the High Court had lost the trust of major parts of

in the GSS interrogations); HCJ 6698/95, *Kaadan v. Israeli Land Administration* 54(1) 258. The ruling prohibiting discrimination against Arabs being accepted as members of a Jewish settlement; Zvi Noah, the issue of the constitution, had excited the public in the last few years. Is there really a judicial "law revolution" as the high court president, Aharon Barak, claims, or does the constitution still await its legislation? *Globes*, February 7, 2001.

[7] See Member of Knesset Prof. Yuli Tamir's speech: "Unlike other countries, we have no process of hearing that provides the public with knowledge about who the people are and their judicial record. As a former member of a committee that appointed judges, I can say that the members of the committee know very little of the judges they choose. This process should be brought to a public discussion and we should not be afraid of it. I am saying this especially to the people in my own camp." From protocols /constitutional committee/ 6351 Jerusalem, April 1, 2003; see also basic law proposition: judging (amendment by the committee to appoint judges for the High Court) filed with the Chairman of the Knesset and brought to the Knesset on June 9, 2003. Thus, one of the principles for selecting judges for the High Court would be that they represent the "proper proportion of different sectors of the Israeli society." Explanation of the proposition: "The choice of judges for the high court should be made by a special committee." See also the discussions of the public committee aimed at completing the legislation, as well as the wording of the existing basic laws designed to obtain broad public acceptance for an Israeli constitution: Yaakov Neeman – chair, Chaim Corpo, Uriel Lin, Uriel Raichmann, Eyal Arad, Yaffa Zilbershatz and Tamir Shaanan, as well as constitutional committee discussions in this respect, protocol num. 204, Law and Constitution Committee (April 14, 2004).

[8] Zvi Noah, the issue of the constitution, had excited the public in the last few years. Is there really a judicial "law revolution" as the high court president, Aharon Barak claims, or does the constitution still await its legislation? *Globes*, February 7, 2001.

the public. On the other hand, Josef Lapid (Shinui – non-religious party) expressed strong objection to the creation of a constitutional court of law and accused the religious Knesset members of "a vicious intent to sabotage the legal system" (Alon, *Ha'aretz* 2000).

8.5. THE ACTIVITIES OF INTEREST GROUPS

Various groups took part in the struggle over the constitutional court of law, contributing to the importance and power of the issue. Among these groups were the representatives of the Government Quality Movement that opposed the initiative. Lawyer Shmuel Shenar, vice president of the movement, explained: "One of the problems we see in the proposition is the composition of judges. The composition proposed for the constitutional court of law is political" (Alon, *Ha'aretz* 2000). The idea of creating a separate constitutional court of law was born in the lobby for the Israeli constitution. To convince the Knesset members that they were right, the lobby launched two campaigns. The first was distributing explanation sheets to Knesset members, substantiating the position of the lobby. The second was the sending of delegations of Knesset members to parliaments and constitutional courts of law in Europe to study their methods. The purpose of the lobby was to expose the Knesset members to the complexity of the issue and the variety of possibilities and solutions. Knesset member Eliezer Cohen, who founded the lobby in the Knesset for the purpose of completing the constitution (Alon, *Ha'aretz* 2000), was one of the Knesset members sent to study the issue both in Israel and abroad (Lex, *BESHVAA – an ultra-orthodox newspaper* 2003).

Another group that influenced the debate was the legal community. It had doubts about the question of whether a constitutional change had actually occurred in Israel or whether the constitution was still waiting to be legislated.[9] It is in light of these circumstances that we may understand Cohen's proposal: "... only the Knesset has the authority to legislate a constitution in Israel" (Noah, *Globes* 2001), which led to the debate as to whether there was a need for a constitutional court of law (Noah, *Globes* 2001).[10] The Israeli Bar Association took the side of the High Court's

[9] See the position of Judges Aharon Barak and Mishael Hashin in the case of United *HaMizrahi Bank Ltd. and others v. Communal Village Migdal and others*; PD 49 (4) 221.

[10] Thus, for example, Prof. Ruth Gavison expressed an opinion contrary to that of High Court President Judge Aharon Barak: "We refer to a special court of law whose only authority is this [to cancel laws – A.M.] as in European countries, and it does not

president and objected to the creation of a constitutional court of law.[11] Senior members from the legal community participated in a discussion held by the Knesset's constitutional committee on July 2, 2001 on the issue and opposed the proposal.

As public discussion increased, the legal community held a series of conferences on the topic. For example, the Israeli Institute of Democracy held a conference in November 2001 at Ben-Gurion University. A few months later, the Hebrew University and the University of Haifa held similar conferences regarding the issue of the constitutional court of law. These conferences examined different models of judicial criticism.

8.6. IN THE POLITICAL ARENA: THE ROLE OF THE CHAIR OF THE CONSTITUTIONAL COMMITTEE

As usual, after the proposal passed the first reading, it was sent to the constitutional committee of the Knesset for discussion. The chair of the committee, Ofir Pines (Paz), took the initiative of inviting those who opposed the creation of a constitutional court of law, including the High Court's president, to a series of six discussions dealing with the legal proposals. In the end, the constitutional committee suggested that the Knesset remove the bill from its schedule. Why did the committee take such a stand? It seems that Ofir Pines's position as chair of the committee had a significant influence on the removal of this issue. Knesset member Bibi charged that, "Judge Barak worked hand in glove with Pines" (Lex, *BESHVAA – an ultra-orthodox newspaper* 2003). He went on to say, "Before the voting, there was a general gathering of Likud" (Lex, *BESHVAA – an ultra-orthodox newspaper* 2003).[12] Zvi Hendel (HaIchud HaLeumi – rightist party) said, "Prime Minister Ariel Sharon, Knesset member Yuval Shteinitz and many others who voted in favor of the proposition, now voted against it" (Lex, *BESHVAA – an ultra-orthodox newspaper* 2003). Hendel could not explain what made them change their minds at the last moment; however, he believed that the pressure put on the Knesset members by the legal community played a

constitute a reduction in honor," cited in Zvi Noah, The Struggle for a Constitution, *Globes*, February 7, 2001.

[11] Yoav Itzhak, "High court judges recruited senior academics in order to help them prevent the founding of a constitutional court of law," Web site, http://www.nfc.co.il (July 3, 2001).

[12] See also: Yoav Itzhak, November 5, 2001, Web site, http://www.nfc.co.il. "The constitutional committee voted against the constitutional court."

TABLE 8.1. *The level of public trust in governmental institutions, 1995–2000*

Trust/mistrust	2000 survey of the entire public (%)	2000 survey of the adult Jewish public (%)	1995 survey conducted by Peres and Yaar-Yochtman among the adult Jewish public (%)
IDF	76	83	90
The High Court	61	63	85
The Knesset	14	13	41
The Government	16	16	40
Parties	11	11	21

Source: Knesset measurement – the public perception of the legislating authority. (http://www.knesset.gov.il/mmm/data/docs/mdd.htm)

part in it (Lex, *BESHVAA – an ultra-orthodox newspaper* 2003). Knesset member Michael Eitan (Likud) was also unable to explain the choice of his peers. "I cannot explain why people would reverse their decisions," he said (Lex, *BESHVAA – an ultra-orthodox newspaper* 2003).

It is possible that what influenced the initiators of the political process to found a constitutional court of law was their impression of the level of trust the public had in governmental institutions. Measurements of public trust in governmental institutions show that there was a significant decline in the level of trust between 1995 and 2000. The level of public trust in the High Court declined significantly between 1995 and 2000, from 86 percent to 61 percent (see Figure 8.1). Such a dramatic decline supplied those who opposed the High Court with a justification for launching initiatives aimed at changing the High Court's role. However, during the same time period, trust in the Knesset members declined in an even more drastic fashion. As Table 8.1 shows, while in 1995 more than half of the public did not trust the Knesset (41%), in 2000, the percentage of the public that still trusted the Knesset had fallen to 14 percent. It seems that the dismal position of the Knesset in the public's eyes gave the High Court the ammunition it needed to oppose the proposal to create a constitutional court of law.

In the debate surrounding the initiative to create a constitutional court of law we should not ignore the desire of the Knesset members to be re-elected. The logic of the constitutional court's opponents was simple though implicit: The creation of a prestigious institution by a declining one would cause a further deterioration of the Knesset and its representatives in the eyes of the public.[13] This logic may explain why the politicians decided in the end to vote against the constitutional court of law. It also explains the stand of Knesset member Cohen (Halchud HaLeumi – rightist party) whose proposal for a constitutional court of law provided an antidote to voters' dissatisfaction with the High Court's decisions. Constitutional interpretation of issues involving values, morals, and ideology should be dealt with by people other than judges.[14] Thus, his bill to remove certain types of decisions from the High Court's purview increased his chances of being re-elected.

8.7. THE POLITICIANS – THE PRIME MINISTER'S STAND

There are people who think that because Ariel Sharon was not interested in starting another battle with the judicial authority, the proposal for the constitutional court was eventually abandoned. The rationale for this suggestion makes the following argument. In parliamentary systems in general, and in the Israeli one in particular, prime ministers have a great deal of power and status. This is the opinion of Asher Arian, David Nachmias, and Ruth Amir in their book *Governability and the Executive Authority*. They say that "prime ministers are the primary political players in Israel... generally it is the prime minister who decides the daily agenda" (Arian, Nachmias, and Amir, 2002: 45). As a part of the decline of political parties (Korn, 1998) and the rise of the value of "the new politicians" who were supposed to be attentive to the needs of the voters (Galili, 2004), Sharon decided to order his party to vote against the proposal and remove it from the daily agenda. By doing so, he appealed to the political center,[15] a move that helped him tremendously in the

[13] Tova Tzimuki, Why Did Justice Barak Call the Knesset Members? *Yedioth Aharonoth* June 11, 2000; see the speech of Judge Aharon Barak: "The High Court has no sword nor purse. All it has is the public trust... the Israeli society is divided – Right and Left; Orthodox and non-religious Jews; Arabs and Jews; Oriental and European Jews. One of the greatest achievements of the state is its law and its judges. All must be done to keep them intact; they must be assisted, promoted and developed. This is to be done by the government and the Knesset, the lawyers chambers and each and every Israeli citizen" (Barak, High Court, http://www.court.gov.il, part of the speech given during the lawyers chambers convention in Eilat, Israel, May 15, 2001).

[14] The position of Knesset member Eliezer (Chita) Cohen, 2003. *Law and Government (Mishpat Umimshal)*, 6 (2): 351.

[15] Note that the conflict between the Supreme Court and the politicians (Israeli Knesset members) revolves around more than just the activism of the Supreme Court in relation to the Knesset. It is also a conflict about the interpretation of values under dispute in

2003 elections, when the number of his party members doubled. Knesset member Michael Eitan was the only one of the Likud members who voted against the majority of his party: "I supported the proposition to found a constitutional court of law, and I was very angry at our ministers and the government for voting to remove the issue from the daily agenda without first holding a discussion on it. That is why I let myself vote against the general position of the party members" (Lex, *BESHVAA – an ultra-orthodox newspaper* 2003).

Israeli society and involves issues of trust, dignity, and accountability. As polls in this chapter show, public trust in the Supreme Court is far more pervasive than public trust in politicians. Therefore, concurring with the Supreme Court is much more compelling for politicians than adopting the position of the rightist or religious parties. Moreover, a poll conducted by Gad Barzilai, Zeev Segal, and Efraim Yaar (1991) showed that the Israeli public disliked attempts by politicians or judges to change the separation of powers in Israel. In the case described in this chapter, the public feeling was that the rightists and religious politicians wanted to punish the Supreme Court by curbing its power (Barzilai, G. Yuchtman-Yaar, E. and Segal, Z. 2004. *The Israeli Supreme Court and the Israeli Public*, Tel-Aviv: Tel Aviv University Press).

9

The Rule of "Who Governs?" as Electoral Capital (1999–2007): The Supreme Court as an Agenda Setter in Israel

9.1. THE SUPREME COURT VERSUS THE POLITICAL SYSTEM: A BALANCE OF POWER (1999–2007)

Since 1997, the Court has made several activist moves in which it invalidated various Knesset laws. For example, in 1999, the High Court panel of eleven judges ruled that a clause to a law that contradicted the Basic Law: Dignity of Man and Liberty was invalid (*Sagi Tzemach*, first filed in 1995). In March 2002, in the *Oron v. Chairman of the Knesset* case (first filed in 1999), the Court ruled that an amendment to the Bezeq Law, which was designed to legitimize the pirate broadcast signals of Channel 7, was invalid, claiming that it violated the Basic Law: Freedom of Occupation. Three years later, in September 2005, the High Court ruled invalid the Intifada Law (an amendment to the Civil Damages Law), which denied Palestinians who live in the occupied territories the right to sue for damages in Israel (*Adalla and others v. Minister of Defense and others*, 2005). An additional ruling was made to abolish a number of clauses in the Disengagement Application Program Law, 2005, known as the Evacuation Compensation Law (*Gaza Coast Regional Council et al. v. The Knesset et al.*, 2005).

However, the politicians have not attempted to hide their intention of limiting the activism of the Court. In 2000, Knesset members decided to submit a law to set up a constitutional court, and in 2002 the Knesset defeated a bill proposing the creation of a constitution. In doing so, the Knesset signaled to the Court that the strategy of constraining steps was not realistic.

In 2007, Justice Minister Daniel Friedman proposed institutionalizing the Court's authority to invalidate a law, a step that would seem to contradict the model (Box 6 in Figure 4.1, Chapter 4). However,

Freidman's proposal had an additional section allowing the Knesset to enact a law that would void a Supreme Court decision. Thus, Friedman sought a middle-of-the-road approach designed to return to the point of equilibrium in which the Supreme Court was careful in its exercise of judicial activism and the politicians refrained from using their right to overturn the Court's decisions except in instances in which they felt such decisions would be harmful to the average voter. Given the circumstances, structures, and cultural conditions in Israel, it seems that this type of equilibrium is here to stay for the foreseeable future.

9.2. THE ISRAELI SUPREME COURT AS A POLITICAL ENTREPRENEUR, PROVIDING AN ALTERNATIVE FORM OF GOVERNABILITY IN CONTROVERSIAL ISSUES

Judicial review of the constitutionality of primary legislation was not explicitly defined in the basic laws and has developed in Israel on the basis of the Supreme Court's interpretation of the constitutional documents. It is through this process that rights such as the freedom of expression, the freedom of election, and the freedom of protest have been established (Kretzmer, 1997).

In the 1970s and 1980s, the Supreme Court began adopting a strategy of increased intervention in the activities of other government agencies in areas where it had heretofore not inserted itself (Mautner, 1993). At the procedural level, the HCJ began to accept cases without rigorous investigation of the doctrines of "standing" and "justiciability," which in the past had been the cornerstones in determining the Court's willingness to hear appeals (Gavison et al., 2000). At the material-content level, in the 1980s and 1990s, the Supreme Court significantly expanded its level of intervention in the activities of administrative agencies. Thus, it ruled that the exemption from military service granted to yeshiva students was not legal. It disqualified interrogation methods used by the General Security Service and, through its intervention, allowed women to be inducted into the Air Force pilot training course. This intervention drew no small amount of criticism from the legal community and members of the public alike. The expression widely used in public and legal discourse to describe these developments is "activism." Among other things, these developments are the result of deep fissures in Israeli society, along with an institutional structure that creates a situation in which the political system finds it very difficult to cope with problems that require the formulation of public policy. The functional failures of the legislative and parliamentary branch lead to an increasing number of appeals to the judiciary branch (Barzilai, 1998; Hofnung, 1999).

The very fact that the Court has the authority to strike down laws is seen by some as dealing a blow to the supremacy of the legislative branch, despite the Knesset's ability to overrule the Court through legislation. However, since the legislation of Basic Law: Human Dignity and Liberty (1992) and Basic Law: Freedom of Occupation (1992), the Supreme Court has invalidated sections of no more than five laws.

A fundamental element of the Israeli system of government is the principle of the separation of powers. Over the years, Israel has undergone a change in terms of how the state is perceived by the Court, moving from a pure separation of powers to a model of checks and balances. In the latter model, the Supreme Court recognized its political power and understood that its legitimacy as a partner in collective social decisions in the State of Israel required it to play a number of roles, including interventional monitoring of the affairs of other agencies. In this regard, the Court was required to intervene in matters that deviated from the traditional pattern of separation of powers, for example, stripping Knesset members of their immunity, overseeing regulations, reviewing political agreements, validating political appointments, and allowing government ministers with indictments pending against them to retain their positions (Claude, 1999).

The judicial branch in Israel has the status of first among equals relative to the other branches of government. Thus, for example, it enjoys a substantial degree of independence from political influence. Judges on the Supreme Court are appointed by the Judicial Selection Committee, composed of representatives of all three branches of government, ensuring a professional and apolitical selection process (Shetreet, 1994).

The Israeli Supreme Court serves a wide variety of functions. First of all, it is the highest court of appeals in the Israeli legal system. Furthermore, it is the first venue in which disputes between individuals and the State are heard. This second role has caused the Supreme Court to be viewed by the general public as the watchdog over the rule of law and the champion in the fight against corruption and the protection of human and civil rights. To reduce the heavy burden of fulfilling this role, a reform has been enacted in which cases brought by individuals against the state will now be heard first by lower courts.

The Supreme Court as an alternative governor benefited the unsatisfied citizens (Barzilai, Yuchtman-Yaar, and Segal, 1994; Vigoda-Gadot and

Mizrahi, 2007) as well as the interest of the politicians, as discussed in the next section.

9.3. THE RULE OF "WHO GOVERNS?" AS ELECTORAL CAPITAL

During the 1990s, the number of appeals and bills of rights initiated by judges grew significantly, thus triggering controversies over the role and place of the Supreme Court in Israel. This trend can be exemplified by Court rulings in cases such as the "Torture Case" (*Public Committee against Torture in Israel v. The State of Israel*, 1999) and the "Land Case" (*New Discourse Movement et al. v. Minister of National Infrastructure et al.*, 2002). Furthermore, in many cases, politicians themselves appeal to the Supreme Court, calling for its intervention in the activity of the legislative and executive authorities. By doing so, they actually weaken the political system and hence also weaken their own power. This behavior seems to contradict politicians' self-interest.

Specifically, Court rulings in cases such as the "Moshavim Case" (*United Mizrahi Bank v. Migdal Cooperative Village*, 1995), the "Israel Investment Managers' Case" (*The Israel Investment Managers' Office v. The Minister of Finance*, 1997) and the "Zemach Case" (*Zemach v. The Minister of Defense*, 1999) show the transformation in the delicate relations between the legal and the political systems. In these cases, the Supreme Court, which does not have constitutional authority of any kind, decided to abolish a parliamentary law, thus signaling its own activist approach. This activism was also expressed in the flexible attitude toward the question of standing and the Court's willingness to hear appeals in areas that had been left to social bargaining in the past. This willingness also led to several debated rulings as, for example, in the case of Ka'adan (*Ka'adan v. Israel Land Authority*, 1995), Alice Miller (*Miller v. The Minister of Defense*, 1994), and the recruitment of yeshiva students (*Rubinstein and Ressler v. The Minister of Defense*, 1997, 1998).

The resulting reality is comfortable for some politicians (Dotan and Hofnung, 2001; Voight and Salzberger, 2002; Doron and Meydani, 2007). They can turn issues over to the high court without taking the risk of paying a political price for decisions that upset the institutional status quo. However, the high court has learned that in certain cases, it is better to refrain from ruling and let the Knesset decide particular issues (see, for example, *Pasaro Goldstein v. Minister of the Interior*, HCJ 1031/93; *Lior Horev and others v. Minister of Transportation and others*, HCJ 5016/96; *Israel Investment Manager Department v. Finance minister*, HCJ 1715/97). However, this informal alternative governability may lead to an imbalance hereby elaborated.

10

The Supreme Court of Israel as an Agenda Setter: Three Cases

This chapter demonstrates the relationship between several political players in the Israeli arena with regard to the defense of human rights in Israel through a deep and detailed analysis of three case studies. The first case is a general one pertaining to the activism of the military court in Israel. The second and third cases are specific judicial decisions dealing with a dispute over acceptable interrogation measures for detainees suspected of committing offenses against state security and a dispute over land use, respectively.

In this chapter, we use the framework elaborated in the previous chapters and analyze the strategic calculations of various social groups in turning to the Court, as well as the role of socio-cultural explanations and the ways in which social players act as agents of political and institutional change. Regarding the judicial decisions, the analysis begins with the presentation of the cases and the Court's decision in each case. Next, in line of the framework developed in the previous chapters, we explain the involvement of the various players and the ways in which this involvement as well as socio-political processes influenced the Court's rulings. Thus, the Court's rulings are understood and explained as part of the policy-making process in which the Court acts as a policy maker, resulting in decisions that reflect the scope of specific human rights.

10.1. JUDICIAL ACTIVISM IN MILITARY COURTS: TOWARD A HUMAN RIGHTS APPROACH

Israel's public and its leaders have been torn by two contradictory beliefs. On the one hand, internal and external threats fostered the belief that the state should retain the authority to wage a war against terrorism or, for example, the authority to impose emergency regulations. On the other hand, the desire to be a part of other nations, coupled with a commitment to the universal values of human rights, fostered the belief that the restriction of civil liberties is inappropriate (Hofnung, 1991; Barzilai, 1992). From the 1990s on, legislators adopted an intermediate policy, leading to a decision by the High Court in 1999 that affected judicial activism in military courts. On the one hand, the Rabin government revoked the prohibition against meeting with the Palestine Liberation Organization (PLO). Furthermore, in 1992, as part of the Basic Laws, the government's authority to impose emergency regulations was restricted. On the other hand, the value of human rights was still not the major guiding principle in setting policy because it had to compete with concerns about self-defense, state security, and safeguarding the public against terrorism. Numerous issues still remained unresolved in 2002, when the General Security Service law was passed. The tension between these contrary beliefs is reflected in the Court's perceptions as well. Dafna Barak-Erez (2003: 28) had her say on the subject:

> The courts are afraid to use their supervisory authority in the case of the war on terrorism. It is also possible that the judges are not always sure that one can actively fight terrorism while preserving human rights and the highest democratic standards, despite the fact that the High Court claims this to be its attitude.

The tension between these beliefs continues to this day and contributes to the cultural and structural conditions mentioned earlier. Given the situation in Israel from the 1980s on, described earlier, what particular factors have affected the development of judicial activism in the military courts in the occupied territories? Judicial activism arises from the interplay among a number of groups – politicians, bureaucrats, interest groups, and the Israeli public at large. In each one of the periods described by Benishu (2005), different events, attitudes, and actions influenced the development of judicial activism.

The first period, 1988–1990, saw the establishment of the civil administration, the outbreak of the first Intifada, which lasted until the Oslo Agreement was signed, and the transfer of the civil administration to the Palestinian Authority. Benishu (2005: 310) notes that at the end of this period (1990), a movement toward judicial activism took place.

The second period, 1998–2000, saw the constitutional revolution and the rise of a neo-liberal civil society dominated by interest groups, bureaucrats, the General Security Service (GSS), the Attorney General's office, and the court system. The same period saw allegations of torture, the outbreak of the second Intifada, and the Israeli Defense Force's (IDF) report regarding cooperation with the Palestinians. At the end of this period, says Benishu, especially after 2000, another move toward judicial activism took place (2005: 310).

The third period, 2001–2003, was marked by the October 2000 events against Israeli Arabs, followed by the Or Committee's report, the GSS Law of 2002, the breakdown of the *hudna* (a temporary halt in fighting), and the conclusions of the Lapid Committee. According to Benishu, this period marked another move toward judicial activism, especially after 2003 (2005: 310). In the detailed discussion of the three periods that follows, we will demonstrate how human rights became a guiding principle in the application of the rule of law in a variety of areas, including security. This newly formulated approach was supported by many in the political sphere and was adopted by the military courts in the occupied territories.

10.1.1. The First Period: 1988–1990

The debate about the judicial position and the future of Judea, Samaria, and Gaza was reflected in two actions taken by the Israeli government, actions whose legality was somewhat doubtful under the terms of the Geneva Convention. These two actions were the creation of Jewish settlements in the regions and the expulsion of local residents deemed potential troublemakers (Negbi, 1982; Shelef, 1996). This debate illustrates how the two conflicting demands for maintaining security and safeguarding human rights led to the type of impasse described in the earlier section on non-governability. However, the 1980s did see a positive step toward implementing the rule of law in the region in the form of the creation of the civil administration.

The Civil Administration

From the 1980s to 1994, the civil administration controlled the everyday life of the local population. This body was composed of government officials from different government ministries, civilians who worked in the IDF, and military officers. The idea behind the establishment of this organization was to use people experienced in civilian public administration to manage everyday life in the region, rather than military officers who had no previous experience in this realm. Even though the final decisions on various topics remained in the hands of the military, the introduction of the civilian perspective influenced the actual policy making. Thus, the civil administration replaced the military bureaucracy on issues related to the needs of the Palestinian population. The military confined itself to issues relating to the defense of Israeli citizens.

The First Intifada

From 1987 to the beginning of the 1990s, a violent revolt broke out reflecting the inability of the civil administration to govern the Palestinians in the region in a manner that satisfied them. The Arabs in Judea, Samaria, and Gaza rose up against Israeli rule. The literature about the first Intifada cites a number of factors that contributed to the Palestinians' feelings that Israel was using the residents of the region for its own purposes, without considering their needs. Radicalization in the Israeli right led some in that sector to call for a transfer of population. Palestinians suffered from poverty, unemployment, overcrowded conditions, and felt humiliated by twenty years of martial rule. Moreover, Palestinians felt that their Arab allies had abandoned them. This situation provided fertile ground for the growth of Muslim extremism (Shalev, 1990).

The solutions Israel tried again reflect the contradiction between the desire to ensure the human rights of the Palestinians and the need to provide security for the Israeli population. The non-governability of the Israeli government led first to a wait-and-see approach. Israel expected the riots to cease by themselves. After about one month, when the riots did not end, Israel adopted a rigid, military approach to try to control the Intifada by force. Israel did finally manage to control the mutiny, but in doing so uncovered many operative and tactical problems with the actions of the army and came to understand the economic price of occupying these areas. Furthermore, the humanitarian problems became a topic of daily debate in Israel and the world.

The Intifada led to a political rift in Israel. The rightist parties condemned the military for having failed to end the Intifada, whereas the leftists claimed that the problem was the occupation of the territories. This rift ultimately led to the dissolving of the unity government and the election of Yitzchak Rabin as prime minister in 1992 (Alon, 1995; Bechor, 1996). The Intifada came to an end completely when the Oslo Agreement (1993) was signed, leading to a partial withdrawal of Israel from the territories.

The Oslo Agreements and the Transfer of the Civil Administration to the Palestinians

On August 20, 1993, the "Oslo A" agreement was signed between the State of Israel and the PLO as part of the peace process initiated between Israel and the Palestinians. On September 13, 1993, the agreement was approved in a formal ceremony in Washington. Due to the signing of this agreement, the splits among the Jewish population in Israel have increased, and the peace process was perceived as trans-societal (Gavison, 1998). Israel acknowledged the PLO as the legal representative of the Palestinian people, and the PLO acknowledged Israel's right to exist and renounced terrorism and violence. The agreement centered on Israel's withdrawal from certain areas in Judea, Samaria, and Gaza, and the establishment of the Palestinian Authority. Some strong opponents of the agreement asked the HCJ to declare these negotiations treasonous, in accordance with paragraph 97 (b) of the Penal Law, 1977. The HCJ rejected this appeal, arguing that the law should not limit the government's authority to negotiate as it saw fit.[1] In December 1995, the "Oslo B" agreement was signed, granting the Palestinians the authority to rule in Palestinian cities in Gaza and the West Bank, as well as in 450 settlements. Subsequently, Israel signed the new deployment protocol (on January 15, 1997) and the Wye Agreement (on October 23, 1998). However, the hope that these agreements would lead to peace between Israel and the Palestinians, or at least bring about a temporary calm, dwindled in the following years, mainly because of the increase in Palestinian terrorism at the end of the 1990s.

Initially, the civil administration that replaced the military rule, bringing with it civilian principles of ruling, functioned as a catalyst for nascent judicial activism in military courts in the region. However, the civil administration collapsed. It seems that the non-governability syndrome deeply entrenched in Israeli society was reflected in the complex sphere of handling the territories as well. If we believe that the process in the territories mirrored the processes in Israel, the movement to counter non-governability with judicialization should be evident. Political processes tried to shift the responsibility for daily life to the Palestinian Authority, because in the mid-1990s, it seemed that the civil administration might be replaced. The 1990s reflected Israel's desire for peace and an end to internal and external terrorism. These years were characterized by an

[1] HCJ case 4354/92, *The Temple Mount and Israel Trustees Movement v. the Prime Minister*, ruling 47 (6) 37, 42.

acceleration of non-governability and the use of alternative politics. This period also saw the rise of civic groups that expressed liberal attitudes toward human rights and saw the rule of law as a solution to non-governability and the rigid bureaucratic government. Finally, there was also an increase in judicialization, with lawyers, the HCJ, the attorney general, and the state controller holding center stage in the political arena. Judicialization accelerated in the 1990s, a fact that had consequences in the realm of security.

10.1.2. The Second Period, 1998–2000

Judicial activism that took place in the 2000s, reflected in the rulings of the military courts in the territories, was the result of the judicialization phenomenon. This phenomenon, in turn, was fueled by the constitutional revolution.

The Constitutional Revolution

In 1992, the Knesset passed two Basic Laws, the Basic Law of Human Dignity and Freedom and the Basic Law: Freedom of Occupation. In 1995, these laws were deemed constitutional by Israeli legislation.[2] Acknowledgment of all of the basic laws as constitutional was called "the constitutional revolution" (Barak, 1993a, 1993b), and forms the basis on which the HCJ would interpret legislation. According to Benishu, "We cannot ignore the definite influence that the legislation of the basic law of human dignity and freedom had on the above process. As a result of this legislation of basic laws– such as the right to freedom and dignity – human rights received a constitutional status" (Benishu, 2005: 313; see also Levi, 2002). The constitutional revolution is not a unique product. Leon Shelef notes that, "There is no doubt that in Israel the existence of active organizations, such as the civil rights organization or the government quality movement, initiates the activity that the High Court continues when civilians appeal to it (since it cannot initiate but only respond)" (Shelef, 1996: 94). The activity of these organizations is a part of what is called in the literature "the rise of the neo-liberal civil society due to the existence of an alternative political culture" (Kretzmer, 1993; Meydani and Mizrahi, 2006).

[2] See 6821/93, *Bank HaMizrahi HaMeuhad v. Migdal*, ruling 49 (4), 221.

The Rise of the Neo-Liberal Civil Society – Interest Groups

We now come to our second example of how the Supreme Court in Israel sets the agenda when it comes to human rights. This case revolves around the question of the appropriate interrogation methods that can be used on those arrested by the General Security Service (GSS) on suspicion of planning or engaging in terrorist activities.

NGOs that promote human rights have played a key role in the development of the anti-torture policy in Israel. These groups include lawyers who are well known for their liberal points of view (Kretzmer, 1993; Kremintzer, 1994). Over time, the influence of such groups has increased. These groups function as interpreters of societal values. For example, Betzelem, the human rights organization in Israel, and the Public Committee against Torture in Israel have demanded a more humane public policy, which led to the investigation of interrogation methods used by the GSS. These groups appealed to the HCJ, whose decision in the Interrogation Case led to a partial change in the law.[3] To win their case, Betzelem had to supply information to prove their claims. They determined that between January 1997 and February 1998, 85 percent of those interrogated by the GSS were subjected to some form of torture.

One might see the hundreds of appeals as the HCJ's contribution to the design of Israeli legal culture and the promotion of the rule of law. However, this approach is slow and laborious (Shamir, 1991: 41; Shelef, 1996: 97). Moreover, other human rights organizations did not counter this activity (Yishai , 1986; Dotan and Hofnung, 2001). Instead, the fight moved to a debate between the GSS and the bureaucrats.

The Bureaucrats: The GSS, the Attorney General, the Legal Adviser, and the Court System in the Territories

Bureaucrats, who have their own agenda, influence both policy design and interpretation. With regard to the security regulations in the occupied territories, the relevant players are the GSS, who enforce the regulations, and the attorney general and his or her legal advisors who determine when the GSS has exceeded its bounds. There seem to be opposing interests in this case. The GSS workers would like to be able to apply flexible interrogation techniques to maximize their ability to do their job well. On the other hand, the attorney general would prefer to do away with

[3] HCJ case 5100/94, the *Public Committee against Torture in Israel v. The Israeli Government*, ruling 53 (4), 817.

sectoral-governmental supervision and transfer that power to the general prosecutor's office. In cases where the GSS has all of the evidence and can determine whether it is effective to apply torture, the security forces have a stronger hand than the attorney general.

However, while there are no definite convictions among the public and no clear laws, in reality the GSS and the attorney general interact closely and cooperate, due to mutual interests, interpersonal relationships, and the institutional dependency of these organizations (Kremnitzer and Shapira-Ettinger, 1999; Zecharia, 2003). Barzilai and Nachmias (1998) claim that the understanding that is developing is a "sphere exchange." The legal adviser and the attorney general are pressed to give up their autonomy in spheres such as national security or government crimes in exchange for broad autonomy in the area of ordinary crime.

Regarding the dynamics between the GSS, the legal councilor, and the attorney general, the HCJ has faith in the latter two and frequently uses them as a means of sending messages to the government (Dotan, 1999). This behavior might be explained by a number of theoretical approaches that appear in the study of law and politics, such as the functionalist-legalist approach, which believes that such behavior arises from the existence of lawyers as a profession and is part of structural solidarity (Kelsen, 1945; Schmidhauser, 1992). However, the central role the HCJ plays in designing the political and social routine in Israel is mainly the result of deep and complex social and political processes, not the personality of the judges. The most important intrusion of the court in security matters was its 1999 decision known as the Interrogation Case. This case had tremendous influence on the development of judicial activism in military courts in the territories.

The Interrogation Case

On June 9, 1999, the HCJ handed down its verdict in the case brought by the Public Committee against Torture in Israel and human rights organizations against the government of Israel, the GSS, and others regarding the use of physical means for interrogating suspects in security offences. The court ruled that

> The GSS has no authority to "shake" a person or hold him in the "shebach" position (that includes the combination of means mentioned in paragraph 30), or make him kneel or deprive him of sleep when these actions are not crucial to the interrogation. We also declare that the excuse of "need" in the penal law may not be used as an authority source for the use of such

> interrogation methods and that there is no basis for the directions given to GSS interrogators that allow the use of such methods.[4]

In this ruling, handed down five years after the case was first brought, the use of physical torture was expressly forbidden. However, interrogators who used such methods could plead "need." The ruling relieved interrogators of criminal responsibility in cases where the torture was meant to save lives (Barak-Erez, 2003: 27). Nevertheless, the ruling was a meaningful shift from the policy customary at that time. The previous policy allowed a "moderate amount of physical pressure to be applied, which does not constitute torture and is relative to of the extent of danger."[5]

This ruling reflects the adoption of a liberal approach that stresses the human rights of those being interrogated. Some claim that the ruling was handed down after a number of years of relative quiet by the Palestinians, and that this same relative quiet was the factor that enabled the High Court to adopt such a liberal approach. We maintain that the explanation is more complex than that. We have to consider the ruling in a broader social-cultural-political perspective, as a balance between a number of players. We cannot discuss this activism by the HCJ without considering the judicialization phenomenon, the increase in non-governability, and the rise of the alternative culture represented by liberal civil groups. Can one begin to understand this decision without considering the diminished security threat in the eyes of the public? Can one understand the phenomenon without considering the changes in the Israeli civil management in the occupied territories and the passing of control to the Palestinians? Or without the constitutional revolution? The Oslo agreements? Any complete understanding must take all of these developments into consideration. Moreover, the High Court was aware of the terrorist threat in the Interrogation Case, and yet it still chose to render a precedent-setting ruling, stating

> From the day of its establishment, Israel has been involved an incessant struggle for its existence and security. The terrorist organizations have as their goal the destruction of the state. Terrorist acts and the disruption of regular life are the means they use in order to achieve their goal. They do not differentiate between military and civilian targets. They commit terrorist acts of mass murder in public places, public transportation, squares

[4] HCJ case 5100/94, 4054/95, the Public Committee against Torture in Israel, ruling 53 (4) 817, paragraph 40 (the torture case ruling).

[5] Landoy Committee Report. The committee was appointed by the government under the terms of the 1968 Investigating Committee Law. The report discusses, among other things, the legal status of the GSS.

> and streets, cinema theaters and coffee shops. They do not differentiate between men women and children. They act out of cruelty and without mercy[6] ... the purpose of the interrogation [of terrorist organizations] is aimed at, among other things, gathering information about terrorists and their ways of organizing in order to be able to prevent them from committing terrorist acts.[7]

A year after the ruling was handed down, the second Intifada, called the Al-Aksa Intifada, began. It is interesting to observe that contrary to the claim that relative peace promotes liberal judicial activism, the following facts show that, in fact, revolts lead to precedent-setting actions. The explanation for this cause-and-effect lies in the events as well as the positions of the players, especially politicians.

The Second Intifada

The Al-Aksa Intifada occurred approximately at the time Ariel Sharon visited the Temple Mount on September 28, 2000. This revolt, which included protests by the people, soon shifted into terrorism and guerilla warfare. The Intifada brought about an economic recession in Israel, reaching its peak in 2002 and 2003, and the almost complete destruction of the Palestinian economy. It created extraordinary situations that gave rise to difficult ethical dilemmas that shook Israeli society for a long time. During this period, the IDF sought to establish its ethical code, declaring, among other things, "The IDF soldiers shall act according to the IDF values and orders, while observing the state laws and human dignity, and respecting the state's values as a Jewish democratic state."[8] The IDF's reference to ethical as well as moral elements reflects its shift toward a more liberal position. However, future events, such as the use of suicide bombers, challenged this liberal IDF policy. Israel chose to cope with such activity by broadening the use of "focused liquidations" – planned assassinations of the activists in terrorist organizations. What about the ethical code, then? The focused liquidations issue was debated daily in Israel, especially due to the ethical dilemma involved. In 2004, an article entitled "Waging a Moral War on Terrorism" by Major-General Amos

[6] The description of the phenomenon is mentioned in the 1987 investigating committee report regarding the interrogation methods of the GSS on the subject of terrorist activity. The committee was headed by (former) Judge Landoy, and the statement appears in his book (vol. 1, 1995), 269, 276.

[7] The Interrogation Case, ibid., the opening passage of the ruling.

[8] The official IDF Web site: http://www1.idf.il.

Yadlin, who headed the IDF national defense college, and the philosopher Professor Assa Kasher was published in a national security magazine. It said, "We shall have to put up with the fact of harming the 'human environment' of the military activity objective . . . a man is considered a ticking bomb not only when he makes his way to an Israeli site with an explosives belt on, but also in the early stages of the actual process – when he provides explosives for others or arranges for another's terrorist act etc."[9] It is important to note that Israel to this day vacillates between the need for security and the desire to preserve human rights. Nevertheless, it is clear that since the 1990s, Israel has taken a major step toward a more liberal attitude (at least regarding the formal side of the rule of law). That change in attitude has affected its perceptions of how residents of the occupied territories should be treated and moved it from an approach that stressed the need for military security to one that institutionalizes human rights. The Israeli response to the "Temple Mount affair" and the events of October 2000 illustrates this change in approach.

IDF Report on Cooperation with the Palestinian Authority

On October 1, 2000, during the Intifada, the Palestinians took over the Temple Mount, one of the holiest sites in Jewish tradition. During the skirmish, an IDF soldier, Madhat Josef, was injured. He subsequently bled to death because the Palestinians would not allow him to be taken to a hospital. The IDF refrained from breaking into the site due to Palestinian leader Jibril Ragub's promise to evacuate the soldier.

The parliamentary committee's examination of the events (the Secondary Committee on National Alerts and Ongoing Security headed by Knesset member Uri Ariel from the Ihud Leumi faction) reached the conclusion that Josef's death was a major failure on the part of the IDF. Trusting the Palestinians to evacuate Josef was a mistake bordering on negligence. The IDF, in its turn, claimed through Major-General Eliezer Stern that its conduct was correct despite the fact that it seemed to contradict the basic values of the military according to which wounded soldiers are not to be abandoned. The army's defense of its actions seems worlds away from attitudes that prevailed ten or twenty years before this event.

[9] For criticism, see Pedhatzur, "The IDF Private Philosopher on the civilianization of society movement in Israel," *Haaretz Newspaper*, February 24, 2004, p. 2 (in Hebrew).

10.1.3. The Third Period, 2001–2003

As mentioned earlier, the end of the 1990s was marked by a high degree of non-governability together with a growing judicialization process. The dawn of the new millennium saw the first instances in which liberal civil elements were able to crack the security service's defenses and make their way into the security institutions in Israel. These actions were led by the legal system, spearheaded by the High Court, and won the support of the political system, even if it did not respond to them. On the political level, a number of political groups, supported by the Israeli Democracy Institute, successfully repealed the 2001 law providing for the direct election of the prime minister and championed a return to the previous format in which individuals cast votes for the party of their choice.

In the last of Benishu's periods, three major events demonstrate the change in the attitudes of bureaucrats and politicians toward Arab residents in the country – the events of October 2000 and the subsequent investigation, the GSS Law of 2002, and the collapse of the *hudna* and the Lapid Committee's report on it.

The October (Israeli Arabs) Events 2000 and the Or Committee

The riots of the Al-Aksa Intifida were initially confined to the Palestinians. However, in October 2000, Israeli Arabs held a public demonstration in support of the Intifada. In the ensuing scuffle with police, twelve Israeli Arabs and one Palestinian were killed. Due to the pressure from Israeli Arab leaders, the then Prime Minister Ehud Barak established a committee, headed by Judge Theodore Or, to investigate the events. The committee's conclusions, published in 2003, included criticism of government ministers, police officers, and leaders of the Israeli-Arab public.[10] The committee also recommended that the police modify their methods of responding to demonstrations and make use of less lethal means for dispersing crowds.

The GSS Law

In 2003, three years after the ruling that identified flaws in the GSS's interrogation methods, Israeli legislators considered formalizing laws about

[10] Official investigating committee (2003). The official investigating committee's report was issued after examining the clash between the security forces and Israeli citizens in October 2000.

the GSS. Ultimately, however, they decided not to act on this idea, leaving the HCJ's 2002 ruling in the Interrogation Case as the last public policy for now. By doing so, the legislators implicitly endorsed the more liberal approach of the HCJ. Informally, however, there are those who claim that the GSS continues to apply interrogation methods that include torture, despite the court's ruling (Pachter, 2004).

The Collapse of the *Hudna* and the Lapid Committee Report

In 2003, the Palestinian organizations tried several times to adopt a *hudna* with regard to violence against Israel. None of these attempts succeeded. Due to the collapse of the *hudna*, Israel renewed its focused liquidations policy. Beginning in 2003, the number of successful terrorist attacks and the number of casualties from such attacks declined. However, the biggest change took place in 2004, when the number of the Israelis killed in terrorist attacks fell by 45 percent. Several factors account for the change, including the separation wall built around Samaria, army intelligence, the GSS's knowledge of the region, and the complete control the IDF had in Palestinian cities.

In September 2003, after the submission of the Or Committee's report, the Israeli government decided to accept the personal advice of the committee and establish a Knesset members' committee (headed by Tomy Lapid, the justice minister) to verify the application of the report's recommendations. The Lapid Committee submitted its conclusions in May 2004 and called for strict guidelines about the use of rubber bullets and the requirement to obtain permission from an area commander in order to open fire. During the Or Committee's discussions, the police had created an activation system designed to deal with violations of order, which met most of the committee's recommendations.

From discussions up to this point, one might draw the somewhat ironic conclusion that the more troublesome the events, the more liberal the political decisions – embracing ethical and moral values rather than the actions of the bureaucrats. Perhaps the social phenomena of non-governability, judicialization, and alternative culture, and the vacillation of politicians, bureaucrats, interest groups, and the public at large between the need for security and the desire to honor human rights explain this situation. The solution that was agreed on reflects the lack of a clear political decision as to how the actions of the Arab residents in the occupied territories should be treated. This vagueness highlights the severe non-governability in this field. In the face of the failure of the civil administration and the Palestinian Authority to deal effectively with the civilians in the territories, the Israeli government has chosen to pass the responsibility on to the bureaucrats, the IDF, the Israeli police, the GSS, and the legal advisors and the attorney general, whose job it is to determine when these groups have exceeded their legal authority. In actuality, there is close interaction and cooperation between the groups, arising from similar interests, interpersonal relationships, and the institutional dependency of the organizations on each other.

10.2. THE INTERROGATION CASE (1999)

The ruling in the Interrogation Case, handed down five years after the appeal, was the first time that the HCJ forbade the use of physical pressure in interrogations. However, there was no outright rejection of the possibility of interrogators' claiming "need" in order to gain an exemption from criminal responsibility when such methods were used in order to save lives (Barak-Erez, 2003: 27). Nevertheless, the ruling constituted a change from the earlier policy. That policy had allowed a "moderate degree of physical pressure, commensurate with the danger presented by the detainee, which does not constitute an abuse or torture of the detainee" (*Public Committee against Torture in Israel v. The State of Israel*, paragraph 16). However, the question of what constitutes a moderate degree of physical pressure remained unanswered.

The Court's ruling in the interrogation case cited an existing policy as a reference point. This policy was shaped by the Landau Committee's report (1987). The committee was created by the government in accordance with the Investigating Committee Law, 1968. The Landau report addressed, among other things, the legal standing of the GSS. In the eyes of the committee, one purpose of the GSS in its interrogation of Palestinian detainees was to gather information on suicide bombers and their organizational methods in order to prevent terrorist attacks during their planning stage. The High Court referred to this point in the interrogation ruling as follows:

> Although there is no specific law that authorizes its actions, due to the authority it is endowed with, through a series of specific legislations and due to the general governmental authority, as stated in the Basic Law of Government (paragraph 29 of the old law, paragraph 40 of the new law), the GSS is thereby authorized to interrogate those suspected of subversive activity... if there is a need for information in order to save human lives,

> the interrogator may apply psychological pressure and a moderate level of physical pressure. (*Public Committee against Torture in Israel v. The State of Israel*, paragraph 16)

The application of such physical pressure, which does not constitute an abuse or torture and is commensurate with the danger, constitutes the condition of "need" that protects the interrogator from criminal responsibility. The committee holds that "this conclusion does not contradict international law, and reflects an attitude that fits the rule of law and the need to guard the safety of the country and its citizens" (HCJ ruling, the Interrogation Case, paragraph 16).

In its ruling, the Court explained the changes in its position as follows:

> We have not ruled, until now, on the question of whether the GSS is authorized to use physical interrogation methods in circumstances defined as "need." We did so, partly, because we had not heard broad-based claims that would present the normative picture in full. Now we have received a number of appeals that include comprehensive claims (written and oral) of the representatives of both sides. We thank them. Although some of the appeals are general and others irrelevant, we decided to discuss them, since the law must be determined with regard to this complex issue. We did so first in these appeals. (HCJ ruling, the Interrogation Case, paragraph 16)

This explanation provided by the High Court focuses on a formalistic claim that entails a twofold paradox. First, the paradox lies in the data. According to the report of the Al Hak organization, based on 700 interviews with Palestinians held between May 1988 and May 1992, at least 94 percent of those interrogated experienced torture and abuse that were beyond moderate physical pressure. In an interview for the Kol Israel radio station, cited in the *Ha'aretz* daily newspaper, the late prime minister, Yitzchak Rabin, said that the method of "shaking" was applied to as many as 8,000 detainees. Second, the claim that the Court avoids intervention when the law is not clear seems paradoxical in light of the High Court's ability to develop law independently, as evidenced in past appeals. Is it true that the lack of broad-based claims had prevented the HCJ in the past from developing laws? The Court stresses the normative picture, even though it is known for developing laws and handing down judgments specifically on normative issues, even when the positivistic law does not provide it with adequate tools. For example, in the Yardor case (1964) Justices Agranat and Zusman ignored the majority opinion (as opposed to the dissenting opinion of Chaim Cohen) with regard to election law, as they thought it inappropriate. Agranat echoed the Israeli Declaration of Independence in stressing the principle that Israel is the eternal homeland of the Jews. Zusman emphasized the super-constitutional principles pertaining to Israel as an eternal Jewish state and a struggling democracy. The result of the ruling was that the political party El Ard was disqualified from participating in elections. Another example is the Bergman case, in which Justice Landau broadened the equality provision in the fourth clause of Basic Law: The Knesset to include the right to be elected. He concluded that the finance law had an indirect effect on the clause, thereby harming it. An additional example is the case of Bank Mizrahi. The opinion of President Barak and Justices Zamir, Levin, and Matza on the constitutive authority of the Knesset and HCJ 306/81 Plato Sharon create a test for the deviation from functional authority that broadens the judicial criticism of the Court.

Thus, the law should be understood as a social phenomenon rather than solely a legal one. This examination requires us to abandon the formalistic, legalistic explanation and focus on an inter-disciplinary explanation that combines the cultural, social, and political contexts. This chapter complements the conclusion stated in this book that judges are "political" creatures and are aware that, given external pressure, they must always act such that their autonomy and legitimacy are preserved (see also various articles dealing with politics and government by Liora Bielski, Eitan Barak, Alina Koren, Mordechai Kremintzer, and Keren Shapira-Etinger, Gad Barzilai, Miriam Gur-Arie, Yuval Karniel, Alon Brener, Leon Shelef, Dafna Barak-Erez, and Asher Maoz in Barzilai, 1999). As a result, the Court may bring about change slowly and incrementally (Rosenberg, 1991). Nevertheless, as we show here, the Supreme Court is not a sole player, and its decisions should be understood in the context of interactions between several players: politicians, bureaucrats, interest groups, and the public (other interest groups). Later in this chapter we suggest such explanations.

10.3. THE LAND DECISION CASE (2002)

The third example of a case in which the Supreme Court served as the institution that set the agenda on human rights was The Land Decision Case. This case revolved around a petition filed with the Israeli HCJ in 2000 by the Mizrahi Democratic Rainbow – New Discourse Movement (henceforth: *Keshet* – the Hebrew word for *rainbow*) asking the court to abolish certain decisions (nos. 727, 737, and 717) made by Israel Lands Administration that allowed agricultural settlements, *kibbutzim* and *moshavim* (the Hebrew words for co-operative settlements), to implement many programs that changed the zoning of land from agricultural to non-agricultural use. On August 28, 2002, the Israeli Supreme Court ruled in favor of the Keshet appeal and against the Israel Land Administration's decisions, contending that they were unreasonable. The Court argued that the decisions that were the object of the appeal awarded exaggerated and unjust benefits to certain sectors (the agricultural sector) and were therefore null and void because of extreme non-reasonability and impingement of the principles of justice. The HCJ's decision opened up a public debate about land policy in Israel (*New Discourse Movement et al. v. Minister of National Infrastructure*).

This decision was considered a precedent-setting one, but we may question to what extent it is a precedent. It has been recognized that the HCJ has the power to revoke administrative decisions as well as to abolish laws. What makes this decision a precedent is the explanation used by the Court in determining the reasoning behind its verdict that the decisions made by the Land Administration must be overturned.

The HCJ claimed that according to the law of the Israel Land Administration, the ability to determine fundamental arrangements lies with the land council, and therefore it is a "lazy" law. Thus, the HCJ chose to adopt the existing system and not to overturn the law as it had done before with other acts of the Knesset. However, using what Keshet called a "reasonable approach," the Court finally decided to intervene. In that sense, its action created a seeming contradiction because in the initial stage the Israeli Land Administration accepted the argument made by Keshet and promised that the decisions would be overturned. At that point (in the beginning of the Court's session) there was no conflict to be solved within the Court. Normally, the Court should have issued a verdict granting Keshet its request without further discussion. However, the HCJ decided to take the case and use it to formulate a fundamental value: "The Distribution of Justice." Because the Court did not explain its own behavior, we will use the inter-disciplinary approach developed in this book to do so.

10.4. ANALYZING PUBLIC POLICY IN THE INTERROGATION CASE AND THE LAND DECISION CASE

This section analyzes the Court's 1999 decision about methods of interrogation and its 2002 verdict on the allocation of land as the product of interactions between four main players: politicians, interest groups, bureaucrats, and the general public. Within this framework, we will emphasize structural factors such as non-governability and the culture of alternative politics, which are deeply rooted in Israeli society.

The Relationship between Citizens and Politicians

As stated in Chapter 2, any policy decision made by a politician in connection with human rights is underpinned by the reciprocal relationship between the politician and the electorate. These reciprocal relationships are based on the mechanism of supply and demand. In other words, the public makes demands for a certain policy on human rights, such as a demand that a more just distribution of land in Israel be included in its socio-economic rights, or a demand that a policy on various methods of interrogation used by the GSS be contained within the country's civil rights. The politician will respond positively (i.e., supply) solely to those demands that increase his or her chances of being elected. This explanation is also a key variable in explaining the original three decisions made by the Israel Land Administration (nos. 727, 737, and 717) in the wake of major economic downturns that threatened the solvency of most of the kibbutzim and many of the moshavim. Those decisions allowed the kibbutzim and moshavim to diversify their sources of income by re-zoning their land from agricultural to non-agricultural use, thereby averting an economic and social crisis.

The need for the State's intervention by means of public policy usually emerges when a shortage of a "public good" arises. A public good is defined as a product whose use, from the very moment it has been supplied, may not be curtailed. As a result, it is not possible to collect any real payments for this good, making such payments contingent on continued supply (Weimer and Vining, 1999). A public good can be defined as such because there are no regulations that restrict its use (e.g., air, water, natural areas) or because society has decided not to collect the real cost of using this product from the public. Examples of the latter case include subsidies for education, health care, and security. In actual fact, the decisions about the distribution of land and the interrogation policy basically apply to all citizens, even those who were not involved in these suits.

However, as explained in Chapter 2, individuals usually prefer a passive strategy of non-participation to an active strategy of participation in the provision of public goods. In our two cases, citizens did not participate strongly in the efforts to change public policy about land use or interrogation methods. Given the collective action problem, politicians were not faced with massive social demands to change policy in those areas. In the absence of strong public demands, other social players became central in the process of policy making – the NGOs that acted to advance and promote human rights (Benvenisti, 1999).

Non-Governmental Organizations as Interest Groups Lobbying for Human Rights

The role of NGOs acting to advance and promote human rights is very important in explaining the policy reflected in the HCJ's decisions. These groups, such as the Association for Civil Rights in Israel (ACRI), the Betselem Organization, and the Mizrahi Democratic Rainbow, manage to overcome the problem of collective action, which is typical of the general public, in order to present demands concerning the lack of a human rights policy.

Our third case illustrates this point. The systematic activity of the Mizrahi Democratic Rainbow – New Discourse Movement in appealing to the Court to overturn certain decisions (nos. 727, 737, and 717) made by Israel Land Administration, with recurrent petitions to the HCJ, led to a change in the human rights policy regarding the allocation of land in Israel. The absence of counter-pressure from the kibbutzim and moshavim made politicians feel that being identified with a policy that violated the fair allocation of land was potentially damaging to their chances of being re-elected. In contrast, advocating a different policy could be instrumental to their being elected. However, in Israel of the late 1990s, the political system was characterized by non-governability and a political culture that was dominated by alternative politics as a mode of political participation. Under these circumstances, politicians tended not to make decisions about crucial issues but rather preferred to hand that authority over to another institution (Voight and Salzberger, 2002). Such an institution was usually the one that the public or interest groups identified as a suitable replacement for the government. In our case, that institution was the Supreme Court.

Similarly, as we saw in the second case, groups such as the Association of Civil Rights in Israel, Betselem, and the Public Committee against Torture in Israel, acting as interpreters of social values, demanded a more humanitarian public policy regarding the interrogation methods employed by the GSS. Thus, the systematic activity of the Public

Committee against Torture in Israel in the 1990s, reflected in recurring appeals to the HCJ, and the participation of the Association for Civil Rights in Israel and Betselem, led to a partial change in the Court's policy toward interrogation. The Court refers to this trend in the following comments:

> A number of appeals filed in this court in recent years pertain to the use of physical force during GSS interrogations (see, for example, HCJ 7964/95, Balbisi v. the GSS [unpublished]; HCJ 8049/96, Hamdan v. the GSS [unpublished]; HCJ 3123/94, A-ton v. Director of the GSS [unpublished]; HCJ 3029/95, Arkan v. the GSS [unpublished]; HCJ 5578/95, Hagazi v. the GSS [unpublished]). In all of these appeals we decided upon an immediate discussion. In most of these discussions, the appellants and we were informed that no physical means were used. On this basis, we asked the appellants to retract the appeals (HCJ ruling on the interrogation issue, paragraph 17).

The next sub-section analyzes the behavior of the HCJ as a bureaucratic player.

The Involvement of Bureaucrats

We noted earlier that public policy is shaped by a complex interaction of a number of players. One of those players is the bureaucrat. In this section, we will focus on two types of bureaucrats. One is the typical bureaucrat, a member of the administration who, by virtue of his or her position, allocates budgets to various activities and thus effectively determines whether certain activities will be undertaken. This type of bureaucrat works vis-à-vis the politicians and affects the determination of specific policy. With regard to our cases, we can see the bureaucratic role of the Israel Land Administration controlled by the agenda designed by the kibbutzim and moshavim (Barak-Erez, 2000). With regard to the interrogation policy, we can see the role of the GSS on the one hand and the players such as the attorney general and the state prosecutor, who must decide whether to bring criminal charges, on the other.

These bureaucrats both act in their own interests and influence the interpretational design underpinning the policy. In the case of the land use issue, the Israel Land Administration includes many members of the agriculture sector. In the wake of the decline in agriculture as a profitable sector of the Israeli economy, it was in their interests to re-zone the land from agricultural to non-agricultural use.

In contrast, the composition of the administration affected by the interrogation policy created a potential conflict of interests. The GSS personnel preferred flexible interrogation methods in order to maximize their performance, whereas the attorney general and the state prosecutor had to decide whether to make such practices criminal. The state attorney would have liked to hand responsibility for supervising this area over to the state prosecutor's office. This move would be especially preferable when the GSS possesses evidence to support its consideration of the use of torture; this fact gives the GSS great power relative to the state attorney. However, given the absence of clear-cut beliefs among the public with regard to what should be allowed and what should not, and without clear legislation, strong interactions and cooperation have developed between the GSS and the state attorney. This cooperation derives from their similar interests, inter-relations, and the mutual institutional dependency of these organizations (Zecharia, 2003). In this context, Barzilai and Nachmias (1998) claim that the developing understanding is "the exchange of spheres." The attorney general and the state prosecutor are pressed to surrender their autonomy in areas such as security or governmental offenses in exchange for broader autonomy in handling ordinary crime. As for the dynamic between the GSS, and the attorney general and the state prosecutor's office, the HCJ puts its trust in the latter and frequently passes messages through them to government ministries (Dotan, 1999). Such behavior can be explained by a number of theoretical approaches to law and politics. For example, the functionalist-legalist approach explains this behavior by the fact that the legal profession is built into the structural solidarity (Kelsen, 1945; Schmidhouser, 1992). Indeed, another type of bureaucrat is the Supreme Court, which plays a significant role with respect to the determination of public policy on human rights.

The Involvement of the Supreme Court in Human Rights Policy

The involvement of the Supreme Court as a key bureaucratic player in the determination of public policy is part of a complex mechanism that both influences and is influenced by the political culture in Israel. The Supreme Court's influence is particularly strong at the decision-making stage rather than at the stage of understanding the problem and formulating a position. The Justices of the Supreme Court cannot initiate a hearing but are dependent on whatever petitions are filed in the Court. The pattern of conduct described earlier has also been adopted by the NGOs seeking to promote human rights. The main channel of activity for advancing public policy on human rights is the legal system, as evident, for example, in the public and legal struggle of the ACRI and the Betselem Organization, the Mizrahi Democratic Rainbow, and the Public Commission against Torture in Israel.

In analyzing the decisions of the Supreme Court regarding the land case and the interrogation case, one can see several factors that serve as sources of legitimacy and support for the conduct of the Supreme Court, along with the involvement of ideology and maximization of political power. We will analyze the Supreme Court as a special bureaucrat with a focus on the maximization of legitimacy, the ideological viewpoint of the Supreme Court judges, the legal community's viewpoint, and the power of the Supreme Court (McGuire and Palmer, 1996; Feeley and Rubin, 1998; McGuire and Stimson, 2004).

The Maximization of Legitimacy

When the law is clear and explicit, the courts are required to implement it. In those cases, there is no problem of outside judicial interpretation. However, when the law is silent, the Court needs to adopt a strategic approach in order to handle competing pressures from the surrounding environment. Thus, in the interrogation case the Court said

> Is there an instruction of law that authorizes the investigators of the GSS to execute investigations in the meaning, mentioned before? Such a special instruction, dealing in the inquiry by people of the GSS does not exist. (HCJ ruling, the Interrogation Case, paragraph 19)

As mentioned before, through this intervention in the determination of political values, the Supreme Court advances its power, at least according to the existing rules of game.

Because its public and professional legitimacy are the central sources of the Supreme Court's power, it aims its decisions at certain communities. Such strategic targets include public opinion, human rights NGOs, and the legal community. For example, in the interrogation case, we can identify various considerations in the Court's ruling. Some considerations are strategic, taking into account the positions of the various players, and some are ideological, expressing a conflict in values between security concerns and liberalism. The resulting rulings reflect cautious progress toward liberalism, owing to both the more liberal mental model in place since the 1990s and the fear that the GSS might damage future interrogation policies.

Similarly, we can see that the Supreme Court is aiming its decision at the human rights community, both local and international. As the Court stated:

> This conclusion matches with principles of international contractual law – which Israel confirmed – that prohibits the use of torture as well as cruel or inhuman treatment or degrading treatment. Those prohibitions are absolute. (The Interrogation Case, paragraph 21)

Another community to whom the Court is directing its decision is the legal community, both local and international, particularly the American legal community (Lahav, 1999; Mautner, 2002). For example, immediately after the Court's ruling in the interrogation case was published, it was translated and distributed abroad by the Court's administration. Furthermore, the Supreme Court consistently cites local and international scholars in its verdicts. In the interrogation case, the Court quoted Prof. Mordechai Kremnitzer in favor of judicial review in matters concerning human rights violations of security prisoners. This notion is supported by other renowned jurists such as Ruth Gavison and Alan Dershowitz (in: *Human Rights and Civil Liberties in Israel: A Reader*, 1991). The Supreme Court also quoted Profs. Yitzhak Zamir and Baruch Bracha regarding the principle of administrative legality, and Judge Yaakov Kedmi regarding the nature of interrogation.

In the land case, we can also see several groups to whom the Supreme Court was addressing its verdict: the New Discourse Movement, a non-parliamentary social movement, consisting mainly of academic scholars who were social activists; the company To the Defense of Nature, an institute made up of planning and environmental social activists; and petitioners from the agriculture sector who support the suit. Indeed, the Supreme Court stated that even in the agriculture sector there were fundamental disputes. As noted before, the Supreme Court quoted local and international scholars such as Prof. Daphne Barak-Erez and S. R. Simpson and emphasized the consistency of this verdict with earlier decisions regarding the importance of land in Israel as a national resource.

The Ideological Viewpoint of the Supreme Court Judges

In both cases, the Court clearly expressed its liberal way of thinking and attempted to advance it through its ruling. For example, in the interrogation case, the Court said, "The power of the interrogation harms the freedom of the individual.... There is no legal-administrative vacuum since it is filled with the general principal of freedom." The Court quoted the words of the former president of the Supreme Court, Meir Shamgar, who said: "There are actions that are not within the authority of the government because operating without legal authorization contradicts basic normative principals rooted in our regime. Thus, basic rights are part of our positive law, whether they were included in basic laws or not" (The Interrogation Case, paragraph 19).

This attitude is also evident in the Land Decision case when the Court said

> Land . . . is a national resource . . . social life depends on the ability of the public to use lands, i.e. to build roads, to lay down railways, to regulate means of communication and so on. . . . (The Land Case, paragraph 36)

The Court continues

> The duty to consider just distribution is part of the authority of an administrative agent when deciding upon the allocation of limited resources . . . this duty was expressed in several decisions regarding the freedom of occupation and equal rights and opportunities. (The Land Case, paragraph 39)

The Power of the Supreme Court

The literature is divided as to whether the Supreme Court is motivated by the desire to maximize its power or by its ideological view. However, it seems evident that the judicial activism demonstrated in the interrogation case and the land case places the Supreme Court in the position of an alternative governor or policy maker. As a result of this behavior, during the 1990s, the Israeli Supreme Court became an alternative institution of government with regard to the instilling of values in Israel.

In 2002, the Israeli parliament passed the *Shabak* (the Hebrew word for GSS) Law but did not enact legislation about interrogation (The General Security Service Act, Paragraph 7), thus leaving the decision of the Supreme Court as the last legal source on that issue. This behavior emphasizes the inability of the Knesset to govern in crucial cases as well as its willingness to hand over power and authority to the Supreme Court.

As for the land decision, even today there has been no consensual decision in the political arena that solves the disputes between the two sides. In fact, numerous appeals have been filed with the Supreme Court, but no fundamental decision has been made, thus leaving the land decision from 2002 as the last legal decision on that issue. However, the inability to define "just distribution" in that case no longer exists. The agricultural sector has adopted the tried-and-true method of "do-it-yourself" by creating facts on the ground, and the administrative authorities are having a very hard time stopping them.

10.5. SUMMARY

Both the interrogation case and the land case occurred at the end of the fifth decade in the history of the State of Israel and reflected the central place of the Supreme Court as a policy maker. In both cases, the Supreme Court interfered in the actions of governmental authorities. We maintain that the Court chose to engage in such judicial activism because the non-governability of the political system and a political culture characterized by quasi-exit behavior and alternative politics created a framework in which the Supreme Court acted as a special bureaucrat. Its judicial activism helped the Court maximize its legitimacy and power and brought its ideological viewpoint in line with that of the legal community both domestically and abroad.

In rhetorical public terms, the State of Israel chooses to belong to the community of nations promoting human rights either regarding interrogation methods or in the allocation of land. However, in operative terms, Israeli politicians prefer to leave the implementation of these rights in the hands of the Israeli bureaucracy, headed by the High Court and its representatives, the state prosecutor's office and the attorney general as the watchdogs of the GSS. We saw that, in reality, the GSS and the state prosecutor's office interact and cooperate on the basis of interpersonal relationships, similar interests, and institutional dependency.

As the verdicts in the interrogation case and the allocation of land also demonstrate, the influence of the High Court is limited, because its decisions reflect an existing mental model. Such a mental model is the outcome of learning processes that followed in the wake of structural changes such as the intensification of non-governability and instrumentality. Until this model changes significantly, the HCJ's decisions are an important tool in safeguarding human rights in Israel. These decisions establish normative directions and reflect Israel's democratic character with regard to the value of human rights.

However, as far as the promotion of human rights is concerned, we must note two key factors. First, various entities may interpret the increasingly frequent appeals to the HCJ as a lack of respect for the defined rules of the game. As a result, respect for the law and its public legitimacy may suffer, at least among certain social groups. Second, legal rules that are not supportable on a large scale are rules that are difficult to enforce. According to Barak-Erez (2003: 26)

> If the prohibition against torturing terrorists is not internalized, it is likely that physical force will indeed be employed to interrogate terrorists. In any case, only a small number of these incidents would reach the courts. This does not mitigate the possibility that the potential of legal criticism or trial would have "a chilling effect" on the activity of the General Security Service.

Thus, judicial activism in the cases discussed in this chapter would not necessarily achieve the goal of defending human rights but may intensify the instrumental approach to the law in Israeli society. By positioning itself as a dominant policy maker, the Court also makes itself the target of criticism that may endanger its legitimacy. These issues are discussed in the following concluding chapters.

11

On Law, Society, and Policy Design – toward a Reform in the Relationship between the High Court of Justice and the Knesset

11.1. INTRODUCTION

The debate that took place between the former Justice Minister Daniel Friedman (Kadima) and the High Court of Justice (HCJ) Judge Dorit Beinish about the status of the HCJ and its involvement in public life reflects the problems in the relationship between the Knesset and the Court. In a review presented on April 11, 2008 in a social responsibility gathering at the University of Haifa, the scholars Arie Retner and Meir Yaish pointed out the decline in the number of citizens who trust the legal system. The percentage of Jewish respondents who said they trust the HCJ dropped from 56 percent in 2007 to 48 percent in 2008. In 2000, the percentage of Jewish citizens who trusted the Court was 80 percent. The decline in public trust is indicative not only of the Court's status, but also of a weakening of the stability that had characterized the relationship between the public and the Court. It appears that the institutional arrangement that characterized the relationship between the Knesset and the Court prior to 2000, an arrangement that produced a number of social changes, no longer meets the needs of Israeli society. Various groups have sought to change this institutional arrangement with an eye to reducing the Court's influence in the public realm.

However, in 2007, Minister of Justice Daniel Friedman proposed institutionalizing criticism of the HCJ via legislation. On the face of it, the proposal seemed to imply that the Knesset had backed down from its desire to restrain the Court by accepting the informal arrangement giving the Court the ability to annul laws passed by the Knesset. However, a closer look at the proposal shows a somewhat different story. Friedman stipulated that if the Court annuls a law passed by the Knesset, the parliament could still adopt the law if a majority of sixty-one Knesset members voted for it, thereby overturning the Court's decision. He made other proposals as well, such as establishing a committee to locate precedents handed down by the Court and expanding the committee that appoints judges. These proposals engendered so much resistance that the legal system's representatives, led by the former president of the High Court of Justice, Aharon Barak, criticized Friedman's conduct. These proposals were not adopted. However, Friedman's proposal to limit the tenure of the Court's president and deputies to seven years was accepted by a majority of fifty-one Knesset members. This law is to be implemented after Judge Dorit Beinish's tenure as President of the HCJ is completed. As of this writing, there has been no law passed on judicial criticism. Such legislation awaits future action.

A major question is whether the decline in public trust in the HCJ means that there is a need to craft a new arrangement between it and the Knesset. Another question is what kind of arrangement exists between the two and does it constitute a market failure? If it does, is the market failure the result of the whole arrangement or parts of it? What is the most appropriate arrangement that could solve the market failure problem? These questions are based on the assumption that there is some kind of arrangement between the Court and the Knesset and that it is not stable. Therefore, it must be fixed in a way that will create a new balance of power, one that offers different rewards to those in the private and public sectors as well as the possibility of arriving at different decisions than those made currently. It is clear that the success of each proposed arrangement depends on its matching the major characteristics of the political culture. Otherwise, such a change will be either insignificant or doomed to failure.

What, then, is the current arrangement between the Knesset and the HCJ? Does it reflect only the Court's ability to annul laws, or is it more complex than that? We argue that the relationship is an informal one that reflects the cultural-structural complexity of Israeli society. Historically, it has placed the HCJ at the center of public life. While this arrangement seemed to satisfy the public up until 2000, it no longer seems to do so. Given the current state of their relationship, this chapter proposes a solution based on structural as well as cultural factors.

11.2. THE SHETREET REPORT

As part of the Presidents' Commission for the Examination of the Structure of Governance in Israel (2006), Prof. Shimon Shetreet pointed out the need for a balance of power between the various government authorities. According to Shetreet, this goal could be accomplished by adopting a model of judicial supervision of laws in which the HCJ would be given the authority to indicate that a law contradicted a basic law passed by the Knesset. Following this verdict, the Knesset would decide (preferably during the same session) whether to amend the law so that it matched the basic law it contradicted or leave it as it was despite the contradiction. Shetreet provides a detailed description of the advantages of the proposed model, such as upholding the democratic values of participation. He also claims that the model is being used de facto in the present-day Israeli government system. In most cases in which the HCJ rules that a law contradicts a basic law, it delays its annulment of the law, allowing the Knesset time to amend it. This "declarative model" was adopted in Great Britain in 1998 and implemented in 2000.

Shetreet notes that it might be useful to adopt two additional reforms apart from the aforementioned model: creating a constitutional panel to oversee cases of judicial constitutional criticism and cutting back on the right of standing. He maintains that these precautions might prevent damage to the judicial system and the government incurred through increasing disputes as well as the fear that aggressive laws might be passed against the legal authority. He adds the exposure of the HCJ to greater pressure requires a constitutional defense in the form of strengthening the judges and the Court against attempts to curb the legal system's authority.

11.3. DISCUSSION OF THE LEGAL LITERATURE

The discussion concerning the practice of legal criticism of laws may be divided into three interrelated issues. The first concerns the extent of judicial criticism toward Knesset legislation. Scholars disagree as to whether the Court has the authority to criticize such legislation. They also disagree about the role and status of the HCJ in the political realm and about the need for a constitutional court. For instance, the President of the HCJ, Aharon Barak (2003), maintains that judicial criticism of laws was in fact recognized in the Bank Mizrahi ruling, and that there are forces attempting to alter the current constitutional-institutional structure in Israel. Segal (2003) makes a similar claim, arguing that even though the Knesset has not explicitly recognized the courts' authority to examine its legislation, the HCJ acted correctly when it adopted this authority because it uses judicial criticism with great moderation. Galnoor (2004: 355) tends to differ: "The High Court of Justice must not and cannot change the face of society, and should interfere in exceptional cases. The unconventional weapon of judicial criticism should be kept in a basement and used in cases of trouble only..." Gavison (1997) posits that the activist position adopted by the HCJ might make it look like a political player, resulting in damage to the constitutional process and public trust in the Court.

Another issue concerns the appointment of judges who discuss constitutional issues. Proposals to establish a constitutional court of law include a demand to change the manner in which judges are appointed to this court to ensure professional variety as well as the representation of different groups. Scholars disagree on this point, but most seem to favor retaining the status quo. For instance, Judge Aharon Barak says:

> Our system [judicial appointment] is good since it allows us to balance the professional side: three judges and two lawyers who are the majority; and the political side: two ministers and two Knesset members, one from the coalition and one from the opposition. There are no political party appointments...in that way the court of law differs from the Knesset. The legislating authority is representative...but not the judicial one. It is ruled by principles of professionalism, objectivity as well as the ability to reflect the complexity of society....Indeed the high court of justice is not a representative but a reflecting body whose judges must reflect the complexity of Israeli society and it pluralism...[1]

Another position maintains that to ensure public trust in judging, it is crucial that the panel of judges reflect the multicultural character of Israeli society (Klein, 2003; Mautner, 2003; Shetreet, 2004).

The third issue deals with the extent to which a constitutional court of law is necessary in the judicial-institutional climate of Israel. Although most scholars believe that there is no need to establish a special court for the judicial criticism of laws, each bases his or her position on a slightly different rationale. Aharon Barak, for instance, deals with arguments in favor of establishing a constitutional court of law by claiming: "I believe that we should avoid establishing a special constitutional court of law since this might turn judging into a political enterprise, jeopardize the professionalism of judging, damage the public trust in the judicial system and result in the destruction of the High Court of Justice..."[2] Segal

[1] Ibid., Barak, 2003, pp. 324–325. See also Zamir, The report of the committee regarding the appointment of judges (2001); Rubinstein Amnon and Barak Medina. 2005. *The State of Israel's Constitutional Law*. Tel-Aviv: Shocken Publishers (in Hebrew).

[2] Ibid., Aharon Barak.

(2003) reaches similar conclusions; however, he proposes granting the court the status of an advisor in constitutional matters while the final decision – annulling a law that might damage a basic law – will be made in the Knesset. Dotan (2000) reaches similar conclusions: "[T]he current model, with a few slight changes, in which the criticism of law's legality is conducted in the regular legal system, is a good and adequate model for our constitutional reality." He, therefore, recommends that the High Court of Justice adopt the old strategy of judging in order to increase public trust and to establish a constitutional court of law only when the constitutional situation in Israel is ripe. "There is no reason to race ahead and establish such a court of law *before the completion* (author's emphasis) of essential structural parts meant to be included in a state constitution."[3] Shetreet (2004) speculates that

> [t]here is a need for the High Court of Justice to retain the right to declare that a certain law contradicts a basic law and to rule in such matters in a constitutional panel of judges; however, the final decision as to whether the law should be amended to match the basic law or to annul it altogether should be made by the Knesset. According to this format the High Court of Justice would decide on constitutional matters in a special constitutional panel of judges based on the principle of transparency. In other words, the discussion concerning the validity of laws will be conducted in front of a panel of judges including at least three women, a traditional judge as well as judges from different strata of society.[4]

Klein (2003) also supports this attitude. He believes that the HCJ is the body that should conduct judicial criticism of laws, albeit in a broader format. Soffer and Fishman (2001) take the opposite position. They emphasize the issue of public trust in judicial criticism and claim that leaving judicial criticism about the legality of laws in the hands of the HCJ in its current format will not strengthen the procedural consensus. In other words, adopting an already agreed on rules of the game to obtain court rulings would only weaken the HCJ. They believe that a constitutional court of law must be established to combine the factors of representation and choice by including those who represent the people and professional appointments in the court.

[3] Dotan, Yoav, 2000. Does Israel Need a Constitutional Court of Law? *Mishpat Umimshal* 5, 117.

[4] Shetreet, Shimon, 2004. *On Adjudication: Justice on Trial*. Tel Aviv: Yedioth Ahronot publishers (in Hebrew), pp. 44–45.

11.4. POLICY SCIENCE

The point of view of this chapter is that of policy science. Policy science was established in the 1950s as a scientific research field. It gained momentum mainly in the 1960s in the United States, reflecting the changes that occurred on the national and international levels. These changes did not go unnoticed by academia. Scholars concluded that to understand complex issues, we must consider all of the dimensions, relationships, and mutual dependencies of the issue. To accomplish this goal, scholars developed an interdisciplinary approach that included theories from the fields of political science, economics, sociology, and mathematics (Dror, 2001).[5]

The discipline that deals with the analysis and design of policy outcomes is called public policy evaluation. We distinguish between objective policy evaluation, which is based on social-public parameters, and subjective policy evaluation, which focuses on the personal interests of the various players, especially politicians and bureaucrats, and evaluates the costs or benefits of the policy for each of them.

This chapter emphasizes the structural, social, and procedural factors that create the balance in the interaction between the HCJ and the political system. Shetreet examines the different models of constitutional criticism from a comparative perspective and focuses on the interaction between the judicial and the legislative branches. He also discusses the advantages for democracy included in the declarative model he proposes. Finally, he notes that the relationship between law and politics is not formalist but interdisciplinary (Shetreet, 1998). Therefore, it is impossible to transfer the British model to Israel and expect it work properly; the model has to be compatible with the existing social, cultural, and structural conditions.

11.5. THE CENTRALITY OF THE HIGH COURT OF JUSTICE: NON-GOVERNANCE AND THE CULTURE OF ALTERNATIVE POLITICS

As noted earlier, when faced with the inability to influence the political system through the normal channels available in a democracy, Israelis

[5] Doron, Gideon, 1986. *To Decide and to Implement: Chapters in Public Policy*. Tel Aviv: Kivunim (in Hebrew); Arian, Asher, Nachmias, David and Ruth Amir, 2002. *Governability and the Executive Authority*. Jerusalem: Israel Democracy Institute (in Hebrew); Dror Yehezkel, 2001. *The Capacity to Govern: A Report to the Club of Rome*. London: Cass (first published in a German edition, 1994).

adopted a culture of alternative politics in which they sought other ways of obtaining the goods and services they wanted. A similar process led to the placement of the HCJ at the center of Israeli society (Mizrahi and Meydani, 2003). Given that there was no formal definition of its role, politicians and the public felt free to appeal to the Court when every other avenue of recourse led to a dead end. Therefore, by applying to this institution with increasing frequency, the public attempted to create a de facto reality. The politicians, in turn, petitioned the High Court in an attempt to promote their own interests because they were unable to do so on the parliamentary level. Furthermore, in most cases, the Knesset chose not to exercise its formal authority and accepted the court's rulings as they were given, thereby increasing the power of the HCJ at the cost of the Knesset's ability to govern.

It follows, then, that the deep gaps in Israeli society combined with its institutional structure make it hard for the political system to cope with issues that involve public policy design. Due to this inability to design public policy, the public has adopted a new behavior pattern. When there is a need for a speedy decision, it petitions the High Court or puts pressure on politicians to change the existing institutional structure. Moreover, it sometimes seems that those who petition the HCJ are more interested in influencing the public and political agenda than in the actual rulings that Court hands down (Doron and Lebel, 2005). Galnoor says the following about the relationship between the political system and the court:

> What is to be done in a situation when politicians deviate to the level of jeopardizing democracy? One is assisted by a court of law. In this period of time when democratic values should be axioms . . . these weren't properly internalized. When these values are lacking, the trust in the rules of the game as well as adhering to them is beginning to weaken including the restriction on government actions and the readiness to trust the political process and institutions. In this respect, frequenting the HCJ as a way to keep the rules of the game might have been useful; however, it didn't prevent political corruption . . . of the HCJ . . . isn't the appropriate institution to decide on controversial ideological questions. It is better for the political process to cope with such issues than legislation or rulings; however, this depends on the political culture that makes this possible.[6]

The central place of the HCJ as an agent in designing the social and political agenda in Israel is, therefore, a result of deep and complex social

[6] Galnoor, Itzhak. 2004. Politicization of Public Life in Israel, *Mishpat Umimshal* 7, 355 (in Hebrew).

and political processes. Within these processes, various players in the political and judicial realms try to design a policy that maximizes their benefits.

11.6. AN ARRANGEMENT THAT PROMOTES GOVERNANCE IS NEEDED

Social choice theory teaches us that public policy is the result of the activity of many players. This chapter considers a number of those players: politicians, bureaucrats, interest groups, and the general public. These players function within an institutional structure that makes it hard for the political system to determine policy and implement it. One of the obstacles facing the political system is an alternative political culture. According to this theory, the initiative of individual players can ignite processes that will change the status quo significantly. The initiative of Knesset members Bibi and Cohen to establish a constitutional court of law (2000) is a case in point. Their proposal reflects an attempt to alter the rules of the game that are, according to them, unfair to certain groups. The proposal has been removed from the public agenda, but it seems to have had a strong effect.

The activism of the HCJ is the result of the deep gaps that exist in Israeli society, which, together with the institutional structure, make it hard for the political system to cope with issues that involve public policy design. As a response to the resulting lack of public policy in different spheres, citizens have identified the HCJ as an institution that can solve their problems by putting pressure on the politicians or by legal rulings. The increasing rate of petitions filed with the HCJ is not necessarily a function of a policy that "everything can be judged." Barak says in the Resler decision, "There is law and there are criteria of law everywhere."[7] They are a function of deep and complex social-political processes that led to the development of the institution that designs the social-political agenda in Israel. Note that agenda design differs from determining actual policy. There is a gap between the public perception of the HCJ's role as public policy maker and its actual activity. The HCJ, in fact, reflects the social preferences in Israel as a result of which it promotes changes in a slow and additive way. In this regard, despite the formal power of the Knesset, in most cases it chooses not to interfere with the HCJ's rulings.

[7] HCJ 910/86 *Resler v. Minister of Security* IsrPD 42 (2) 441.

Thus, the weakness of the politicians as well as their inability to rule promotes the centrality of the HCJ in public life.

For some politicians, the reality thus created is comfortable; they can let the HCJ deal with issues without paying the political price involved in decisions that disrupt the institutional status quo. However, the HCJ learned that in some cases it is better to avoid ruling and put the decision back into the hands of the Knesset.[8] Nonetheless, when the Knesset fails to determine policy in a given case, the HCJ is bound to "take responsibility" and to rule. Such rulings necessarily have an effect that might harm certain groups leaving their members dissatisfied with the policy. In the long run, the representatives of those who have been disappointed by the Court's verdicts may use strategies to push the Court not to rule on cases that disrupt the status quo.[9] If this strategy does not work, they might try to alter the rules of the game in a way that serves them best.

This chapter deals with public debate and the process of public policy making. It does not attempt to prove or disprove certain claims used by spokesmen on either side of the debate concerning institutionalization of the interaction between the HCJ and the Knesset and the establishment of a constitutional court of law. In this regard, the literature proposes a court of law with a panel (of judges) that has several characteristics: transparency (who is to determine the transparency?); legitimacy of the institution (in whose eyes?); and the social role of the institution (measured using which social dimension?). Usually there are no clear-cut answers, and therefore finding a solution to a public problem entails defining the problem itself first. However, even after the problem has been defined, one must remain consistent in order to arrive at a solution. This chapter has demonstrated that the problem is, in fact, a social-cultural one; therefore, the solution will not be found in arrangements that do not correspond to the dynamics of Israeli society, including all of its groups.

Shetreet posits that the declarative model functions de facto in the current Israeli government system. In most case, when the HCJ decides that the Knesset has passed a law that contradicts a basic law, it postpones the annulment of law and gives the Knesset the necessary time to amend it. Note that the salience of the Court's ruling is greater when the High Court of Justice has to interfere in the decisions of different bodies, not

[8] See HCJ 1031/93 *Pasaro (Goldstein) v. Minister of the Interior* IsrPD 49 (4) 661; HCJ 5016 *Lior Horev and others v. Minister of Transportation and others* IsrPD 51 (4) 91; HCJ *Israel Investment Managers' Chamber v. Minister of Finance* IsrPD 51 (4) 367.

[9] HCJ 5364/94 *Velner v. Avoda Party Chairman* IsrPD 49 (1) 758.

when it annuls a law made by the Knesset (i.e., see the yeshiva students' recruitment affair, the GSS interrogation techniques case, the Alice Miller affair).[10] The book also points out the lack of public policy (meaning the sub-optimal existence of policy in the eyes of the public). In this regard, the HCJ is not the sole player, but only one of the players. Thus, any accurate examination of the situation must take the behaviors of all of the players into account.

The centrality of the HCJ seems to be indicative of the major problem, that of the non-governance of the political system. Therefore, the solution we should adopt must first and foremost be one that promotes the ability of the political system to govern.[11] The establishment of a political system capable of promoting public policy in issues fundamental to society has become a critical mission in Israel. Until that mission is accomplished, the interests of the politicians will determine the character of the mechanisms designated to provide public policy. These interests will probably encounter a certain level of resistance from other interest groups dissatisfied with the quantity and quality of policy supply, leading to a continuation of the stalemate.

11.7. A SUMMARY – A PROPOSED INSTITUTIONAL ARRANGEMENT

Introduction

1. The relationship between the HCJ and the Knesset reflects an institutional societal arrangement.
2. The arrangement in Israel is not defined and is, to some extent, unstable.
3. Any proposed policy must be appropriate to the conditions of the given society as well as its culture and structure in order to have a reasonable chance of success.

[10] The controversial HCJ rulings were not focused on petitions to annul the law but on administrative petitions; see: HCJ 3872/93 *Mitral Ltd. v. Prime Minister and Minister of Religion and others* IsrPD 47 (5) 491; HCJ 1031/93 *Pasaro (Goldstein) v. Minister of the Interior* IsrPD 49 (4) 661; HCJ 721/94 *El-Al v. Danilovitch* IsrPD 48 (5), 749. HCJ 6698/95 *Aadel Kaadan v. Israel Land Administration* IsrPD 54 (1) 258.

[11] Moshe Gorali, *Haaretz*, "The return to a single ballot already appears to be a mistake," January 3, 2003; See the opinions of Asher Arian, Gad Barzilai, Amnon Rubinstein, Arik Carmon, Claude Klein, and Dafna Barak-Erez regarding the change in the election system; they reflect a leading argument that maintains that social and cultural problems are not solved by election systems or constitutional or judicial formulae.

Structure and Culture

4. Non-governance as well as an instrumental political culture characterizes Israel society. This inability to govern has made the HCJ a trustworthy alternative to the normal channels of governance in the eyes of the public.

A Change in Public Trust

5. Since 2000, there has been a decline in public trust in the HCJ, arising from both disagreement with the Court's rulings and its involvement in controversial matters in which it adopted a liberal policy that does not correspond to beliefs common in Israeli society. This decline of trust has led to a desire to institutionalize the HCJ's place in the political system in Israel.

Disagreement between the HCJ and the Knesset

6. There is disagreement over whether the HCJ has the right to nullify a law passed by the Knesset. There must be a clear definition of the parameters of each institution when it comes to legislation.

   a. *Nullifying a law that contradicts a basic law*

In Israel a non-formal agreement was reached in which the HCJ is authorized to nullify a law according to the "restriction paragraph."

Violation of Freedom of Occupation

4. There shall be no violation of freedom of occupation except by a law befitting the values of the State of Israel, enacted for a proper purpose, and to an extent no greater than is required, or by regulation enacted by virtue of express autorisation in such law." Basic Law: Freedom of Occupation (amendment 1994).[12]

[12] Such a paragraph also appears Basic Law: Human Dignity and Liberty:

> What happens when there is a contradiction between a basic law and an ordinary law passed after the basic law was passed? The answer to this question hasn't yet been given in any law (the Basic Law: Legislation will deal with it), but the High Court of Justice has, in recent years, related to it in several rulings: On September 24, 1997, the HCJ with a make-up of 11 judges cancelled in a precedental ruling several

Although formally the Knesset in the most limited case has the right to overrule the HCJ's ruling by a majority of sixty-one members, in accordance with the "overcoming paragraph" in Basic Law: Freedom of Occupation amendment 1994:

> 8. A provision of a law that violates freedom of occupation shall be of effect, even though not in accordance with section 4, if it has been included in a law passed by a majority of the members of the Knesset, which expressly states that it shall be of effect, notwithstanding the provisions of this Basic Law; such law shall expire four years from its commencement unless a shorter duration has been stated therein.[13]

The institutionalization of judicial criticism of laws reflects developments in recent decades. The "overcoming paragraph" has been in place since 1994. The Knesset has already accepted restrictions on its power and acknowledged that basic laws have a fundamental essence.

6. *Nullifying a policy that contradicts a Basic Law*

Many of the HCJ's rulings deal with revoking policies that conflict with central values of Israel society. Examples of such rulings include importing non-kosher meat [prior to legislation], recruiting women pilots, allowing women to pray at the Western Wall, GSS interrogation techniques, recruiting yeshiva students [prior to legislation] and allowing Arabs to purchase property in Jewish areas. In these cases, the HCJ nullified the policy based on the principle of human honor and dignity, arguing

instructions in the law for regulating the occupation of investment consultancy. In the opinion of the High Court, they contradict the Basic Law: Freedom of Occupation 'to a degree which supercedes [sic] that required to realize the goal of the law.' On October 14, 1999, the HCJ ruled, once again with a make-up of 11 judges, that an article in a law, which contradicted the Basic Law: Human Dignity and Liberty, was null and void. The article in question was article 237a(a) of the Military Judgement Law, that enabled a military policeman to detain a soldier for four days without first bringing him before a judge. (Basic Laws – Introduction – the Knesset Web site: http://www.knesset.gov.il/description/eng/eng_mimshal_yesod.htm).

[13] It should be noted that regarding the question of the superiority of the basic laws over other laws, there are differences of opinion. Some claim that the basic laws are not superior to an ordinary law, unless they include a specific stipulation to the contrary. These base their position on the argument that because a basic law is passed by an ordinary majority (i.e., a majority of those voting), such a majority cannot grant superior status to a piece of legislation. Others claim that the superiority of basic laws stems from the fact that they are the product of the Knesset acting as the Constituent Assembly, and that from their mere definition as "basic laws" one may conclude that they are constitutionally superior. (Basic Laws – Introduction – the Knesset Web site: http://www.knesset.gov.il/description/eng/eng_mimshal_yesod.htm).

that such policies damage the democratic values of the state, specifically through discrimination. Before nullifying the law, it gave the Knesset sufficient time to modify it. In at least two cases – importing non-kosher meat and recruiting yeshiva students – the Knesset decided contrary to the HCJ's recommendations.

We can see that institutionalizing the HCJ's right to overturn laws would not solve these cases once they get to the HCJ. Therefore, in this case, it is better to adopt the arrangement proposed by Judge Barak in the Resler – Yeshiva students case as well as in the Shetreet Report's declarative model: The HCJ declares that a certain policy harms a given value and lets the Knesset handle it without nullifying the law.

Limiting Public Petitioners' Standing Rights

7. The aforementioned analysis showed that petitioning the HCJ reflects a social – institutional process that developed over a number of decades. However, one cannot ignore the decline of public trust in the HCJ. This is a worrisome fact that requires attention. There is a disagreement in the literature about the role of the HCJ in determining values. The traditional approach adopted by Ruth Gavison maintains that values are the provenance of the Knesset and the public, not a bureaucratic body (Gavison, 1998).[14] A more liberal approach adopted by Judge Aharon Barak posits that when the government cannot govern, the HCJ's role is to intervene and instill values (Barak, 1998).[15] We should be able to find a compromise somewhere between those two approaches. In times of paralyzing non-governance and an alternative political culture, the accepted models of social consensus, such as referendums, do not yield immediate results. However, they might have an effect on creating and promoting an essential culture of political participation in the long run. The question is how a society should behave when an institution like the Knesset, whose representatives are elected by the people, chooses not to decide on various matters because its electorate's preferences are unclear. The limitation of standing rights according to law is an "up-down" behavior that disregards the informal institution that has been developing since the 1970s. This compels the HCJ to behave very carefully. In this regard, Shetreet's proposal of "fine tuning" becomes relevant. It attempts to prevent friction

[14] Ruth Gavison, 1998. *The Constitutional Revolution – A Reality or a Self-Fulfilling Prophecy?* Jerusalem: Israel Democracy Institute (in Hebrew).

[15] Aharon Barak, 1998. The Role of the Supreme Court in a Democratic Society. *Israel Studies* 3(2), 6–29.

between the judicial and legislative authorities. Fine tuning of the judicial role in society as well as the limits between the judicial branch and other branches, he says, must be determined by the courts themselves, just as the expansion of judicial criticism was determined by the court.

Non-Governmental Organizations and the HCJ

8. Non-governmental organizations that seek to promote human rights through the HCJ may impede the opportunity to establish democratic, liberal norms in Israeli society. Basing their activity almost solely on the judicial branch or preferring it over putting pressure on the legislative and executive authorities damages the principle of the separation of powers, one of the tenets of liberal democratic society. In fact, NGOs both allow and demand that the Supreme Court function as a policy maker without there being any defined rules that authorize it to do so. Such behavior may be interpreted by other groups as a disregard of the defined rules of the game, resulting in legitimizing disrespect for the law. Moreover, directing its efforts primarily toward the judicial authority and preferring it to other authorities or to public activity might create a feeling that human rights are a matter of concern only to a narrow, elitist group with clearly defined social characteristics. Such an attitude might significantly slow down the internalization of democratic norms and sabotage the ability of these organizations to provide a good basis for civil society in Israel (Gavison, 1991; Meydani and Mizrahi, 2006).

A Constitutional Court of Law – Yes or No?

9. The well-known claim against a special constitutional court of law, supported by Aharon Barak for instance, is the fear that politicization of the judicial system might endanger its professional standing and damage public trust in it. The contrary claim is no less convincing. Those who support the move emphasize the public trust issue in judicial criticism about the legality of laws. They also maintain that if this function remains in the hands of the HCJ in its present format, its status as a valued solver of disputes is bound to weaken. A constitutional court of law that combines representatives chosen by the people and appointments based on professional qualifications is considered a good solution. What, then, is the correct course of action?

Many have focused on issues such as technical and judicial ones, but the real point is that a constitutional court of law would not solve the social problems of non-governance and the alternative political culture that have transformed the HCJ into an alternative to the Knesset. As Knesset member Shaul Yahalom (Mafdal) notes: "It is unacceptable that the authority to rule, after a process of legislation, on the legality of a given law is in the hands of the High Court of Justice, which is not a representative body. The constitutional council might reduce the number of petitions filed with the HCJ; however, this will not strengthen the perspective that is so important to us." Thus, the new constitutional court of law will be unable to cope with the existing problems. Every decision that contradicts the desires of a particular group would lead to major criticism and demands to reduce the Court's power. Given the structures of the state as it is, a constitutional court of law would not solve the problem of political non-governance. At most, it might serve as a mechanism for handing down judgments. These verdicts, however, would encounter a certain level of resistance from different interest groups that are dissatisfied with the quality and quantity of services provided by the policy it adopts. Thus, we must look for other solutions that promote the ability of the political system to govern so it can determine public policy in matters that are important to Israeli society.

A Series of Institutional Amendments

10. The problem of non-governance must be solved. It is also necessary to make a number of changes to the nation's institutions. The changes must be made slowly, while the values of democratic culture are being internalized. For instance, one of the major problems is the inefficiency of the legal system. The Or Committee (1997) discussed the situation and arrived at a number of recommendations, including increasing the tenure of judges, re-organizing the courts and their authority, and shortening the duration of procedures.

Ultimately, the public must decide on its own values. It should be allowed to do so by creating new rules of the game. Promoting reform is essential, but it must be carried out slowly, with the participation of the public through large public committees and hearings.

12

Conclusion and Normative Implications

The central role of the Israeli Supreme Court as a policy maker can be primarily explained by the strategic calculations of many groups in Israeli society. The atmosphere of an alternative political culture (quasi-exit behavior) is a necessary condition for this situation. The views and attitudes of specific judges, which explain the degree of judicial activism, create the sufficient conditions for judicial activism.

Many groups within the Israeli public turn to the Court as a part of an alternative political culture (quasi-exit) strategy, thus giving it the opportunity to become a policy maker. In response, the HCJ advances its organizational and political interests by adopting the alternative political culture's (quasi-exit) strategy of encouraging appeals. This, in turn, further encourages social players to adopt such quasi-exit behavior in the form of appeals to the Court, which, in turn, trigger the quasi-exit behavior of the HCJ in a never-ending cycle. Through this on-going cycle, social players and the HCJ threaten politicians, leading them to make institutional reforms.

More generally, we explained that inefficient political systems are likely to produce a form of political participation characterized by quasi-exit. When political inefficiency and the inability to produce policy decisions increase significantly, and democratic forms of participation as well as liberal values are not deeply rooted in the population, the public is likely to look for an alternative decision maker. One such alternative is the military elite. Indeed, in many cases when an inefficient democratic system collapses, a military regime or another form of authoritarian regime based on the support of the military elite is imposed. Another possible center of power is the Supreme Court – especially in systems where the Court's authority is not clearly defined and it enjoys public legitimacy. Under such circumstances, citizens and politicians may regard the Court as a potential supplier of efficient public policies.

From a normative perspective, judicial activism that results from quasi-exit behavior has both positive and negative aspects. On the one hand, like the military elite, the Supreme Court is a bureaucratic organization, meaning that its members are not elected by the public. Thus, appealing to either the military or the Court can potentially damage the principle of democratic representation. However, to become such a policy maker, the Supreme Court depends on citizens' appeals, through which they express their preferences, while the military elite usually forces a military regime on the people. It follows that the Supreme Court can be an agent of peaceful institutional change. This possibility may justify judicial activism under the previously mentioned conditions.

On the other hand, a political culture that is characterized by quasi-exit reflects an instrumental view of the law, because most of the alternative channels for supplying public goods are either semi-legal or illegal. Thus, when increased judicial activism occurs in such a political culture, in the absence of formal authorization for the Court to do so, it weakens rather than strengthens the foundations of democratic values and the respect for the law. In other words, such a process is likely to strengthen the instrumental view of democracy but weaken liberal and democratic values. On the other hand, restraining judicial activism may increase the sense of deadlock among citizens as far as policy decisions are concerned, thus weakening support for the democratic regime as a whole, perhaps in favor of an authoritarian regime that can create policy decisions. It follows that those who want to defend democracy should be interested in fundamental institutional reform within the democratic rules that will improve the ability of the political system to reach policy decisions.

Furthermore, because the HCJ acts as a bureaucratic organization to advance its own interests, it attempts to strengthen its position in the bargaining over institutional arrangements. To do so, it has a clear interest in encouraging appeals, thus increasing its dominant position in the political structure. By doing so, the Supreme Court is not only threatening politicians but also signaling the possible compromise that will satisfy its interests. Given that it gradually became clear that almost any decision made by the government or the parliament was likely to be brought to the HCJ by some dissatisfied group, politicians started to consider the possible position of the HCJ in any decision-making process. In that way the quasi-exit behavior of the Israeli public maximized the influence of the HCJ on processes of policy making. The impact of these processes on the Israeli constitutional order is a subject for further research.

This book also attempts to explain the reciprocal relationship between the Supreme Court and the Israeli political system based on a public-choice rationale bounded by the non-governability of the political system and an alternative political culture. Both are formal and informal variables affecting the behavior of several political players within the Israeli arena. The analysis illustrates the usefulness of such a model for analyzing long-term socio-political processes and explaining the actions of the players. In that regard, such a model can serve as a bridge between rationale-choice institutionalism, which focuses on static interactions at the micro level, and historical institutionalism, which emphasizes macro-level socio-political processes (Weingast, 2005).

The theoretical model and the empirical analysis focused on the direct reciprocal relationship between the Supreme Court and politicians in Israel. Social factors such as the public's positions, the activities of interest groups, the processes of cultural change, and structural-institutional changes have found expression in the interests and preferences of the players. For example, the fact that politicians are dependent on public support and that the Israeli public prefers a balance between the powers influenced the order of politicians' preferences. Furthermore, the combination of these factors goes a long way to explaining the unique balance of powers between the Supreme Court and the political system defined in this book as a middle-of-the-road approach in Israel.

In this book, we identified a general trend of judicial activism that has taken a middle-of-the-road approach, both by the Supreme Court and the political system. The Court has displayed juridical activism on certain issues such as human rights and religion, while at the same time exercising judicial self-restraint with regard to issues of security and the functioning of the Knesset. This cautious approach is evidenced by the response of the Supreme Court to various petitions, a response that also safeguards the Knesset's special position as the shaper of values in Israel. The Knesset, too, has adopted a middle-of-the-road approach, evidenced by selectively permissive legislation alongside petitions to the Supreme Court on some matters.

However, since the 1990s, we have witnessed a change in the relationship between the Supreme Court and the Knesset. Unlike previous patterns of conduct, the Court has begun to flex its muscles, invalidating laws and making decisions about ethical issues such as the drafting of yeshiva students and General Security Service interrogation techniques that it had previously avoided. Surveys show a marked decline in public trust in the Supreme Court (Vigoda-Gadot and Mizrahi, 2007), inviting various politicians to attempt to institutionalize a different structural arrangement in the relationship between the Supreme Court and the Knesset.

Indeed, there are indications that in recent years, the Supreme Court has tried to circle around this kind of equilibrium to obtain immediate gains or to determine its space for maneuvering. In any case, these attempts were designed to position the Court at an optimal starting point for the expected bargaining process over structural changes in the legal system, the legal status of the Supreme Court, and its power. In the absence of a change in the rules of the game, it is expected that the Supreme Court will restrain its involvement and role to avoid creating a situation in which legislation is enacted that will harm it. Nevertheless, any institutionalization of the Supreme Court-Knesset relationship that strays from formal institutional regulations is unlikely to be accepted by the legislators in Israel. The analysis in this book suggests that the process will result in a middle-of-the-road approach that will be adopted by the Supreme Court and the politicians.

This book also contributes to the process of designing public policy on human rights. Such public policy involves the work of many players: politicians, bureaucrats, interest groups, and the public. All of these function as part of an institutional structure, partly legal and partly social, in the determination of the outcome of human rights in Israel in a wide range of fields, such as the general political structure of the State of Israel; its economic and cultural development; the implementation of the right to self-determination; the synthesis between religion and democracy in Israel; freedom of religion and conscience; the protection and enforcement of fundamental human rights such as the right to life and equality before the law; the right to human dignity and liberty; freedom from torture and from cruel, inhuman, or degrading treatment or punishment; freedom of movement; the right to a fair trial; the right to privacy; freedom of opinion and expression; freedom of assembly and association; prohibitions against propaganda relating to racial, national, or religious hatred; and protecting the rights of minorities, children, and the family.[1] This book demonstrates that human rights laws in Israel try to strike a balance between democracy and religion, between the lack of

[1] The Combined Initial and First Periodic Report of the State of Israel Concerning the International Covenant on Civil and Political Rights (ICCPR), July 15, 1998.

a clear constitution and statements about human rights that are partial in nature, and between political instability and judicial activism. The liberal attitude expressed by the Supreme Court since 1992 has caused some Knesset members to seek the creation of a constitutional court of law. Their proposition was an attempt to change the rules of the game, which they contended were unfair to certain parts of the public. The proposal was removed from the public agenda, but the message seems to be clear that its removal will not be for long.[2]

Within these political and social processes, we also examine the role of the Israeli Supreme Court based on shared mental models and political entrepreneurship by adopting hypotheses and concepts taken from the institutional literature to develop a procedural model for analyzing formal political rule changes in a democratic system. Thus, the role of the Israeli Supreme Court is a result of the deep splits that exist in Israeli society. These splits, coupled with the institutional structure, make it difficult for the political system to cope with issues that require the shaping of public policy. As an answer to this difficulty, which creates a lack of public policy in many spheres, the public has identified the High Court as an institution that can provide solutions by applying pressure on politicians or by handing down legal rulings. As long as the institutional reality of non-governability and an alternative political culture dominate the political sphere, the High Court will retain its political role as an informal public address for interest groups and politicians seeking decisions for controversial issues.

This informal "Who governs?" rule of the game is comfortable for both sides. The Supreme Court can maximize its power while the politicians can turn issues over to the High Court without taking the risk of

[2] See, for example, HCJ 1030/99 *Oron v. Knesset Speaker*, PD 56(3) 640: Cancellation of a law that granted broadcast licenses without a tender to radio stations operating for more than five years. The verdict was handed down in light of the violation of competitors' freedom of occupation. See also HCJ 8276/05 *Adalah – The Legal Center for Arab Minority Rights in Israel et al. v. the Minister of Defense* (not yet published): The Supreme Court accepted a petition to void Amendment No. 7 of the Civil Wrongs (Liability of the State) Law, which denies subjects of an "enemy state" and members of "terrorist organizations" the right to compensation for injuries they sustain at the hands of security forces. The amendment also denies Palestinians the right to sue for compensation if they are injured in an area outside Israel declared a "conflict zone" by the Defense Minister, except for a few exceptions. See also HCJ 1661/05, *The Gaza Coastal Regional Council v. The Knesset et al.*, PD 59 (2) 481: The Israeli Supreme Court canceled several provisions of the disengagement law, such as those that denied the evacuees the right to sue under general law or limited the minimum age for receiving grants to twenty-one.

paying a political price for decisions that upset the institutional status quo. However, the Supreme Court has learned that in certain cases, it is better to refrain from ruling and let the Knesset decide particular issues. In cases where the Knesset is unable to set policy, the High Court has to take responsibility and hand down a ruling. Such rulings run the risk of being only partially acceptable. They might harm certain groups and leave their members dissatisfied with the new policy. Therefore, representatives of such groups might try to stop the High Court from ruling on issues that upset the status quo.[3] If that approach does not work, the representatives try to change the rules of the game in their own favor.

[3] See, for example, the Velner case: *Velner v. The Chairman of the Israeli Labor Party*, HCJ 5364/94.

Bibliography

Aaron, Richard I. 1995. *John Locke*. London: Oxford University Press.

Aharoni, Yair. 1998. "The Changing Political-Economy of Israel." *Annals of the American Academy of Political and Social Science* 555: 127–146.

Ainsworth, Scott and Itai Sened. 1993. "The Role of Lobbyists: Entrepreneurs with Two Audiences." *American Journal of Political Science* 37: 834–866.

Amit-Kohn, Uzi et al. 1993. *Israel, the "Intifada" and the Rule of Law*. Tel Aviv: Ministry of Defense Publications.

Anderson, James E. 1979. *Public Policy-Making*. New York: Rinehart and Wilson.

Appleby, Paul H. 1949. *Policy and Administration*. Tuscaloosa: University of Alabama Press.

Arian, Asher. 1997. *The Second Republic – Politics in Israel*. Chatham, NJ: Chatham House.

Arian, Asher, David Nachmias, and Ruth Amir. 2002. *Executive Governance in Israel*. Jerusalem: the Israel Democracy institute. (In Hebrew).

Arian, Asher and Michal Shamir (eds.) (1999) *The Elections in Israel – 1996*. Albany: State University of New York Press.

Arian, Asher and Michal Shamir (eds.) (2002) *The Elections in Israel – 2001*. Jerusalem: Israel Democracy Institute. (In Hebrew).

Aristotle. 1975. *Aristotle's Politics*. Books 1–2. Translated by H. Y. Ruth. Jerusalem: The Magnes Press. (In Hebrew).

Arrow, Kenneth. 1963. *Social Choice and Individual Values*. New York: Wiley.

Austen-Smith, David. 1998. "Allocating Access for Information and Contributions." *Journal of Law Economics and Organization* 14: 277–303.

Avineri, Shlomo. 1986. *Res Publica: Lectures on Political Thought*. Bnei-Brak: Sifriat Poalim. (In Hebrew).

Avnor, Hanna. 1998. "When I Was Sitting in Judgment, I Was Afraid of the Moment I'd Have to Say: Life Sentence." *Orech Hadin* 5: 23.

Axelrod, Robert. 1984. *The Evolution of Cooperation*. New York: Basic Books.

Barak, Aharon. 1987. *Judicial Discretion*. Tel-Aviv: Papyrus, Tel-Aviv University. (In Hebrew).

Barak, Aharon. 1992. *Interpretation in Law*. Jerusalem: Nevo. (In Hebrew).

Barak, Aharon. 1993a. Judicial Philosophy and Judicial Activism. *Iyunei Mishpat* 17, 3: 475–501. (In Hebrew).
Barak, Aharon. 1993b. The Role of the Supreme Court in a Democratic Society. *Hapraklit* 41, A–B: 5–12. (In Hebrew).
Barak, Aharon. 1993c. The Constitutional Revolution: Protected Human Rights. *Mishpat Umimshal* 1, 1: 9–10. (In Hebrew)
Barak, Aharon. 1998. Those Who Practice Law. *Din Udvarim* 29. (In Hebrew).
Barak, Aharon. 2000. The Parliament and the Supreme Court: A Glimpse to the Future. *Hapraklit* 45, A: 5–12. (In Hebrew).
Barak, Aharon. 2003. The Supreme Court as a Constitutional Court, 6 *Mishpat Umimshal* 315–329, CA 1908/94 Mizrahi Bank v. Migdal [1995] IsrPD 49, 4: 221.
Barak-Erez, Dafna. 2000. Land in Israel between Public Management and Privatization: Distribution of Justice in the Administrative Procedure. In Menachem Mautner, ed. *Justice Distribution in Israel*. Ramot: Tel Aviv University. (In Hebrew).
Barak-Erez, Dafna. 2003. *Key Cases: Landmarks in the High Court Activity*. Tel Aviv: The Department of Security. (In Hebrew).
Barro, Robert. 1973. The Control of Politicians: An Economic Model. *Public Choice* 14: 19–42.
Barzilai, G. 1998. Courts as Hegemonic Institutions and Social Change. *Politics* 3: 31–51. (In Hebrew).
Barzilai, G. 1999. Courts as Hegemonic Institutions: The Israeli Supreme Court in a Comparative Perspective. *Israel Affairs* 5: 15–33.
Barzilai, Gad. 1992. *A Democracy in Wartime: Conflict and Consensus in Israel*. Tel-Aviv: Sifriat Poalim. (In Hebrew).
Barzilai, Gad. 2002. Justices as Policy-Makers. In D. Korn, ed. *Public Policy in Israel: Perspectives and Practices*. Lanham, MD: Lexington Books, pp. 71–77.
Barzilai, Gad. 2003. *Communities and Law: Politics and Cultures of Legal Identities*. Ann Arbor: University of Michigan Press.
Barzilai, Gad and David Nachmias. 1998. Governmental Lawyering in the Political Sphere: Advocating the Leviathan. *Israel Studies* 3, 2: 31–45.
Barzilai, Gad, Ephraim Yuchtman-Yaar, and Zeev Segal. 1994. *The Israeli Supreme Court and the Israeli Public*. Tel-Aviv: Tel Aviv University Press. (In Hebrew).
Baum, Lawrence. 1976. Implementation of Judicial Decisions: An Organizational Analysis. *American Politics Quarterly* 4: 86–114.
Baum, Lawrence. 1989. *The Supreme Court*. Washington, DC: CQ Press.
Baum, Lawrence. 1997. *The Puzzle of Judicial Behavior*. Ann Arbor: University of Michigan Press.
Bechor, Guy. 1996. *Constitution for Israel*. Jerusalem: Keter Press Enterprises.
Becker, Theodore L. 1964. *Political Behavioralism and Modern Jurisprudence*. Chicago: Rand McNally.
Bendor, Ariel. 1988. Justiciability in the High Court of Justice. *Mishpatim* 17: 592–636. (In Hebrew).

Bendor, Jonathan B. 1990. Formal Models of Bureaucracy: A Review. In Naomi B. Lynn and Aaron Wildavsky, eds. *Public Administration: The State of the Discipline*. Chatham, NJ: Chatham House.

Bendor, Jonathan, Serge Taylor, and Ronald van Gaalen. 1985. Bureaucratic Expertise versus Legislative Authority: A Model of Deception and Monitoring in Budgeting. *American Political Science Review* 79: 1041–1060.

Bendor, Jonathan, Serge Taylor, and Ronald van Gaalen. 1987a. Stacking the Deck: Bureaucratic Missions and the Search for Alternatives. *American Political Science Review* 81: 873–896.

Bendor, Jonathan, Serge Taylor, and Ronald van Gaalen. 1987b. Politicians, Bureaucrats, and Asymmetric Information. *American Journal of Political Science* 31: 796–828.

Benvenisti, Eyal. 1999. Exit and Voice in the Age of Globalization. *Michigan Law Review* 98: 167–212.

Black, Donald. 1972. The Boundaries of Legal Sociology. *Yale Law Journal* 81: 1086–1100.

Blackstone, William. 1979. *Commentaries on the Laws of England*. Chicago: Chicago University Press.

Brams, Steven J. 1994. *Theory of Moves*. Cambridge: Cambridge University Press.

Breton, Albert. 1995. Organizational Hierarchies and Bureaucracies: An Integrative Essay. *European Journal of Political Economy* 11: 411–440.

Browne, Angela and Aaron Wildavsky. 1983. Implementation as Exploration. In Jeffrey L. Pressman and Aaron Wildavsky, eds. *Implementation*. Berkeley: University of California Press.

Bruno, Michael. 1993. *Crisis Stabilization and Economic Reform: Therapy by Consensus*. Oxford: Oxford University Press.

Buchanan, James, Richard Tollison, and Gordon Tullock (eds.) 1980. *Towards a Theory of Rent-Seeking Society*. College Station: Texas A&M Press.

Burke, Edmund. 1965. *Reflections on the Revolution in France*. Chicago: Chicago University Press.

Chernichovsky, Dov. 1991. *Lessons of the Crisis in the Israeli Health-Care System: Key Principles and Proposals for Reform*. Jerusalem: JDC-Brookdale Institute. (In Hebrew).

Christopoulos Dimitrios C. 2006. Relational Attributes of Political Entrepreneurs: A Network Perspective. *Journal of European Public Policy* 13, 5: 757–778.

Claude, K. 1999. Separation of Powers in a Democracy. In Cohen-Almagor, R., ed. *Basic Issues in Israeli Democracy*. Tel Aviv: Sifriat Poalim, pp. 111–128. (In Hebrew).

Coate, Stephen and Stephen Morris. 1995. On the Form of Transfers to Special Interests. *Journal of Political Economy* 103: 1211–1235.

Cohen, Haim. 1992. Expulsion as Required. *Mishpat Umimshal* 1, 2: 471.

Cohn, Margit and Kremnitzer, M. 2005. Judicial Activism: A Multidimensional Model. *Canadian Journal of Law and Jurisprudence* 18: 333–356.

Constable, Marianne. 1994. *The Law of Other – The Mixed Jury and Hanging Conceptions of Citizenship, Law and Knowledge*. Chicago: Chicago University Press.

Cornell, Clayton and Howard Gillman (eds.) 1999. *Supreme Court Decision Making, New Institutionalist Approaches*. Chicago and London: University of Chicago Press.

Cowan, Thomas A. 1958. Group Interests. *Virginia Law Review* 44: 331–345.

Dahl, Robert. 1961. *Who Governs?* New Haven, CT: Yale University Press.

Dahl, Robert. 1963. *Modern Political Analysis*. Englewood Cliffs, NJ: Prentice-Hall.

Dayan, Ilana. 1995. The Amnesty of the GSS Officials. In David Heshin, ed. *The Courts – Fifty Years of Judicature in Israel*. Tel-Aviv: The Ministry of Defense Publication, pp. 148–152. (In Hebrew).

Descartes, René. 1994. *Meditations on First Philosophy*. Translated by Joseph Or. Jerusalem: Magnes Press, Hebrew University. (In Hebrew).

Descartes, René. 1999. *Discourse on Method*. Translated by Joseph Or. Jerusalem: Magnes Press, Hebrew University. (In Hebrew).

Dor, Gal and Menachem Hofnung. 2006. Litigation as Political Participation. *Israel Studies* 11, 2: 131–157.

Doron, Gideon. 1986. *To Decide and to Implement*. Tel-Aviv: Kivonim. (In Hebrew).

Doron, Gideon. 1988. *Rational Politics in Israel*. Tel-Aviv: Ramot, Tel-Aviv University. (In Hebrew).

Doron, Gideon and Udi Lebel. 2005. *The Politics of Bereavement, 2nd edition*. Tel-Aviv: Ha Kibbutz Hameuhad. (In Hebrew).

Doron, Gideon and Assaf Meydani. 2007. Establishing a Constitutional Court? An Alternative Political Culture Approach – the Israeli Case. *Policy and Society* 26: 105–124.

Doron, Gideon and Itai Sened. 2001. *Political Bargaining: Theory, Practice, and Process*. London: Sage Publications.

Dotan, Yoav. 1996. General Petitioning and Judicial Politics in the High Court of Justice. *Iyunei Mishpat* 20: 93. (In Hebrew).

Dotan, Yoav. 1999. Do the "Haves" Still Come Out Ahead? Resource Inequalities in Ideological Courts: The Case of the Israeli High Court of Justice. *Law & Society Review* 33: 1059–1080.

Dotan, Yoav. 2000. Does Israel Need a Constitutional Court of Law? *Mishpat Umimshal* 5: 117–163. (In Hebrew).

Dotan, Yoav. 2004. Pre-petitions and Constitutional Dilemmas Regarding the Role of Government Lawyers. *Mishpat Umimshal* 7, 1: 159–205. (In Hebrew).

Dotan, Yoav and Menachem Hofnung. 2001. Interest Groups in the Israeli High Court of Justice: Measuring Success in Litigation and in Out-of-Court Settlements. *Law and Policy* 23: 1–27.

Dotan, Yoav and Menachem Hofnung. 2005. Legal Defeats – Political Wins: Why Do Elected Representatives Go to Court? *Comparative Political Studies* 38, 1: 75–103.

Downs, Anthony. 1957. *An Economic Theory of Democracy*. New York: Harper and Row.

Downs, Anthony. 1967. *Inside Bureaucracy*. Boston: Little and Brown.

Dror, Yehezkel. 1989. *Memorandum for the Israeli Prime Minister: To Build a State*. Jerusalem: Academon, Hebrew University. (In Hebrew).

Dror, Yehezkel. 2001. *The Capacity to Govern: A Report to the Club of Rome*. London: Portland.
Durkheim, Emil.1958. *Professional Ethics and Civic Morals*. Glencoe, IL: Free Press.
Dworkin, Ronald. 1980. *Taking Rights Seriously*. Cambridge, MA: Harvard University Press.
Easton, David. 1953. *The Political System*. New York: Alfred A. Knopf.
Edelman, Martin. 1992. The Judicial Elite of Israel. *International Political Science Review* 13: 235–248.
Edelman, Martin. 1994. *Courts, Politics, and Culture in Israel*. Charlottesville: University of Virginia Press.
Edelman, Martin. 1995. Israel. In Neal Tate and Torbjorn Vallinder, eds. *The Global Expansion of Judicial Power*. New York: New York University Press, pp. 403–415.
Ehrlich, Eugen. (2002). *Fundamental Principles of the Sociology of Law*. New Brunswick: Transaction Publishers.
Eisenstadt, Shmuel N. 1989. *The Transformation of Israel Society*. Jerusalem: Magnes Press, Hebrew University. (In Hebrew).
Ekelund, Robert B. and Robert D. Tollison. 1980. Economic Regulation in Mercantile England: Hecksher Revisited. *Economic Inquiry* 18: 567–599.
Elmore, Richard. 1979. Backward Mapping: Implementation Research and Policy Decisions. *Political Science Quarterly* 94, 4: 601–616.
Epstein, Lee, Daniel E. Ho, Gary King, and Jeffrey A. Segal. 2005. The Supreme Court During Crisis: How War Affects Only Non-War Cases. *New York University Law Review* 80, 1: 1–116.
Epstein, Lee and Jack Knight. 1998. *The Choices Justices Make*. Washington, DC: CQ Press.
Epstein, Lee, Jeffrey A. Segal, Harold J. Spaeth, and Thomas G. Walker. 1994. *The Supreme Court Compendium: Data, Decisions, and Developments*. Washington, DC: CQ Press.
Epstein, Lee and Thomas G. Walker. 1995. *Constitutional Law for a Changing America: Rights, Liberties, and Justice*. Washington, DC: CQ Press.
Eskridge, Jr., William N. and J. Ferejohn. 1992. The Article I, Section 7 Game. *The Georgetown Law Journal* 80: 523–564.
Eskridge, Jr., William N. and Philip P. Frickey. 1994. Foreword: Law as Equilibrium. *Harvard Law Review* 108: 26–108.
Etzioni-Halevy, Eva. 1997. *A Place at the Top: Elites and Elitism in Israel*. Tel-Aviv: Cherikov. (In Hebrew).
Evan, William M. 1980. *The Sociology of Law*. New York: Free Press.
Feeley, Malcolm M. and Edward L. Rubin. 1998. *Judicial Policy Making and the Modern State: How the Courts Reformed America's Prison*. New York: Cambridge University Press.
Flemming, Roy B. and Dan B. Wood. 1997. The Public and the Supreme Court: Individual Justice Responsiveness to American Policy Moods. *American Journal of Political Science* 41: 468–498.
Foeler, Lon. 1964. *The Morality of Law*. New Haven, CT: Yale University Press.

Galnoor, I. 2004. The Judicialization of the Public Domain in Israel. *Law and Government* 7, 1: 355–386. (In Hebrew).
Gans, Haim. 1989. *Essays on the Theory of Law*. Tel-Aviv: Dyonon. (In Hebrew).
Gardiner, John A. (ed.) 1977. *Public Law and Public Policy*. New York: Praeger.
Gavison, Ruth. 1997. The Constitutional Revolution: A Description of Reality or a Self- Fulfilling Prophecy? 28 *Mishpatim*, 21–44. (In Hebrew).
Gavison, Ruth. 1998. *The Constitutional Revolution: A Reality or a Self-Fulfilling Prophecy*. Jerusalem: The Israel Democracy Institute. (In Hebrew).
Gavison, Ruth. 2009. Can Courts Bring about Social Change? A Review of the Second Edition (published in 2008) of Gerald Rosenberg's Book *The Hollow Hope*. *Ma'asei Mishpat Law Review* 2: 15–32. (In Hebrew).
Gavison, Ruth, Mordechai Kremnitzer, and Yoav Dotan. 2000. *Judicial Activism: For and Against*. Jerusalem: Magnes, Hebrew University. (In Hebrew).
Gely, Rafael and Pablo T. Spiller. 1990. A Rational Choice Theory of Supreme Court Statutory Decisions with Applications to the State Farm and Grove City Cases. *Journal of Law, Economics and Organization* 6: 263–300.
Geva-May, Iris, and Aaron B. Wildavsky. 1997. *An Operational Approach to Policy Analysis: The Craft – Prescriptions for Better Analysis*. Boston: Kluwer.
Gidron, Benjamin, Michal Bar, and Hagai Katz. 2003. *The Third Sector in Israel: Between Welfare State and Civil Society*. Tel Aviv: Hakibbutz Hameuchad. (In Hebrew).
Gilman, Howard. 1996–1997. The New Institutionalism, Part 1. More and Less Than Strategy: Some Adventages to Interpretive Institutionalism in the Analysis of Judicial Politics. *Law & Courts*, Winter: 6–10.
Goggin, Malcolm L., Ann O. M. Bowman, James P. Lester, and Laurence J. O'Toole, Jr. 1990. *Implementation Theory and Practice: Toward a Third Generation*. Glenview, IL: Scott Foresman/Little Brown.
Gough, John W. 1950. *John Locke's Political Philosophy*. Oxford: Oxford University Press.
Gross, Meron and Yoram Shachar. 1999. The Assignment of Panels in the Israeli Supreme. Court: A Quantitative Analysis. 29 *Mishpatim*: 567–585. (In Hebrew).
Gunningham, Neil and Robert A. Cagan. 2005. Regulation and Business Behavior. *Law and Policy* 27, 2: 213–218.
Harris, Michael, Y. Katz, Gideon Doron, and A. Woodlief. 1997. Ideology and Privatization Policy in Israel. *Environment and Planning A – Government and Policy* 15: 363–372.
Hausgger, Lori and Lawrence Baum. 1999. Inviting Congressional Action: A Study of Supreme Court Motivations in Statutory Interpretation. *American Journal of Political Science* 43: 162–185.
Helmke, Gretchen and Steven Levitsky. 2004. Informal Institutions and Comparative Politics: A Research Agenda. *Perspectives on Politics* 2: 725–740.
Higley, John and Lowell G. Field. 1980. *Elitism*. London: Routledge.
Himma, Kenneth E. 1998. Functionalism and Legal Theory: The Hart/Fuller Debate Revisited. *De Philosophia* 14: 2.
Hirschl, Ran. 1992. *Controlling the Consciousness and the Law*. M.A. thesis. Tel-Aviv: Tel-Aviv University. (In Hebrew).

Hirschl, Ran. 2001. The Political Origins of Judicial Empowerment through Constitutionalization: Lessons from Israel's Constitutional Revolution. *Comparative Politics* 33, 3: 315–335.

Hirschl, Ran. 2004. *Towards Juristocracy: The Origins and Consequences of the New Constitutionalism*. Cambridge, MA and London: Harvard University Press.

Hirschman, Albert, 1970. *Exit, Voice & Loyalty*. Cambridge, MA: Harvard University Press.

Hobbes, Thomas. 1985. *Leviathan*. Translated by Joseph Or. Jerusalem: Magnes Press, Hebrew University. (In Hebrew).

Hofnung, Menachem. 1991. *Israel Security Needs vs. the Rule of Law*. Jerusalem: Nevo. (In Hebrew).

Hofnung, Menachem. 1997. Authority, Influence and Separation of Powers – Judicial Review in Israel in Comparative Perspective. *Mishpatim* 28: 211–238. (In Hebrew).

Hofnung, Menachem. 1999. Israeli Constitutional Politics: The Fragility of Impartiality. *Israel Affairs* 5: 34–54.

Hofnung, Menachem and Keren Weinshall Margel. 2010. Judicial Setbacks, Material Gains: Terror Litigation at the Israeli High Court of Justice. *Journal of Empirical Legal Studies* 7, 4: 664–692.

Holmes, Oliver W. 1952. *Collected Legal Papers*. New York: Peter Smith.

Holmes, Oliver W. 1984. *The Common Law*. Boston: Little Brown.

Horowitz, Dan and Moshe Lissak. 1990. *Trouble in Utopia*. Albany: SUNY Press.

Howlett, Michael, and Evert Lindquist. 2004. Policy Analysis and Governance: Analytical and Policy Styles in Canada. *Journal of Comparative Policy Analysis Research and Practice* 6, 3: 225–251.

Huller, Mike. 1997. Twilight Law and Order. *Haglima* 13: 4–6. (In Hebrew).

Hume, David. 1982. *An Enquiry Concerning the Principles of Morals*. Translated by Joseph Or. Jerusalem: Magnes Press, Hebrew University. (In Hebrew).

Jabbari, David. 1992. From Criticism to Construction in Modern Critical Legal Theory. *Oxford Journal of Legal Studies* 12, 4: 507–542.

Kairys, David (ed.) 1990. *The Politics of Law: A Progressive Critique*. New York: Pantheon Books.

Katzelson, I. and B. R. Weingast. 2005. Intersections between Historical and Rational Choice Institutionalism. In I. Katzelson and B. R. Weingast, eds. *Preferences and Situations: Points of Intersection between Historical and Rational Choice Institutionalism*. New York: Russell Sage.

Kelsen, Hans. 1945. *General Theory of Law and State*. Cambridge, MA: Harvard University Press.

Kendall, Willmore and George W. Carey. 1968. The Intensity Problem and Democratic Theory. *American Political Science Review* 62: 5–24.

Kilwein, John C. and Richard A. Brisbin. 1997. Policy Convergence in a Federal Judicial System: The Application of Intensified Scrutiny Doctrines by State Supreme Courts. *American Journal of Political Science* 41: 122–148.

Kingdon, John. W. 1995. *Agendas, Alternatives and Public Policies*. 2nd Edition. New York: HarperCollins.

Klein, Claude. 2003. Constitutional Court of Law: Things Aren't Really That Bad! *Mehkarei Mishpat* 19: 497–521. (In Hebrew).

Knaani, David (ed.) 1967. *Encyclopedia of Social Sciences*. Tel-Aviv: Sifriat Poalim.

Korn, Dan. 1994. *Time in Gray: National Unity Governments 1984–1990*. Tel Aviv: Zemora-Bitan. (In Hebrew).

Kramer, Fred A. 1977. *Dynamics of Public Bureaucracy*. Cambridge, MA: Winthrop.

Kremnitzer, Mordechai. 1999. The Supreme Court and Public Policy Shaping: Equality between the Sexes. In David Nachmias and Gila Menahem, eds. *Public Policy in Israel*. Jerusalem: The Israel Institute for Democracy.

Kretzmer, David. 1993. Judicial Review over Demolition and Sealing of Houses in the Occupied Territories. In Itzhak Zamir, ed. *Klinghoffer Book on Public Law*. Jerusalem: Hebrew University. (In Hebrew).

Kretzmer, David. 1997. The Path to Judicial Review in Human Rights Cases: From Bergman and Kol Ha'am to Mizrahi Bank. *Mishpatim* 28: 359–385. (In Hebrew).

Lahav, Pnina. 1989. The Power and Position of the Supreme Court in the First Decade of Its Existence. *Iyunei Mishpat* 14: 479–501.

Lahav, Pnina. 1999. *Israel in the Law*. Tel Aviv: Am-Oved. (In Hebrew).

Landau, Martin. 1969. Redundancy, Rationality and the Problem of Duplication and Overlap. *Public Administration Review* 29 (July/August): 346–358.

Landau, Moshe. 1996. The Supreme Court as Constitution Namer for Israel. *Mishpat Umimshal* 3, 2: 697. (In Hebrew).

Landes, W. M. and R. A. Posner. 1975. The Independent Judiciary in an Interest-Group Perspective. *Journal of Law and Economics* 18: 875–911.

Landoy, Moshe. 1994. A Constitution as the Supreme Law for the State of Israel. *Hapraklit*: 342–352.

Lawrence, S. E. 1992. A Book Review: The Hollow Hope: Can Courts Bring about Social Change? by Gerald N. Rosenberg. *The American Political Science Review* 86, 3: 812–813.

Lehman-Wilzig, Sam N. 1991. Loyalty, Voice and Quasi-Exit. *Comparative Politics* 24: 97–108.

Lehman-Wilzig, Sam N. 1992. *Wildfire: Grassroots Revolts in Israel in the Post-Socialist Era*. Albany: SUNY Press.

Levi-Faur, David, Sheffer Gabriel, and Vogel David (eds.) 1999. *Israel: The Dynamics of Change and Continuity*. London: Frank Cass Publishers.

Levinthal, Daniel. 1988. A Survey of Agency Models of Organizations. *Journal of Economic Behavior and Organization* 9: 153–185.

Llewellyn, Karl N. 1962. *Jurisprudence: Realism in Theory and Practice*. Chicago: University of Chicago Press.

Locke, John. 1997. *The Second Treatise of Civil government*. Translated by Joseph Or. Jerusalem: Magnes Press, Hebrew University. (In Hebrew).

Lohmann, Susanne. 1993. A Signaling Model of Information and Manipulative Political Action. *American Political Science Review* 87: 319–333.

Lohmann, Susanne. 1995. Information, Access, and Contributions: A Signaling Model of Lobbying. *Public Choice* 85: 267–284.

Lohmann, Susanne. 1998. An Information Rationale for the Power of Special Interests. *American Political Science Review* 92: 809–827.

López, E. J. 2002. The Legislator as Political Entrepreneur: Investment in Political Capital. *Review of Austrian Economics* 15, 2–3: 211–228.

Machiavelli, Niccolo. 1961. *Political Writing*. Translated by Ephraim Shmueli. Jerusalem: Schocken. (In Hebrew).

Mackinon, Catharine A. 1989. Toward Feminist Jurisprudence. In Catharine A. Mackinon, ed. *Toward a Feminist Theory of the State*. Boston: Harvard University Press.

Macpherson, Crawford B. 1962. *The Political Theory of Possessive Individualism: Hobbes to Locke*. Oxford: Oxford University Press.

Mantzavinos, Chrysostomos. 2001. *Individuals, Institutions and Markets*. Cambridge: Cambridge University Press.

Mantzavinos, Chrysostomos, Douglass North, and Syed Shariq. 2004. Learning, Institutions and Economic Performance. *Perspectives on Politics* 2: 75–84.

Marks, Brian A. 1988. A Model of Judicial Influence on Congressional Policymaking: Grove City College v. Bell. *Working Papers in Political Science, P-88-7*. Stanford: The Hoover Institution, Stanford University.

Marmor, Andrei. 1997. Judicial Review in Israel. *Mishpat Umimshal* 4, 1: 133. (In Hebrew).

Marshall, Thomas R. 1989. *Public Opinion and the Supreme Court*. New York: Longman.

Mautner, Menachem. 1993. *The Decline of Formalism and the Rise of Values in Israeli Law*. Tel-Aviv: Ma'agalay Da'at. (In Hebrew).

Mautner, Menachem. 2002. Law and Culture in Israel: The 1950s and the 1980s. In Ron Harris, Alexander Kedar, Pnina Lahav, and Assaf Likhovski, eds. *The History of Law in a Multi-Cultural Society: Israel 1917–1967*. Dartmouth: Ashgate, pp. 175–217.

Mautner, Menachem. 2003. The Selection of Judges to a Supreme Court in a Multi-Cultural Society. *Mehkarei Mishpat* 19: 423–439. (In Hebrew).

McGuire, Kevin T. and Barbara Palmer. 1996. Issues, Agendas, and Decision Making on the Supreme Court. *American Political Science Review* 90: 853–865.

McGuire, Kevin T. and James A. Stimson. 2004. The Least Dangerous Branch Revisited: New Evidence on Supreme Court Responsiveness to Public Preferences. *Journal of Politics* 66: 1018–1035.

Medina, Barak. 2007. Four Myths about Judicial Review (In Response to Robert Bork's and Richard Posner's Criticism of Aharon Barak's Judicial Activism). *Din Udvarim, Haifa University Interdisciplinary Law Review* 3: 399–426. (In Hebrew).

Mensch, Elizabeth. 1990. The History of Mainstream Legal Thought. In David Kairys, ed. *The Politics of Law*. New York: Pantheon Books.

Meridor, Dan. 1995. The Constitutional Revolution Was Affected by the Knesset, Not by the Courts. *Halishka* 24: 20–26. (In Hebrew).

Meydani, Assaf and Shlomo Mizrahi. 2006. The Politics and Strategies of Defending Human Rights: The Israeli Case. *Israel Law Review* 39, 1: 39–56.

Migdal, Joel. 2001. *Through the Lens of Israel: Explorations in State and Society*. Albany: SUNY Press.

Mill, John S. 1966. *On Liberty*. Translated by Arie Simon. Jerusalem: Magnes Press, Hebrew University. (In Hebrew).

Mill, John S. 1993. *Utilitarianism*. Translated by Joseph Or. Jerusalem: Magnes Press, Hebrew University. (In Hebrew).

Miller, Gary and Terry Moe. 1983. Bureaucrats, Legislators, and the Size of Government. *American Political Science Review* 77: 297–322.

Mishler, William and Reginal S. Sheehan. 1993. The Supreme Court Decisions. *American Political Science Review* 87, 1: 87–101.

Mitchell, William C. and Michael C. Munger. 1991. Economic Models of Interest Groups: An Introductory Survey. *American Journal of Political Science* 35, 2: 512–546.

Mizrahi, Shlomo and Assaf Meydani. 2003. Political Participation via the Judicial System: Exit, Voice, and Quasi-Exit in Israeli Society. *Israel Studies* 8, 2: 118–139.

Monsen, Joseph R. and Mark W. Cannon. 1965. *The Makers of Public Policy*. New York: McGraw Hill.

Montesquieu, Charles L. 1949. *The Spirit of the Laws*. New York: Hafner Library of the Classic.

Murphy, Walter F. 1964. *Elements of Judicial Strategy*. Chicago: University of Chicago Press.

Nachmias, David and Eran Klein. 1999. *The Arrangement Law: Between Economics and Politics*. Jerusalem: The Israel Institute of Democracy. (In Hebrew).

Nachmias, David and Itai Sened. 1999. Governance and Public Policy. In David Nachmias and Gila Menahem, eds. *Public Policy in Israel*. Jerusalem: The Israeli Democracy Institute, pp. 11–31. (In Hebrew).

Nagel, Stuart S. 1994. Systematic Policy Evaluation. In Stuart S. Nagel, ed. *Encyclopedia of Policy Studies*. New York: Marcel Dekker.

Naor, Arye. 2001. *Greater Israel: Belief and Policy*. Haifa: Haifa University Press. (In Hebrew).

Negbi, Moshe. 1982. *Justice under Occupation: The Israeli Supreme Court versus the Military Administration in the Occupied Territories*. Jerusalem: Cana. (In Hebrew).

Neumann, Franz L. 1957. *The Democratic and Authoritarian State*. Glencoe, IL: Free Press.

Niskanen, William A. 1971. *Bureaucracy and Representative Government*. New York: Aldine-Atherton.

Nonet, Philippe. 1976. For Jurisprudential Sociology. *Law and Society Review* 10: 525–545.

Olson, Mancur. 1965. *The Logic of Collective Action*. Cambridge, MA: Harvard University Press.

Oz-Salzberger, Fania and Eli Salzberger. 1998. The Secret German Sources of the Israeli Supreme Court. *Israel Studies* 3, 2: 159–192.

Parosh, Adi. 1993. Judicial Activism, Legal Positivism and Natural Law – Justice Barak and the Doctrine of the Omnipotent Knesset. *Iyunei Mishpat* 17, 3: 863–866. (In Hebrew).

Parsons, Talcott. 1962. The Law and Social Control. In William M. Evan, ed. *Law and Sociology*. New York: The Free Press.

Pedhatzur, Reuven, "The IDF Private Philosopher on the civilianization of society movement in Israel," *Haaretz Newspaper*, February 24, 2004 p. 2 (in Hebrew).

Peltzman, Sam. 1976. Toward a More General Theory of Regulation. *Journal of Law and Economics* 19: 211–240.

Penei-Gil, A., A. Yaniv, and Y. Tunik. 1998. The Supreme Court Has Stepped Out of Consensus: An Interview with the Chairmen of the Knesset Dan Tichon. *Orech Hadin* 6: 16. (In Hebrew).

Perelman, Chaim. 1984. *Logique Juridique: Nouvelle rhétorique*. Jerusalem: Magnes Press, Hebrew University. (In Hebrew).

Peres, Shimon. 1995. The Program Is Tested in Its Implementation, from Multiple Discourse: The 10th Anniversary of Israel's Economic Stabilization Program, *The Economics Quarterly*, December. (In Hebrew).

Plamenatz, John. 1949. *The English Utilitarians*. Oxford: Basil Blackwell.

Posner, Richard A. 1971. Taxation by Regulation. *Bell Journal of Economics and Management Science* 2, 1: 22–50.

Posner, Richard. 1972. *Economic Analysis of Law*. Boston: Little Brown.

Pound, Roscoe. 1943. A Survey of Social Interest. *Harvard Law Review* 57: 1–39.

Pound, Roscoe. 1999. *American National Biography* 17: 760–763.

Powell, W. W. and P. J. DiMaggio (eds.) 1991. *The New Institutionalism in Organizational Analysis*. Chicago and London: University of Chicago Press.

Pritchet, C. Herman. 1948. *The Roosevelt Court: A Study in Judicial Politics and Values, 1937–1947*. New York: Macmillan Co.

Rabushka, Alvin and Kenneth A. Shepsle. 1972. *Politics in Plural Societies: A Theory of Democratic Instability*. Columbus, OH: Charles E. Merrill.

Razin, Assaf and Ephraim Sadka. 1993. *The Economy of Modern Israel: Malaise and Promise*. Chicago: University of Chicago Press.

Riker, William. 1980. Implications from the Disequilibrium of Majority Rule for the Study of Institutions. *American Political Science Review* 74: 432–447.

Riker, William. 1984. The Heresthetics of Constitution-Making: The Presidency in 1787, with Comments on Determinism and Rational Choice. *American Political Science Review* 78: 1–16.

Rist, Ray C. 1995. Introduction. In Ray C. Rist, ed. *Policy Evaluation*. Aldershot: Edward Elgar.

Rocamora, Joel. 2000. Formal Democracy and Its Alternatives in the Philippines: Parties, Elections, and Social Movements. Paper presented at the conference "Democracy and Civil Society in Asia: The Emerging Opportunities and Challenges," Queen's University, Kingston, Ontario, August 19–21, 2000.

Rosenberg, Gerald A. 1991. *The Hollow Hope – Can Courts Bring about a Social Change?* Chicago: University of Chicago Press.

Rousseau, Jean J. 1984. *Du contrat social ou principes du droit politique*. Translated by Joseph Or. Jerusalem: Magnes Press, Hebrew University. (In Hebrew).

Rozen Zvi, A. 1993. Culture of Law. *Iyunei Mishpat* 17, 3: 689–716. (In Hebrew).

Rubinstein, Amnon. 1980a. *Judges of Israel*. Tel Aviv: Am Oved. (In Hebrew).

Rubinstein, Amnon. 1980b. *Constitutional Law of the State of Israel*. Tel-Aviv: Schocken. (In Hebrew).

Rubinstein, Amnon. 1996. *Constitutional Law of the State of Israel*. 5th Edition. Tel-Aviv: Schocken. (In Hebrew).

Rubinstein, Amnon and Barak Medina. 2005. *Constitutional Law of the State of Israel, Vol. 1*. Tel-Aviv: Schocken. (In Hebrew).

Salisbury, R. H. 1969. An Exchange Theory of Interest Groups. *Midwest Journal of Political Science* 13: 1–32.

Salzberger, Eli. 2003. Temporary Appointments and Judicial Independence – Theoretical Analysis and Empirical Findings from the Supreme Court of Israel. *Mehkarei Mishpat* 19: 541–568. (In Hebrew).

Salzberger, Eli M. and Alexander Kedar. 1998. The Quiet Revolution – More on Judicial Review According to the New Basic Laws. *Mishpat Umimshal* 4, 2: 489. (In Hebrew).

Schmidhauser, John R. 1992. Introduction: The Impact of Political Change upon Law, Courts, and Judicial Elites. *International Political Science Review* 13, 3: 223–233.

Schneider, M. and P. Teske. 1992. Toward a Theory of the Political Entrepreneur: Evidence from Local Government. *American Political Science Review* 86: 737–747.

Schubert, Glendon. 1965. *The Judicial Mind: The Attitudes and Ideologies of Supreme Court Justices, 1946–1963*. Evanston, IL: Northwestern University Press.

Schubert, Glendon. 1974. *The Judicial Mind – Revised: Psychometric Analysis of the Supreme Court Ideology*. New York: Oxford University Press.

Schubert, Glendon. 1985. *Political Culture and Judicial Behavior*. Lanham, MD: University Press of America.

Schubert, Glendon A. and David J. Danelski. 1969. *Comparative Judicial Behavior*. New York: Oxford University Press.

Schumpeter, J. A. 1942. *Capitalism, Socialism and Democracy*. New York: Harper & Brothers.

Schwartz, Edward P., Pablo T. Spiller, and Santiago Urbiztondo. 1994. A Positive Theory of Legislative Intent. *Law and Contemporary Problems* 57: 51–74.

Segal, Jeffrey A. 1997. Separation-of-Powers Games in the Positive Theory of Congress and Courts. *American Political Science Review* 91: 28–44.

Segal, Jeffrey A. and Harold J. Spaeth. 1993. *The Supreme Court and the Attitudinal Model*. New York: Cambridge University Press.

Segal, Zeev. 1998. Shadows Surrounding the Rule of Law – Along with the Bar-On Affair and its Outcome. *Mishpat Umimshal* 4, 2: 587. (In Hebrew).

Segal, Zeev. 2000. The High Court of Justice – The Court as a Shaper of Society. In Hannah Herzog, ed. *Society in the Mirror*. Tel-Aviv: Ramot Publishing, Tel-Aviv University. (In Hebrew).

Segal, Zeev. 2003. Activating Judgment Day Weapon in Judicial Criticism. *Mishpat Umimshal* 6: 337–349. (In Hebrew).

Sened, Itai. 1995. Equilibria in Weighted Voting Games with Side-payments in Two-Dimensional Spaces. *Journal of Theoretical Politics* 7: 283–300.

Shachar, Yoram and Meron Gross. 1996. The Rejections and Acceptance of Appeals to the Supreme Court. *Legal Research* 13; 329–341. (In Hebrew).

Shachar, Yoram, Meron Gross, and Chanan Goldshmidt. 2004. 100 Leading Precedents of the Supreme Court – Qualitative Analysis. *Mishpat Umimshal* 7: 243–303.

Shachar, Yoram, Meron Gross, and Ron Harris. 1996. Anatomy of Discourse and Dissent in Israel's Supreme Court. *Tel Aviv University Law Review* 20, 3: 749–795. (In Hebrew).

Shaham, David. 1998. *Israel – The 50 years*. Tel-Aviv: Am Oved. (In Hebrew).

Shamir, Ronen. 1990. Landmark Cases and the Reproduction of Legitimacy: The Case of Israel's High Court of Justice. *Law and Society Review* 24: 781–805.

Shamir, Ronen. 1991. Litigation as Consummatory Action: The Instrumental Paradigm Reconsidered. *Studies in Law, Politics and Society* 11: 41–67.

Shamir, Ronen. 1994a. Discretion as Judicial Power. *Theory and Criticism* 5: 7–23. (In Hebrew).

Shamir, Ronen. 1994b. Without Limits: On the Supreme Court's Deportation Decision. *Plilim* 26, 6: 59–66. (In Hebrew).

Shamir, Ronen. 1995. Jewish Society and Democratic Fundamentalism. *Iyunei Mishpat* 19, 3: 699–712. (In Hebrew).

Shapiro, Yonathan. 1977. *Democracy in Israel*. Ramat-Gan: Masada. (In Hebrew).

Shapiro, Yonathan. 1984. *An Elite without Successors: Generations of Political Leaders in Israel*. Tel-Aviv: Sifriat Poalim. (In Hebrew).

Sheingate, A. D. 2003. Political Entrepreneurship, Institutional Change, and American Political Development. *Studies in American Political Development* 17: 185–203.

Sheleff, Leon. 1992. The Green Line Is the Border of Judicial Activism: Queries about Supreme Court Judgment in the Territories. *Iyunei Mishpat* 17, 2: 757–809. (In Hebrew).

Sheleff, Leon. 1996. *The Rule of Law and the Nature of Politics*. Tel-Aviv: Papyrus–Tel-Aviv University. (In Hebrew).

Shepsle, Kenneth and Barry Weingast. 1981. Structure-Induced Equilibrium and Legislative Choice. *Public Choice* 37: 503–519.

Sheptler, Michael. 1970. Passing Thoughts on Constitutional Queries." *Hapraklit* 26: 6. (In Hebrew).

Shetreet, Shimon. 1994. *Justice in Israel: A Study of the Israeli Judiciary*. Dordrecht: Martinus Nijhoff.

Shetreet, Shimon. 1998. *The Good Land between Power and Religion*. Tel-Aviv: Yedihot Hachronot. (In Hebrew).

Shetreet, Shimon. 2004. On Adjudication – the Justice System in Law. Tel-Aviv: Yedioth Aharonoth. (In Hebrew).

Shprinzak, Ehud. 1986. *Everyman Whatsoever Is Right in His Own Eyes: Illegalism in Israeli Society*. Tel Aviv: Sifriat Poalim. (In Hebrew).

Shtruzman, Uri. 1998. Mister Chairman of the Knesset, for Your Consideration. *Orech Hadin* 5: 30. (In Hebrew).

Sidgwick, Henry. 1962. *The Methods of Ethics*. Chicago: University of Chicago Press.

Smith, Rogers. 1988. Political Jurisprudence, the "New Institutionalism," and the Future of Public Law. *American Political Science Review* 82, 1: 89–109.

Soffer, Oren and Gabriela Fisman. 2001. Judicial Review in a Polarized Society. *Iyunei Mishpat-Tel Aviv University Law Review* 24, 3: 663–694. (In Hebrew).
Sommer, Udi. 2010. A Strategic Court and National Security: Comparative Lessons from the Israeli Case. *Israel Studies Forum* 25,2: 54–80.
Sowell, Thomas. 2001. *A Conflict of Visions*. Jerusalem: Shalem. (In Hebrew).
Stigler, George J. and C. Friedland. 1962. What Can Regulators Regulate? The Case of Electricity. *Journal of Law and Economics* 5: 1–16.
Strauss, Leo. 1959. *The Political Philosophy of Hobbes*. Chicago: Chicago University Press.
Tapp, June Lovin and Felice J. Levine. 1974. Legal Socialization: Strategies for an Ethical Legality. *Stanford Law Review* 27: 1–72.
Tate, N. and T. Vallinder (eds.) 1995. *The Global Expansion of Judicial Power*. New York: New York University Press.
Taylor, Michael. 1987. *The Possibility of Cooperation*. Cambridge: Cambridge University Press.
de Tocqueville Alexis. 1962. *L'ancien Régime et la Révolution*. Translated by Ada Tzemach. Jerusalem: Bialik Institute. (In Hebrew).
Tribe, Laurence H. 1985. *Constitutional Choices*. Cambridge, MA: Harvard University Press.
Tsoker, Dedi. 1998. Who Will Interpret the Basic Laws? *Orech Hadin* 3: 12. (In Hebrew).
Tullock, Gordon. 1980. Why So Much Stability. *Public Choice*. 21: 2–23.
Turk, Austin T. 1976. Law as a Weapon in Social Conflict. *Social Problems* 23: 276–291.
Unger, Roberto M. 1975. *Knowledge and Politics*. New York: Free Press.
Vigoda-Gadot, Eran and Shlomo Mizrahi. 2005–2006. National Assessment Project of Public Administration (NAPPA) Haifa University. (In Hebrew).
Vigoda-Gadot, E. and S. Mizrahi. 2007. *The Performance of the Israeli Public Sector: A Citizens Survey and National Assessment*. The Division of Public Administration and Policy, School of Political Sciences, University of Haifa. (In Hebrew).
Vigoda-Gadot, Eran and Fany Yuval. 2000–2004. National Assessment Project of Public Administration (NAPPA) Haifa University. (In Hebrew).
Viscusi, K.W. (ed.) 2002. *Regulation through Litigation*. Washington, DC: American Enterprise Institute–Brookings Institution.
Voight, Stefan and Eli M. Salzberger. 2002. Choosing Not to Choose: When Politicians Choose to Delegate Powers. *KYKLOS* 55, 2: 289–310.
Von Neumann, John and Oskar Morgenstern. 1947. *The Theory of Games and Economic Behavior*. Princeton, NJ: Princeton University Press.
Weber, Max. 1947. *The Theory of Social and Economic Organization*. Glencoe, IL: Free Press.
Weber, Max. 1962. Bureaucracy. In Max Weber, *Essay in Sociology*. New York: Oxford University Press.
Weimer, David L. and Aidan R. Vining. 1999. *Policy Analysis: Concepts and Practice*. Upper Saddle River, NJ: Prentice Hall.
Weingast, B. R. 2005. Persuasion, Preference Change, and Critical Junctures: The Microfoundations of a Macroscopic Concept. In I. Katznelson and B. R.

Weingast, eds. *Preferences and Situations: Points of Contact between Historical and Rational Choice Institutionalisms*. New York: Russell Sage Foundation.
Wildavsky, Aaron B. 1979. *Speaking Truth to Power: The Art and Craft of Policy Analysis*. Boston: Little, Brown.
Witkon, Alfred. 1965. *Politics and Law*. Jerusalem: Hebrew University. (In Hebrew).
Witkon, Alfred. 1982. *Law in Developing Israel*. Jerusalem: The Jubilee Book of Pinchas Rosen. (In Hebrew).
Yadlin, Omri. 2002. "Judicial Discretion" and "Judicial Activism" as a Strategic Game. *Bar-Ilan University Law Review* 19, 2: 665–720. (In Hebrew).
Yishai, Yael. 1986. *Interest Groups in Israel: The Test of Democracy*. Tel-Aviv: Am Oved. (In Hebrew).
Yogev, Abraham. 1999. Order in the Chaos: Israel Education Policy in the Post-Modern Era. In David Nachmias and Gila Menachem, eds. *Public Policy in Israel*. Jerusalem: The Israeli Democracy Institute. (In Hebrew).
Zakariah, Fareed. 1997. The Rise of Illiberal Democracy. *Foreign Affairs* 76, 6: 22–43.
Zalmanovitch, Yair. 1998. Transitions in Israel's Policy-Making Network. *Annals of the American Academy of Political and Social Science* 555: 193–208.
Zamir, Yitzhak. 1993a. Judicial Review of Statutes. *Mishpat Umimshal* 1, 2: 395–410. (In Hebrew).
Zamir, Yitzhak. 1993b. Judicial Activism – A Decision to Be Decided. *Iyunei Mishpat* 17, 3: 647–658. (In Hebrew).
Zamir, Yitzhak. 1996. *Administrative Authority, Vol. 1*. Sarigim: Nevo Publishing Co. (In Hebrew).
Zamir, Yitzhak and Moshe Sobel. 1999. Equality Before the Law. *Mishpat Umimshal* 5, 1: 165. (In Hebrew).
Zinger, Roni. 2004. Guarding Home by Private Police. *Ha'aretz Daily* 13.8.04: B1. (In Hebrew).
Zweig, David. 2002. *Democratic Values, Political Structures, and Alternative Politics in Greater China, Peaceworks No. 44*, Washington, DC: United States Institute of Peace.

NEWSPAPER ARTICLES

Adeto, Edna. "Barak: The court shouldn't be the generator of consensus; the solution should be social and political." *Yedioth Achronot* 3.8.1997. p. 7. (In Hebrew).
Adeto, Edna. "The Supreme Court criticized the IDF for withholding information from bereaved families." *Yedioth Achronot* 17.9.1998. p. 12. (In Hebrew).
Adeto, Edna and Gabi Biron. "The Supreme Court president invited the Chairmen of the Knesset for a clarification meeting." *Yedioth Achronot* 6.7.1998. p. 7. (In Hebrew).
Alon, Gideon. "Beilin welcomes Judicial Review." *Ha'aretz* 16.12.1999, A11. (In Hebrew).
Alon, Gideon, "The constitutional committee accepted two out of the three basic laws." *Ha'aretz* 18.9.2000.

Alon, Gideon. "Religious Knesset Members Attack the High Court: Does not represent the People." *Ha'aretz* 29.8.2001.

Arlozorov, Merav. "The brokers' war." *Globes* 9.2.1997. (In Hebrew).

Baron, Gadi. "Judges object linking their salaries to the index." *Yedioth Achronot* 25.5.2001. (In Hebrew).

Benvenisti, Eyal. "The pact between the High Court of Justice and the Knesset." *Ha'aretz* 14.01.2000, B12. (In Hebrew).

Daklo, Shmuel. "11 Supreme Court Judges extended the appointed time for Investment managers' temporary license." *Globes* 3.6.1998, p. 22. (In Hebrew).

Dayan, Arie. "Beit Alfa under Fire." *Ha'aretz* 13.7.2001, p. 6b. (In Hebrew).

Eldar, Arye. "Thus buried the Human Rights governorship in the Minister's drawer." *Ha'aretz* 27.3.2002, p. b2. [In Hebrew].

Friedman, Sara. "Who will judge the Judges?" *Maariv* 3.3.1998, p. 10. (In Hebrew).

Goldberg, Michal. "9 Supreme Court judges will judge MK Deri immunity." *Yedioth Achronot* 8.7.1998, p. 6. (In Hebrew).

Goldberg, Michal and Roni Shaked. "Tomorrow, 9 Supreme court judges will discuss the legality of special investigation methods." *Yedioth Achronot* 19.5.1998, p. 6. (In Hebrew).

Kim, Hanna. "The Odd Couple." *Ha'aretz* 1.10.1997, p. A22. (In Hebrew).

Lex, Ofra, "Aharon Barak's nightmare." *At Seven (BESHVAA – an ultra-orthodox newspaper)*, 3.1.2003.

Lider, Zvi. "74 Investment managers had Joined the Investment Managers Bureau." *Ha'aretz*. 9.2.1997. (In Hebrew).

Magen, Hadas. "A. Barak: whoever claims political matters shouldn't be put in judgment, doesn't understand law." *Globes* 3.6.1998(a), p. 22. (In Hebrew).

Magen, Hadas. "Hanegbi calls Nethanyahu to dismiss Yiga'al Bibi." *Globes* 11.6.1998(b), p. 21. (In Hebrew).

Mittelman, Shmuel. "The Supreme Court declined Pdsako Petition for compensation on the basis of the peace agreement." *Maariv* 24.9.1998. (In Hebrew).

Mittelman, Shmuel. "The Supreme Court judges are also unsatisfied with the Yovel association." *Maariv* 5.5.1998. (In Hebrew).

Mittelman, Shmuel. "11 Supreme Court judges gather today to discuss Yeshiva students' enlistment." *Maariv* 19.5.1998. (In Hebrew).

Mittelman, Shmuel. "Judge Barak: The state wants the Supreme Court to do the unpleasant job." *Maariv* 21.5.1998, p. 9. (In Hebrew).

Mittelman, Shmuel. "Supreme Court's patience has reached its end." *Maariv* 21.12.2000. (In Hebrew).

Noah, Zvi. "The struggle for the constitution." *Globes* 7.2.2001.

Segal, Zeev. "The Transfer Government is exempt of judicial review." *Ha'aretz* 26.1.2001. (In Hebrew).

Shahar, Ilan. "The balance of terror between the Supreme Court and the Knesset remains." *Ha'aretz*. 7.1.2001, p. 1a. (In Hebrew).

Shahar, Ilan. "MKs are willing to lose in the Supreme Court for the sake of some publicity." *Ha'aretz* 13.11.2000, p. 1a. (In Hebrew).

Sheleg, Yair. "The Supreme Court has opened the doors – a symbiosis between the Supreme Court and public petitioners." *BaMachane* 8.8.1997, p. 54. (In Hebrew).

Tzimuki, Tova. "Hanegbi to propose conferring powers on Barak with respect to the courts." *Yediot Aharonot* 5.1998, p. 5 (In Hebrew).

Tzimuki, Tova. "Judge Barak tries to promote court's reform by a rare visit to the Knesset." *Yediot Acharonot* 20.5.1998, p. 14. (In Hebrew).

Tzimuki, Tova. "The Constitution commission is trying to cut back on Judge Barak's authorities." *Yediot Acharonot.* 15.12.1998, p. 22. (In Hebrew).

Tzimuki, Tova. "Why did Judge Barak phone called MKs?" *Yediot Acharonot* 11.6.2000. (In Hebrew).

Tzimuki, Tova and Edna Adato. "For the first time, a commissioner dealing with complaints against judges will be appointed." *Yediot Acharonot* 11.6.2000, p. 14. (In Hebrew).

Tzimuki, Tova and Edna Adato. "Mina Tzemach says the Judges' survey is not statistically representative." *Yediot Acharonot* 9.1.2001. (In Hebrew).

Tzimuki, Tova and Michal Goldberg. "The secrets behind the gown." *Yediot Acharonot* 26.1.2001. (In Hebrew).

———. "Just to talk: Judge Barak invited Orthodox reporters for a meeting." *Kol Ha'Ir*, 4.5.2001. (In Hebrew).

Online Newspapers

Pachter, Avraham. "The Supreme Court against the General Security Service – 5 years after." *NFC*, www.nfc.co.il Yoav Itzchak editor. 19/9/2004.

ISRAELI SUPREME COURT DECISIONS

HCJ 1/48. *Neiman v. Military Governor of the Occupied Area of Jerusalem.*

HCJ 1/49. *Bejerano v. Minister of Interior.*

HCJ 1/50. *Grossman v. Chief Military Attorney.*

HCJ 46/50. *Sobachi el-Eyovi v. Minister of Defense.*

HCJ 288/ 51, 33/52. *J'amal Machmud Azlan v. Commander and Military Governor of Galilee Area.*

HCJ 65/51. *Jabotinsky v. Weizman.*

HCJ 210/52. *Merkaz Rehitei Lekol v. The Minister of Trade and Industry.*

HJC 73/53. *Kol Ha'am Company v. Minister of Interior.*

HCJ 86/58. *Boganim v. Commander in Chief.*

HCJ 10/59. *Viki Levi v. Tel-Aviv Region Rabbinic Court.*

HCJ 72/62. *Rufeisen v. Minister of Interior.*

HCJ 243/62. *Filming Studios in Israel v. Gerri and the Film Review Board.*

HCJ 228/63. *Azuz v. Ezer.*

HCJ 58/68. *Shalit v. Minister of Interior.*

HCJ 222/68. *Hugim Leumi'im v. Minister of Police.*

HCJ 62/69. *Asraf v. Eilat's Religious Council.*

HCJ 98/69. *Bergman v. Minister of Finance and State Comptroller.*

HCJ 302/72. *Sheikh Soliman Hussein Oda Abo Chilo v. State of Israel.*
HCJ 148/73. *Kaniel v. Minister of Justice.*
HCJ 455/74. *Bara'ad v. Meder.*
HCJ 469/74. *Gonen v. Yom Kippur War Committee of Inquiry.*
HCJ 56/75. *Motti Askenazi v. Minister of Defense.*
HCJ 789/78. *Ofek v. Minister of Interior.*
HCJ 355/79. *Katalan v. Israel Prison Service.*
HCJ 802/79. *Samara v. Commander of Judea and Samaria District.*
HCJ 390/79. *Dyokat v. Government of Israel.*
HCJ 320/80. *Koasma v. Minister of Defense.*
HCJ 118/80. *Grinstein v. the Chief Military Attorney.*
HCJ 246/81. *"Agudat Derekh Eretz" et al. v. Broadcasting Authority et al.*
HCJ 652/81. *Sharid v. Chairman of the Knesset.*
HCJ 141/82. *Rubinstein v. Chairman of the Knesset.*
HCJ 243/82. *Zichroni v. Governing Council of the Broadcasting Authority.*
HCJ 200/83. *Waatad v. Minister of Finance.*
HCJ 7/83. *Biaras v. Rabbinic Court.*
HCJ 153/83. *Levi v. Police Commander of the Southern District.*
HCJ 73/85. *Kach party v. Chairmen of the Knesset.*
HCJ 620/85. *Mia'ari v. Chairmen of the Knesset.*
HCJ 428/86. *Barzilai v. Government of Israel.*
HCJ 910/86. *Ressler v. Minister of Defence.*
HCJ 153/87. *Leah Shakdiel v. Minister of Religious Affairs et al.*
HCJ 753/87. *Poraz v. Mayor of Tel-Aviv.*
HCJ 142/89. *Laor movement v. Chairman of the Knesset.*
HCJ 610/89. *Bachri v. Commander of IDF forces in Judea and Samaria area.*
HCJ 242/90. *Al-Kazaf v. Commander of IDF forces in Judea and Samaria area.*
HCJ 1601/90. *Meshulam Shalit v. Shimon Peres and others.*
HCJ 4919/90. *Miller v. Minister of Defence.*
HCJ 168/91. *Morcus v. Minister of Defence.*
HCJ 1414/91. *Federman v. Minister of Defence.*
HCJ 4481/91. *Bargil v. Government of Israel.*
HCJ 510/92. *Turkman v. Minister of Defence.*
HCJ 4353/92. *Temple Mountain and Eretz Yisrael Faithful Movement v. Prime Minister.*
HCJ 4562/92. *Zanberg v. Israel Broadcasting Authority.*
HCJ 1843/93. *Pinchasi v. Knesset of Israel.*
HCJ 3872/93. *Miteral v. Prime Minister and Minister of Religion.*
HCJ 4267/93. *Amitai – Citizens For Order in Administration v. Prime Minister.*
CV (Civil Appeal) 6821/93 *United Bank Hamizrahi LTD v. Migdal, Cooperative Village*
HCJ 721/94. *El-Al Israel Airlines v. Johnthan Danielowitz.*
HCJ 2910/94. *Ernst Yefet v. State of Israel.*
HCJ 4541/94. *Alice Miller v. Minister of Defence.*
HCJ 4676/94. *Miteral et al. v. Knesset of Israel.*
HCJ 5100/94. *Public Committee against Torture in Israel v. The State of Israel.*
HCJ 5364/94. *Velner v. Chairman of the Labor Party.*

HCJ 5503/94. *Segal v. Chairman of the Knesset.*
HCJ 698/95. *Ka'adan v. Israel Land Administration.*
HCJ 6055/95. *Sagi Tzemach v. Minister of Defence.*
HCJ 4712/96. *Meretz Party v. Commander of Jerusalem District.*
HCJ 5016/96. *Horev v. Minister of Transportation.*
HCJ 5268/96. *Pinchasi v. Government Legal Adviser.*
HCJ 2205/97. *MK Adiso Massala v. Minister of Education and Culture and Shmuel Shnitzer.*
HCJ 1715/97. *Investment Mangers Bureau v. Minister of Finance.*
HCJ 2534/97. *Yahav v. Attorney General.*
HCJ 2367/97. *The Movement for Quality Government v. Government Legal Adviser.*
HCJ 3267/97. *Ressler v. Minister of Defence.*
HCJ 335/98. *Hoffman v. Director General of the Prime Minister's Office.*
HCJ 3966/98. *Amitai – Citizens For Order in Administration v. Knesset Committee.*
HCJ 102/99. *Mishgav v. Knesset of Israel.*
HCJ 3959/99. *The Movement for Quality Government v. Committee for Punishment Consideration.*
HCJ 1248/99. *Plonit v. Commander in Chief.*
HCJ 244/00. *New Discourse Movement et al. v. Minister of National Infrastructure et al.*
HCJ 450/97. *Tnufa, Manpower Services v. Minister of Labor and Social Affairs.*

Index